THE
COMPLETE
IDIOT'S
GUIDE® TO

Being a Cheapskate

by Mark W. Miller

alpha
books

A Division of Macmillan General Reference
A Simon & Schuster Macmillan Company
1633 Broadway, New York, NY 10019-6785

Macmillan Publishing books may be purchased for business or sales promotional use. For information please write: Special Markets Department, Macmillan Publishing USA, 1633 Broadway, New York, NY 10019.

International Standard Book Number: 0-02-862726-1

Library of Congress Catalog Card Number: 98-89951

01 00 99   8 7 6 5 4 3 2 1

Interpretation of the printing code: the rightmost number of the first series of numbers is the year of the book's printing; the rightmost number of the second series of numbers is the number of the book's printing. For example, a printing code of 99-1 shows that the first printing occurred in 1999.

Printed in the United States of America

Note: This publication contains the opinions and ideas of its author. It is intended to provide helpful and informative material on the subject matter covered. It is sold with the understanding that the author and publisher are not engaged in rendering professional services in the book. If the reader requires personal assistance or advice, a competent professional should be consulted.

The author and publisher specifically disclaim any responsibility for any liability, loss or risk, personal or otherwise, which is incurred as a consequence, directly or indirectly, of the use and application of any of the contents of this book.

Alpha Development Team

Publisher
Kathy Nebenhaus

Editorial Director
Gary M. Krebs

Managing Editor
Bob Shuman

Marketing Brand Manager
Felice Primeau

Editor
Jessica Faust

Development Editors
Phil Kitchel
Amy Zavatto

Production Team

Development Editor
Doris Cross

Production Editor
Michael Thomas

Copy Editor
John Carroll

Cover Designer
Mike Freeland

Photo Editor
Richard H. Fox

Technical Editor
Nancy Dunnan

Illustrator
Paul Malamphy

Book Designers
Scott Cook and Amy Adams of DesignLab

Indexer
Tim Wright

Layout/Proofreading
Tricia Flodder
Cheryl Gibbons
Mary Hunt

Contents at a Glance

Contents

Foreword

One of the best things you can do in your financial life is to become smarter about your spending. In *The Complete Idiot's Guide to Being a Cheapskate*, Mark Miller provides hundreds of ways to save money every day, on items large and small.

You need this book if, like so many millions of Americans, you feel as if you're stuck on an earning/spending treadmill—never able to save enough money no matter how much comes through the door. The best remedy for that feeling is specific advice about saving money on big-ticket budget-busters (mortgages and other debt, insurance, taxes, and major purchases) and on those smaller items that, taken together, can also wreak financial havoc. Example: Many Americans spend $2,000 a year on cappuccino. That's fine if you're rich, but a bad idea if you're not.

Unlike works by the more fanatical advocates of frugality, this book can actually help real people solve real-world problems without ruining their enjoyment of life. In these pages you will *not* learn how to reuse garbage bags nine times or how to make wind chimes out of used juice-can lids. Instead, you will simply learn how to save money in every aspect of your life.

Becoming an intelligent cheapskate should be everyone's goal. The label "cheapskate" doesn't mean you're a miser. Misers never have fun with their money. Cheapskates, on the other hand, get more pleasure out of every dollar they earn because they are able to save more for what they really want—recreation, vacations, home remodeling, or investing in the future.

That's the right way to live. What's wrong is to waste money in dozens of ways and never have enough to realize your dreams.

Enjoy your life as a cheapskate!

Andrew Feinberg

Author of *Downsize Your Debt: How to Take Control of Your Personal Finances*

Introduction

Several years ago I was out of work, broke, and doing odd jobs to make ends meet. I was driving a used Honda Accord that was rusting from the inside out and had had its rear end smashed up in an accident several months earlier. I couldn't afford to get it fixed, and around town, people were calling it the Honda Accordion. Things couldn't have been worse, and all I could think about was the good days a few years back when I had been a financial adviser. Yes! Believe it or not, I'd made a good living teaching other people all the strategies and techniques of saving and investing, and never applied them myself.

In desperation, I started putted what I knew about being a cheapskate into practice in my own life. I had dreams no sane person could have believed would come true, and I started to work and save to make them happen. Within a couple of years everything I'd wanted—the house, the car, the travel to exotic places—was a reality. And I had $40,000 in the bank. Are you amazed? So was I, and today I feel fortunate to be able to help people get out from under the pressures of the almighty buck. You can take responsibility for how you live into your own hands; that's what being a cheapskate is all about. The techniques in this book can change your financial life forever, and you don't have to be a money guru to have them work for you. All you have to do is get started!

How To Use This Book

This book is divided into six parts, each focusing on one of six different aspects of how to be a cheapskate.

Part 1: "So, You Want To Be a Cheapskate?" is about how money—having it and not having it—affects every part of your life. You'll discover how cheapskates save and invest so they can gain the financial freedom to control their lives. You'll learn the planning techniques and buying tricks they use, so you can put them into practice yourself.

Part 2: "Guerrilla Shopping Strategies," teaches you how to shop like a cheapskate by foiling supermarket schemes to get you to pay more, avoid traps when you buy a car, and where to shop for just about anything.

Part 3: "Save Cash All Over Your Place," can show you how to keep your dream of owning a house from turning into a nightmare. What to look for in a house, how to get the best mortgage, handle maintenance problems, and keep utility costs down are some of the things you'll learn in these chapters.

Part 4: "Finally, Time to Lounge Around," takes you out of all that and on to fun and affordable vacations, out to eat at half the cost, and to more sports events and performances that you ever thought you could fit into your budget. You'll also learn how to celebrate birthdays for far less, and avoid the holiday season spending frenzy.

Part 5: "More Down-and-Dirty Tactics," teaches you even more about saving money on the kids without selling them short, ways staying in good health can save you a bundle, and how you can pull off seeing your kids through college.

Part 6: "Cheap Money Management," gives you the grand scheme for a solid financial future. You'll learn how to save on a regular basis, and then ease into investing by starting small, and learning how to manage your money. Save on banking fees, and even taxes, too.

Extras

The Complete Idiot's Guide to Being a Cheapskate includes four special sidebars that contain tips, advice, and cautions no cheapskate should be without:

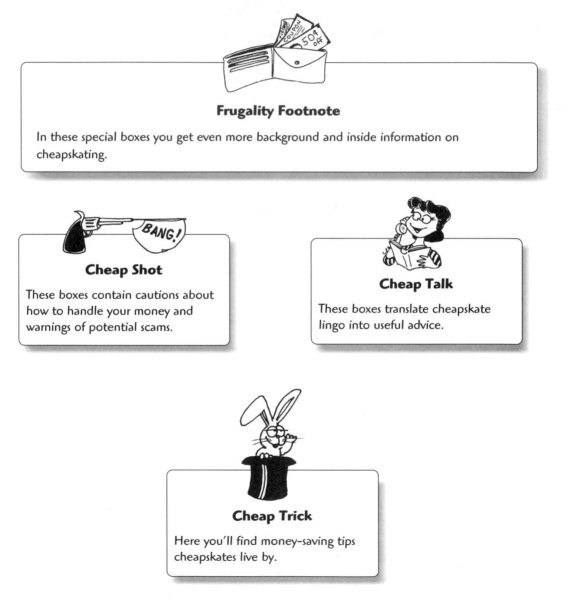

Frugality Footnote

In these special boxes you get even more background and inside information on cheapskating.

Cheap Shot

These boxes contain cautions about how to handle your money and warnings of potential scams.

Cheap Talk

These boxes translate cheapskate lingo into useful advice.

Cheap Trick

Here you'll find money-saving tips cheapskates live by.

Part 1
So, You Want To Be a Cheapskate?

Money is not just something to shop with. It affects just about everything we do in our lives. Having enough of it gives us the freedom to control our own destiny—freedom from stress, freedom to choose where we live, send our kids to college, travel, buy the things we want, and live comfortably in our retirement. When we are good stewards of the money we receive, we can transform the way we and our families live our lives.

Being a cheapskate is not about pinching pennies or hoarding cash under your mattress. It's about learning habits that give you financial control, so you can change your future for the better.

In Chapter 1, you'll get inside the mind of the real cheapskate and find out what your cheapskate potential is. You'll learn about how cheapskates save money and strategize for the future in Chapter 2, and, if you decide you want to be a cheapskate, Chapters 3 and 4 will help you put debt behind you and start on the road to financial freedom. The first step in taking control and becoming the world's greatest cheapskate is very simple—just get started!

Chapter 1

What Being a Cheapskate Means

> ## In This Chapter
>
> ➤ What's a cheapskate?
>
> ➤ More money isn't the answer
>
> ➤ A little pain, a lot of gain
>
> ➤ A pop quiz to test your cheapskate I.Q.
>
> ➤ The twenty biggest money wasting mistakes you can make

What do you think of when you hear the word "cheapskate"? The buddy who always has to leave the table just before the dinner check arrives? Your roommate who borrows the car and never "has time" to stop off and refill the gas tank? How about your neighbor, who drives all over town to find that one-cent-cheaper can of tuna. Or your eccentric aunt who'd rather make Christmas ornaments out of dryer lint than buy ready-made ones at Kmart?

Well, they probably all qualify for the term. But before you look down your nose at them, think of this: Today, the cheapskate is really the wise miser, saving with zeal and still living in style. It's the "in" thing to do. And they have a long history: Think Ben Franklin, J. Paul Getty, and Sam Walton. Wealthy men all, and they still opted for cheap transportation and $5 haircuts—they knew the value of a dollar, and when to save it.

Cheap Talk

Cheapskate n. chep-skat (long e and a); a miserly or stingy person; *esp* one who tries to avoid his share of costs.

It all boils down to what you think money's there for—is it for taking care of the day-to-day details, or for covering the costs of things you *really* care about? Franklin, Getty, and Walton understood the difference: They knew that saving money on some things gave them the financial freedom to spend on the things that mattered: themselves, their families, and their communities. Now, *that's* what being a cheapskate is all about: being a smart money manager who has cash left at the end of the day to use the way *you* want to.

The bottom line? If you want to have more money without taking that second (or third) part-time job, then you'd better learn to be a cheapskate. In this book, you'll learn how to do it right. You'll learn everything you need to know about turning saved pennies into dollars—thousands of them.

So, You Want to Be a Cheapskate?

Cheap Trick

If you want to be a great cheapskate, treat saving money as a challenge, not a chore. The goal is to save as many pennies as you can, and to the victor goes the (monetary) spoils. Sacrifices won't seem so much like sacrifices, after all.

Being a "true" cheapskate is not for the faint of heart. You have to have the right stuff. I could tell you that there's absolutely no pain involved in learning how, but that would be a lie. You'll have to make some sacrifices. You'll need to develop a little discipline. But it's nothing you can't handle—and if you really get into it you may even find the challenge of cheapskate-living fun. Not to mention that it'll all pay off in the end—big time.

Get ready for lots of practical advice on becoming a champion cheapskate. And the first piece of advice is this: Don't focus on what you can't HAVE... focus on what you can DO. If you doubt your ability to follow through on the suggestions in this book, keep in mind that they're all tried and true—real people have successfully done them all. If they could do it, so can you. All you need is the will to succeed, and a desire for a lot more extra cash.

Take the Cheapskate Quiz

Okay, time to roll up your sleeves and get started down the road to saving bundles of cash. But before you start, here's a quick quiz that'll help you figure out your cheapskate I.Q. No cheating, now!

Cheapskate Pop Quiz

1. I try to put money aside every month, but it's so hard.   Yes   No
2. I don't have time to shop around when I spend money.   Yes   No
3. It's a hassle to perform regular maintenance on my car and my house.   Yes   No
4. Are you kidding? I can't possibly pay off my credit card balance at the end of each month. Yes   No
5. I'm uncomfortable buying used cars and appliances because they often break.   Yes   No
6. I always seem to have too much month left at the end of the money.   Yes   No
7. I haven't read too many books about money in my life.   Yes   No
8. I'm always buying things on sale. I save money that way.   Yes   No
9. What's all this fuss about the lottery? It's good, cheap fun.   Yes   No
10. I generally buy clothes made by my favorite designers.   Yes   No
11. If I only had a little more money, it would solve a lot of problems.   Yes   No
12. If I didn't get my next paycheck, I would be hard-pressed to pay bills.   Yes   No
13. I don't have much respect for people who always try to save a measly dime.   Yes   No
14. Researching the best values on big-ticket stuff like cars and computers just confuses me. Yes   No
15. My checkbook sometimes looks like Egyptian hieroglyphics.   Yes   No
16. I don't know what the interest rate is on my credit card unpaid balances.   Yes   No

How Do You Stack Up?

Now it's time to grade your test. Simply add up the number of "yes" responses. Your grade is indicated on the key below.

Cheapskate Grading Sheet

Number of "yes" responses	Cheapskate Level
0 to 3	You are a cheapus maximus, otherwise known as the elite of the cheapskate species.
4 to 7	Not too bad. You have a good foundation, but there is always room for improvement.
8 to 11	Spendthrift alert! Time to start pinching those pennies, reining in those rubles, and manage those marks. Read on to learn how.
12 to 16	You've scooted right past spendthrift and need a crash course in cheapskate-ology. Not to fear, help is here.

Hey, Are You Calling Me a Cheapskate?

If you want to know the meaning behind your score, here's a quick explanation of the questions in the quiz you just took. Once you understand the reasoning behind them, you'll start to learn what it means to think like a cheapskate.

Question #1. Champion cheapskates don't find it hard to save every month. They save because they know the value of a buck and want to maximize their money. They all save at least 10 percent of their gross income, and most save between 15 and 20 percent. If you are just starting out, $5 to $10 a week is a great start.

Question #2. "I don't have the time" is probably the lamest excuse anyone can give for not saving money. Sure this is a busy world, and you have a busy life, but we all manage to find the time to do what we think is important. If you think you "don't have the time" to save, you haven't made saving a priority.

Question #3. Champion cheapskates know that by keeping their big ticket stuff in tip-top shape they're saving money hand over fist. They keep cars and appliances running great and perform all routine maintenance around the house to keep it looking super. Why? First, they want their expensive purchases to last forever. Second, when it comes time to sell, they'll get top dollar.

Frugality Footnote

Compared to how people live in many places in the world, you live like royalty, even if you think you're broke. We live in such a wealthy society that it's easy to lose perspective: Over 25% of the world's population lives on less than the equivalent of $200 per year, and over 90 million people survive on $75 per year! Don't ever forget how much *more* money you have even now.

Question #4. Do you want to get 18 percent on your money? Just pay off your credit cards religiously. Cheapskates know that the credit cards companies *want* you to carry a large unpaid balance on your card. They *love* it if you only make minimum payments. That's what they collect all that lovely interest on. The credit card is one of the biggest wastes of money ever invented.

Question #5. The idea that "used" means "likely to breakdown" is a total myth. Cheapskates always buy quality used merchandise because they know they can save up to 75 percent off new. But they're not idiots: They thoroughly evaluate the merchandise before they buy. And they know that if something *does* go wrong, the amount they saved up front will pay for the repairs ten times over.

Question #6. The first law of the cheapskate is "live beneath your means." A cheapskate knows how to budget appropriately and never find him- or herself getting panicky about finances at the end of the month.

Question #7. Cheapskates are *always* looking for new ideas on how to save. They read books, magazines, newsletters, and newspapers to get money saving ideas on a regular basis. It's all part of the challenge of saving.

Question #8. *Whenever* you buy something, you're spending money. I don't care how much you saved on the purchase, you still spent *some* money. Cheapskates don't buy just because they see a great deal. They don't buy just because they find something they *want*. The only buy because they absolutely *need* something. And they never fall for store come-ons and marketing tricks.

Question #9. The lottery and sweepstakes that require you to buy something to enter are two of the biggest wastes of money in the world. Think of them as taxes on the stupid. Sure, they *look* like cheap fun, but for many they're just a way to blow hundreds of dollars per year on a pipe dream. Cheapskates realize that their odds of winning are so astronomically poor that they refuse to waste their money to play.

Question #10. Designer label clothes and tennis shoes are some of the highest mark-up products around. Buying designer knockoffs or generic brands is how the smart shopper beats the Madison Avenue fat cats when buying clothing. And there are plenty of shops that carry designer labels with minor imperfections—that slightly crooked seam can mean major savings. Another excellent source for designer threads: thrift shops and tag or garage sales.

Question #11. This should already be familiar territory for you: More money doesn't mean a darn thing if you just go out and spend it. In fact, it can get you into bigger trouble if you use it to rack up more debt.

Question #12. The wise penny-pincher always has at least three months' income of ready cash in case of emergency. And it's a sure bet that losing your job counts as an emergency.

Question #13. Get a clue. You only save dollars by starting with saving dimes (and even pennies). If you think people who try to save money are fools, I guarantee that all you have to do is look in the mirror to see a person who is broke!

Question #14. Research may be difficult, but the cheapskate learns how to use buying guides, the Internet, and other free resources at the library to make the most informed buying decisions possible. Why be the only one on your block who shelled out cold hard cash for the Super-Duper Whatchamacallit that all the buying services rated as a total dud?

Question #15. Time really *is* money—and cheapskates always take the time to get their finances organized, so they don't get caught off guard with unexpected expenses or wrong balances.

Question #16. Most people get their new credit card and think it's free money. Weeks later, they don't even realize they are paying loan-shark rates to use that "free money." Cheapskates only use credit cards in an emergency and pay them off immediately. But if you asked them the credit card interst rate, they could still tell you.

There's Always Room for Improvement

A wealthy Texas entrepreneur named Max Hudson has experienced many financial hardships in his life. He failed at over ten businesses, declared bankruptcy twice, and lost everything he had on three different occasions. Half of what he experienced would have sent most of us to our graves. Max's problem wasn't his ability to make money; he had proven he could make any amount of the green stuff he wanted in real estate. Max was such a respected entrepreneur that Texas bankers used to pound down his door wanting to give him money. If this was true, why did he fail so may times?

Cheap Trick

Subscribing to money-saving newsletters or periodicals is a great way to keep up to date on the latest and greatest cheapskate strategies. My favorites are *Your Money* magazine, *Kiplingers Personal Finance* magazine, and *Moneysworth.* You can also visit local libraries, share subscriptions with friends, or go online to find out about the best deals in the country.

His problem was the way he handled his finances. It was simple for him to make money, but not so simple for him to keep it. He just didn't know how to be a cheapskate. He would spend and spend thinking that there would always be new income to take care of new expenses. He never took into account the ups and downs in the real estate market, and he never tried to regulate his spending accordingly. In other words, he lived like most Americans, only on a larger scale.

But after a downturn in which Max lost about a million dollars and was once again on the brink of financial collapse, he decided he wanted to end this "riding high in April, shot down in May" cycle. After reading about saving money in a local paper, Max decided to explore his saving strategies. Somewhere in the article he came across the idea that saving *smarter* was the only way to solve his financial woes. And he was right. Nine months later, he was back on top in the real estate market, but for the first time in his life, he also had several hundred thousand dollars in the bank and was planning to scale back his lifestyle even further. Max has decided to retire in ten years to the Cayman Islands, and he is well on his way.

Like Max, you can change your whole financial life around just by getting the right information and making a few changes in your spending habits. You may not be on the brink of financial collapse like our friend Max, but there's probably a lot of room for improvement in your saving strategies. If you learn how to become a cheapskate you may just change the course of your financial future. And if even Max could learn to rein in his former freewheeling, crazy lifestyle, you can do it, too.

More Money Isn't the Answer

Does your financial situation resemble the maiden voyage of the Titanic? When the passengers first saw this mighty ship, they said over and over, "It will never sink." When it was actually sinking, there were still people on deck saying the same thing, denying it to the end. But even the best built ships are vulnerable if they hit an obstacle and spring a leak.

Does this sound familiar? You just got a big raise at work or inherited a chunk of cash and said to yourself, "Finally, now I have all the money I need. It's smooth sailing from here." Suddenly there's lots more money available, and you figure, why not enjoy it? Well, it's likely that you suddenly found yourself living beyond your means. Maybe you tried to postpone the inevitable by paying off your credit card bills with other credit cards, or maybe you tried to take out a home equity loan to cover your debts—deep down, you knew your ship was sinking.

Cheap Talk

A *home equity loan* is a loan from a bank or other financial institution that uses your equity in your house as collateral. People often use the money from these loans to pay off bills or finance a "needed" family purchase. But remember—if you miss payments you could end up losing your house.

The problem for most people is that once their budget springs a leak, they don't find out where the problem is and plug it up. Instead, they look for other ways to solve the problem: paying their bills (or, worse, buying groceries) on their credit cards, or trying to get a debt consolidation loan. But doing this is kind of like bailing more sea water *into* the Titanic. You manage to cover today's expenses, sure—but at the cost of ever more debt you'll have to pay later on.

There have probably been many times in your life when you've had more money than usual. The question is, what the heck happened to it? If you're like most of us, you probably let it just slip through your fingers, never to be seen again. But the key cheapskate concept to understand is that you *always* have "more" money. Right now, no matter how much money you have, there are ways you can make more of it stay with you, frittering less of it away.

Instead of drowning yourself in debt or spending endless hours carrying a second job, why not try to keep your budgetary ship from sinking by plugging the money leaks? Learning to be a cheapskate can be your financial life preserver. You can solve your problems by living within your income and making the right cheapskate choices.

Making the right choices early will prepare you for the obstacles that lay in your path.

Frugality Footnote

The majority of all successful cheapskates have a belief that no matter how little money they have in their bank account, they will get by just fine.

Even if they live very frugally, they feel comfortable with where they are, and they aren't constantly trying to outdo their neighbors with unneeded purchases, acquired only for their status-symbol value. Their main focus is simplicity in lifestyle because they know that this approach will lead to lasting wealth.

A Cheap Attitude Is Everything

"Your attitude determines your altitude," said author and motivational speaker, Zig Zigler.

He was right, especially in matters of money. Your attitudes about money will determine your financial outcomes. If you were raised to believe that money was the root of all evil, chances are you've lacked money all your life, and it's probably caused major challenges for you. You may also hold the limiting belief that you are unworthy of money. Conversely, if you were raised to believe money is good and can be used positively for your family and community, you probably have more than the average Jane or Joe.

The truth is that the only thing that can stand in the way of your becoming a successful cheapskate is a negative attitude about saving.

If you've been laboring under negative attitudes about your relationship to money, it's okay. Remember that our beliefs are simply generalizations about what we *think* is true. Fortunately, you have the power to change your attitudes with what's in that six inches between your ears. The fact that you bought this book is a sign in itself that you want to make some changes in your financial situation. So now here's one very important change to make: you need to develop a cheapskate's

Cheap Trick

Cheapskates are masters at communicating about money. They teach themselves words and phrases that help them. Some are, "Are you having any sales soon?," "Is this the absolute rock-bottom price?," "Is there anything else you haven't told me about this product?," and "How long does the warranty on this TV run?"

10

attitude. This means that you'll have to alter any limiting beliefs you may have about money. That's easy to do, if you have the motivation, and a little bit of the right information.

Most of the world's best cheapskates have a great attitude about money. It excites them to think about saving and accumulating cash. Their sense of self worth is increased when they know that they've saved on something they absolutely needed, or when they've invested wisely. They share a strong sense of proper financial stewardship, which makes them do whatever it takes to guard against the unwarranted waste of even one dollar.

Making Uncommon Cents

During my second year in college, I had about $6,000 in a savings account that I was just itching to spend. I was fixated on a sharp sapphire-blue Camaro that I felt was a great investment. My father had other ideas. He sat me down and tried his best to explain to me the value of a dollar—and especially the value of $6,000.

Dad grew up in a small Missouri town outside Kansas City called Liberty. When he was young, not many people in Liberty had much money. It was a town of hard-working folks who definitely knew the value of a buck. He was brought up in a family that saved as much as it could and took a vacation only once in a while. It was in this environment that he learned to respect people's opinions about money, and they learned to trust him enough to let him handle it for them.

He took a job as a teller with a large bank in Kansas City and worked his way up to be a vice president. He then began to invest in several profitable community banks throughout the state of Missouri. He attained this stature primarily because of his ability to get along with others and his small-town common sense about money. For years, we were never short of money, and lived a far more comfortable life in the nice part of Kansas City than he had been accustomed to while growing up in Liberty.

My Dad wanted me to use that $6,000 I had socked away to cover my college expenses—our arrangement was that he paid for tuition, room, and board, and I was responsible for all my incidentals. But as a college student, I wasn't thinking about saving. I bought the sporty car, and it turned out that he was right. I had a rough time paying my bills that year—those incidentals sure did add up. When I went to my father on my knees to ask him to help, he wouldn't give me an extra nickel, and every time I got into the car, I felt guilty. Eventually, I felt guilty enough to sell it—at a hefty loss!

Cheap Shot

Watch out when you get a lump sum of money. Most Americans immediately figure out ways to spend money received as a windfall. Instead, park the money in the safest and highest paying interest-bearing account for several months while you think of ways you can invest and save wisely. If you must spend some, blow 10% and invest the rest.

The moral of my story? After spending money unwisely, you'll end up kicking yourself and wishing you had it back. After all, money is oh-so-easy to spend, but very hard to make. So when you get some cash, you should do your best to keep it in your pocket. The best cheapskates have learned how to do the right thing with their money.

Cheapskate Hall of Shame

So, how did you score on that pop quiz? If you didn't do well, never fear—you can still learn to be a great cheapskate. All you've got to do is be willing to try. And the first thing to learn about are some commonly encountered hazards to avoid. These are so easy to fall into that you can end up wasting money without even realizing it. Take a look at this list of mess-ups and see if you've ever made any of them yourself.

Top Twenty Biggest Wastes of Money

1. Buying lottery tickets and entering sweepstakes
2. Purchasing a new car every two years
3. Investing in or anything you may be clue-less about such as whole life insurance, pork bellies, options on stocks, or land in Transylvania.
4. Buying credit life insurance
5. Purchasing extended warranties on appliances and electronics
6. Taking action on a "hot" stock tip
7. Lending money to friends
8. Shopping on QVC or the Home Shopping Channel
9. Claiming the wrong amount of deductions on your W-4s
10. Getting suckered into "get rich quick" opportunities
11. Paying fees on your checking account
12. Using credit cards like a regular loan
13. Buying name brands on a regular basis
14. Keeping money in low-interest savings accounts
15. Buying anything at convenience stores
16. The car dealer extras
17. Shopping at ritzy clothes and grocery stores
18. Paying an annual fee on a credit card
19. Failing to check the total on your restaurant tab
20. Buying food and drinks at the movies or ball games

The Least You Need to Know

➤ Becoming a cheapskate is really not that hard. You can learn how to make more without earning more, just by following the habits of champion cheapskates.

➤ Your primary focus shouldn't be making "more" money. If you haven't made a commitment to also live within your means, you'll only wind up spinning your wheels.

➤ Use some common sense about how you spend money. You'll need to assess your spending habits and attitudes to determine how much you need to change your lifestyle.

➤ No matter how bad a cheapskate you are now, you can become the best saver that ever lived just by making a decision to do it, and then learning how.

➤ Avoiding the biggest saving mistakes is an easy way to start on the road to becoming a champion cheapskate.

Chapter 2

Daily Lifestyles of the Rich and Cheap

In This Chapter

➤ The daily life of a cheapskate

➤ Learn to curb the spending urge

➤ Master the monthly savings method

➤ Caution: Salestalk ahead

➤ How inflation deflates your funds

➤ Financial freedom means a better life

➤ The cheapskate hall of fame

It's not how much you make; it's how much you spend. That's what being a cheapskate is all about. You don't have to make a fortune to have financial security, a nice home, enough for the kids' education, and a comfortable retirement; all you have to do is spend less and save more. Even if you make a lot of money, if you don't learn to be cheapskate, you can easily wind up broke.

Drop In on a Cheapskate's Day

How do cheapskates with modest incomes achieve financial security and even wealth? Check out these cheapskate habits. How many of them do you practice on a regular basis?

Cheap Shot

This is a serious caution: People who don't get into the habit of spending much less than they earn and saving on a consistent basis will never achieve any form of financial success. There are no exceptions to this rule!

1. Cheapskates never forget that every dollar they accumulate can be exchanged for something of value.

2. They never stop learning about how money works and how to spend as little and save as much of it as possible. Reading, researching, and finding new savings ideas go with the cheapskate way of life.

3. Contrary to popular belief, cheapskates have imagination and spontaneity. A cheapskate with a sense of adventure will go on a spur-of-the-moment cruise, for example, if it's a great last-minute deal. Cheapskates have the foresight to be ready to jump at a good opportunity when they see it.

Frugality Footnote

Cheapskates are big into networking with fellow cheapskates to get new and better ideas about saving money. If they're out of their territory or in a new location, it's the first thing they do to find out where to get the best bargains. Savvy cheapskates also get on the Internet to research and chat about the latest money-saving techniques.

4. They may not be the neatest people in the world, but cheapskates are well-organized when it comes to money. They've learned that keeping files, planning shopping excursions, making lists, and using coupons saves them a lot of time and money.

5. Cheapskates ask a lot of questions, and they're not shy about it, particularly when they're shelling out their hard-earned money. When they get answers that their gut tells them just don't add up, they'll cut and run.

6. They never buy the first item they see. Cheapskates always shop around, and around, and around until they find the best deal on a similar product.

7. Cheapskates are never afraid to ask for a discount, even when there's no reason to think they'll get one. They save thousands of dollars a year that way, and also add to their lists of best places to shop.

8. They know when to say no. If they don't really need something, or the timing isn't right for buying it, cheapskates have great sales resistance.

9. Cheapskates have plans. They sit down and set financial goals for themselves and their families, and they stick to them. Whether they follow a strict budget or religiously save a certain amount every month, or both, they have a financial plan of action. Some work with a financial adviser to create the kind of financial underpinning that will enable them to meet their goals.

10. Cheapskates save and invest regularly and focus most of their attention on their financial future. Almost everything they do has some bearing on their money situation, not just for tomorrow, but down the road. By always strategizing for the future, they know what the smart moves are for today.

How to Become a Spenderbender

Cheapskates keep from overspending the same way dieters lose weight; they tighten their belts. Saving does take discipline, but if you hold onto the image of how good it'll feel to have some financial security, you can do it. Just break down your spending habits into bite-sized portions and they'll be easier to reform.

The Spending Habit: Bend, Don't Break

Most people try to lose weight on crash diets. "Okay, tomorrow I'm going to stop eating so much," you may say. Tomorrow rolls around and you eat a piece of dry toast for breakfast, and skip lunch; by dinnertime you're ready to eat the refrigerator! That's when you say to yourself, "I can't do this diet thing. It's too hard. I'm a worthless chocaholic." That's not the way to make any progress.

Cheap Trick

Ease into taking control of your spending by doing more thinking about how much you really need the products and services you're used to, and what other options there are. You'll probably end up crossing some things off your list altogether.

It's much the same with spending and saving. If you try to change all your financial habits in one day, you're setting yourself up for failure. Going cold turkey and denying yourself every opportunity to spend doesn't work. What does work is a lot of practice at learning how to spend smarter.

Cheap Shot

Don't ever think of a sale as license to spend. No matter how good a buy it is, first stop and ask yourself if you really need it (or if it'll make a good gift) and, if not, walk away from it.

Start learning how to spend smarter by looking at alternative ways to shop and save. Keep spending; just do it differently. Cheapskates never buy anything over $50 or $100 without first checking at least one or two other similar products and stores. Be willing to take a little time to research what you're buying and, if you use just this one method, you'll be saving thousands over the years.

Take the time to find things on sale; there's always a sale somewhere. Look in the local papers and call some stores in the Yellow Pages. If you save $20 or $30, it's worth the effort.

Retrace Your Spending Steps

To get a fuller picture of your current buying habits, retrace your spending over the last several months and determine which purchases have enhanced your life and which you could have lived without. I bet a lot of what you bought is sitting around in a closet or already up in the attic. Just think, you could have increased your bank balance by a few hundred bucks instead.

Once you stop buying on impulse and start thinking about what you spend and how, spending more wisely will get easier and easier. It's just a matter of getting used to asking yourself, "Do I really need this?" and, if the answer is yes, "Can I get it cheaper somewhere else?"

How Much Savings Is Enough?

You can do a lot for yourself and your family by getting into the habit of salting away some money every month. Even if it's not much, if you start now, it can add up and make a big difference tomorrow.

How much you should save every month depends on a number of factors including your age, assets, income, expenses, and goals. Saving is much easier when you have some concrete objectives in mind.

Think through your short- and long-term goals for the next twenty years. They could be things such as buying a new home or car, retirement, and in a broader sense, complete financial freedom—however you define it. Then decide how you can allocate what you save to meet those goals.

The average cheapskate should save about 10 percent of his or her annual pre-tax income up to the age of 35. As you get older, the percentage should go up to about 15 percent at age 45 and 30 percent at age 55. These figures may seem high, but if you really want financial freedom, you need to put away as much as possible.

Fill out the income/expenses worksheet in chapter 3 to see how your savings stack up to these percentages. If you fall short, try to figure out ways to free up more money to put away. Make the hard choices now and you will have the kind of future you hope for.

A good strategy to help you increase savings in the future is socking away any bonuses, and a percentage of any pay raises you receive. Given enough years, it can compound tremendously, especially if you throw in any other "found money" that may come your way. It's really extra cash that you could have gotten along without, so it's hard to argue against earmarking it for savings.

Cheap Talk

Gross income, also called *pre-tax income,* is what you receive in pay before taxes, social security payments, and any other costs are deducted from it.

Try coming up with regular maneuvers to set even more money aside, things like putting away what you save on a sale item you needed anyway. You don't have to make more to save more if you implement the tips and strategies you find here, but if you do get a raise, remember to put some of it in the bank.

Buyer Beware

Cheapskates are experts in recognizing people and organizations who are out to take advantage of them.

How many times have you heard, "You get what you pay for," but is it always true? Not if you know the tricks many companies use to get you to pay more.

You can get the quality you want and pay less at the supermarket, on car maintenance, home furnishings, insurance, and even luxury vacations when you know the trade secrets the pros never tell us.

Cheap Shot

Beware of insurance companies, banks, car dealerships, and mortgage companies. These are the big four of industries that will take you for a ride (and not in a car) if you're not a savvy cheapskate.

➤ Imagine being able to walk into a car dealership and pay $350 less than what the dealer paid for a new car, and thrill them by buying it.

➤ How about saving $30,000 on your dream home and still getting everything you want?

➤ Would you feel comfortable saving several hundred dollars a year on auto insurance and still be fully covered?

You can learn how to do all of the above and much more in this book through cheapskate strategies that are simple to understand and implement. If you use them, you'll save yourself from getting burned and save thousands in cash over your lifetime.

Caution: Salestalk Ahead

Most salespeople are honest and are held to certain ethical standards by their industry, but every business has its share of con artists, and some have more than others.

Few car salespeople will tell you about a recent recall due to a car's faulty fuel injector; it could mean a lost commission they were counting on.

There aren't many stockbrokers who'll tell you to stay out of the stock market, even if the economic climate clearly warrants it. That means no commissions.

An insurance agent is unlikely to sell you anything but the most expensive policy possible, even when you don't need the benefits. It means more money in his or her pocket.

Frugality Footnote

Most salespeople are not greedy, uncaring people, but individuals just like you and me trying to do the best for themselves and their families. It's simply human nature to care more about their own financial picture than yours.

As the saying goes, "Let the buyer beware." You are the only person who will put your financial interest first; how could it be otherwise? But how do you protect your wallet with so many people trying to grab it?

1. First, arm yourself with the facts. A little knowledge can go a long way when you deal with salespeople. Before you make a major purchase, go down to the local library or get on the Internet and spend an hour researching the product you're buying. It can save you hundreds or thousands of dollars in product costs and commissions.

2. Be aggressive in asking questions, and demand answers in plain English. Don't worry about coming off overbearing. You have the right to ask, and no one to blame but yourself if you walk out feeling as though you've been taken.

3. If you feel confused or pressured, walk away. Give yourself some time to think over your choices; you can always buy later.

Once you get in the habit of making wise spending decisions, it'll seem less of a chore and much more fun than you thought it could be. Yes, cheapskating can be as much fun as rollerskating!

The Incredible Shrinking Dollar

Purchasing-power risk is something all cheapskates understand. It's the effect of inflation on your investments. Even if you own the most conservative investments in the world, if inflation goes up, you can lose more than you think when you go to cash out.

Let's say you purchase a $10,000 5-year certificate of deposit and spend the interest income. Inflation is running about 5 percent per year. When you get your $10,000 back, it buys only $7,800 worth of goods and services. Even if you invested the interest in a safe vehicle, you come out behind.

Frugality Footnote

Investing all your money in debt obligations such as bonds, CD's, and Treasuries exposes you to purchasing-power risk. The bottom line is that, because your interest rate doesn't change, your income remains flat while your cost of living increases. So, investing solely in bonds may not be as conservative as you thought.

Take Stock

Whether you're old or young, you need a component in your portfolio that keeps pace with inflation. Most common stocks do, except in the early stages of heightened inflation, because companies are able to raise their prices to maintain returns on product investments. As profits grow, so do dividends and capital gains to investors, so you're staying ahead of inflation. This growth makes common stock a far superior investment over the long haul than bonds. Since 1928, U.S. stocks have outpaced inflation 100 percent of the time, whereas bonds have outpaced inflation only 28 percent of the time (see Chapter 23 for more details).

The Real Estate Remedy

In some cases, rental real estate can be an even better investment than common stocks to outpace inflation. You can often pass inflationary operating expenses along to tenants. Many investors buy real estate when they expect inflation to rise (which often creates a self-fulfilling prophecy). If you're willing to take on the added responsibilities

and risk associated with owning real estate, you should consider investing some assets in good income-producing property. For an average investor, real estate returns are about equal to stock market returns over time. But if you become a proficient real estate investor, sometimes you can far outpace the return from common stocks, though they have the advantage of being an easier and more efficient way to stay ahead of the game.

Keeping Money in Perspective

We've all heard that "money can't buy happiness." Cheapskates know that it's true, but they also know that it sure can take the stress out of your life, add a little pleasure, and provide a degree of comfort.

Cheap Trick

Gold is often considered an inflation hedge, but its value fluctuates wildly in good and bad times. If you want to own gold, you'd better have a strong stomach. Be prepared to keep gold for at least twenty years to see any kind of true appreciation.

Frugality Footnote

In a recent study, Americans making between $15,000 and $30,000 per year said they would be happier and could fulfill all their dreams if they made between $50,000 and $60,000. When people earning $60,000 a year were asked what their happiness and dream threshold was, they said they would need $125,000. Everyone always needs more money, but is more money really the answer? The real test is what you do with the extra money you make. Most people immediately spend it and increase their standard of living, only to find that they hit a debt ceiling again in no time. Look back at the times in your life when you had "more." Have those times made a lasting impact on your life, or did they just dig you deeper into a hole?

Cheap Shot

Be careful about the balance you have in your life. Making money is important, but it can backfire if you lose sight of why you're doing it.

Although cheapskates are devoted to living within their means and increasing their income, they also have strong feelings about the things money can't buy. This book is about how to save and make more money, but not to the exclusion of a healthy balance between work and play. Cheapskates believe that the purpose of achieving true financial independence is to be able to make more choices about how they live.

Having both money and happiness *is* possible. The key is to strike a healthy balance between your financial life and your "life." Be very careful if your pursuit of wealth and success is driving you too far from the things you value in life. You know what they are; and you know that money can't buy them— only nourish them.

The Cheapskate Hall of Fame

These are some of the best money moves you can make right now. Each is discussed in detail throughout this book:

Top Twenty Best Money Moves

1. Save a fixed amount of money every month
2. Avoid illness by eating right and exercising regularly
3. Shop at warehouse clubs
4. Buy term life insurance instead of whole life insurance
5. Take a Saturday morning to browse neighborhood garage sales
6. Do your own taxes
7. Invest through mutual funds
8. Buy generic and store brands at the grocery store
9. Double-check the word of a commissioned salesperson
10. Buy clothes at thrift stores
11. Get wired to the Internet to find the best deals on everything
12. Invest in common stocks and income-producing real estate
13. Be your own travel agent
14. Find out the dealer's cost of a car before you start negotiations
15. Be debt-free and buy most everything with cash
16. Educate yourself about investing and being your own adviser
17. Find a no-fee checking account
18. Shop at outlet stores
19. Eat most meals at home rather than out
20. Make "extra principal" payments on your mortgage

The Least You Need to Know

➤ To manage your money better, adopt some cheapskate habits, such as getting organized, asking lots of questions, and shopping around for the best quality for the price.

➤ If you currently spend too much, don't go on a non-spending crash diet. Instead, gradually stop spending by looking at alternative ways to shop. Buy what you want, but be a total cheapskate about it.

➤ If you haven't started saving money on a regular basis, begin today. Set aside at least 10 percent of your total income monthly and put it into a good investment. Ten percent is a good start, but cheapskates save about 20 percent.

➤ The only way to make sure you don't get taken by salespeople and companies is to educate yourself about personal finance. Read one book a month on saving money and you'll be light years ahead of the rest of the country.

➤ Always keep the almighty buck in perspective. If you end up worshipping money, you'll miss out on a lot of the best things in life.

Chapter 3

Plan On Paper

In This Chapter

➤ At last, a finance formula that works

➤ Beginning with the future in mind

➤ Goal-setting worksheet

➤ Down with budget drudgery

➤ How to stash more cash

➤ Budget-buster worksheet

When it comes to saving, consistency is everything. That means asking yourself whether you really need that purchase, saving when you shop, and also disciplining yourself to make regular monthly payments to a savings or investment account. If you're not used to saving, it's not easy to get into; when you have extra money, the first thing you think of is how you're going to spend it. Being battered by hundreds of commercials a day doesn't help, but if you keep the long-term payoffs of saving and investing in mind, you can do it. It's the only way to avoid financial stress and realize your goals.

To get to the cheapskate's Promised Land you have to have a game plan—on paper.

➤ The first step is to sit down and set financial goals for yourself and your family.

➤ Once you have established clear and definable goals, backtrack to see what steps you need to take to achieve them.

➤ Put together a budget that you can live with, with the focus on setting aside as much money as you can for the future.

From there, it's just a matter of persistence. The key is to write a detailed plan and refer to it on a regular basis.

Cheap Trick

Let your dreams and goals captivate your attention, and the possibility of achieving them will become more and more real. If you're fortunate, destiny will then take over and change your life forever. Napoleon Hill says, "Whatever the mind of man can conceive and believe, it can achieve."

Begin with the End in Mind

Many people don't save because they simply don't know where or how to start. Napoleon Hill in his book, *Think and Grow Rich,* talks about how important *desire* is in achieving anything in life, especially more money in the bank. Hill's belief is not just a theory; it's based on years spent interviewing some of the wealthiest and most powerful cheapskates in the world.

His book doesn't tell you how you can become an instant millionaire by buying "nothing down" real estate or placing tiny ads in newspapers. It's about making a few sacrifices to create the life you want. If your objective is abundance and prosperity, these simple guidelines can help you achieve true financial independence.

To get started on the road to prosperity, follow these specific steps, and don't cut any corners.

Cheapskate Success Formula

1. If you want something that involves money, you have to have in mind the exact amount it will cost. Whether your money goal is ten months from now or ten years, it doesn't matter. Having some flighty goal such as, "I want lots of money to buy a sports car," just doesn't cut the mustard. Being definite will crystallize your dreams and desires in your mind.

2. Are you ready to give up something for your dreams and desires? You can't just wish something into being. You have to have the will to sacrifice a little for the reward you want. Describe in detail what it is you are willing to do to get your desired outcome.

3. By what date do you want to achieve the objectives of your plan? Be specific.

4. To develop a game plan write down the things you could do today to start on the road to achieving your goals. Don't worry if they don't seem perfect; you can always change your approach as the months go on. Just do something!

5. Review steps one through four and then write out a clear and precise "power statement" that incorporates all the main themes of those steps. Make it as specific as possible and don't worry about how long or short it is. Here's a great guideline to determine if it's powerful enough: It should send chills up your spine! If it doesn't, start over. The object of this exercise is to step back and envision a life way beyond the one you're used to.

6. Read your statement aloud every day until you know it by heart. If you do it for just a month, you'll get used to the idea that you deserve what you desire, and start to do what it takes to make your vision a reality.

Cheap Shot

Cheapskates know that they have to have written plans to have a chance of achieving financial freedom. Be crystal clear about where you want to go financially and get your plan on paper; otherwise, the best you'll do is to just "get by."

What is the most important component in the formula for success? The desire to succeed. If you want something badly enough, you'll do what it takes to get it. If it means staying at work another hour every day, or starting a part-time business, you'll do it. The formula can help make your desires more vivid, and strengthen your belief that you can make them a reality. The mind is a powerful tool; use it to help change your destiny.

Frugality Footnote

Cheapskates know that the success formula works. Try your own variations if you like, but stay within its general framework. Going through the success formula process will speed you toward your goals.

I am living proof that the cheapskate formula works, and it works with just about anything you want or desire in life. Several years ago I sat down and wrote down a series of goals and dreams for my future, within specific time periods—one, three, five, ten, and twenty years. The results were phenomenal. Not only have I attained most of my goals, I've gone farther than I ever imagined I could. I learned that setting high standards moved me further ahead because it expanded my vision of the future. Put this formula to the test, and watch it pay off.

Go For the Goals

Everyone wants financial independence, but most people just daydream about it. If you want to start on the road to achieving it:

Cheap Shot

It's vital that you make a list of things you want to accomplish financially so that you can focus on them every day. If you don't, your money will slip through your hands and you won't even know where it went.

1. Write down specific goals for set time periods: next year, three years from now, five years, ten years, and twenty years. Write down exactly what the goals are and attach dollar figures to them. For instance, "I want a new 2,300-square-foot white colonial house in three years." What will it take to get this? $10,000 or perhaps $20,000 in the bank for a down payment? "I want to send Johnny to Dartmouth College in ten years." This goal might cost $100,000.

2. Put your list on the refrigerator, the bathroom mirror, and where you can see it at the office. Make a smaller version of it for your purse or wallet so you'll see it every time you spend money.

3. Repeat your goals to yourself in the morning and evening. If your dreams are always in front of you, you'll be inspired to do whatever it takes to reach them.

4. Don't worry if what you want seems way beyond your means; dream about it anyway. You never know how or when your financial situation may change for the better.

5. Be flexible as you go through the process; financial goals are not set in stone.

6. Write down obstacles to attaining your goals as well as the means of reaching them.

7. Find a great way to reward yourself when you reach a financial goal. Be creative!

Goal-Setting Jumpstart

To help you get started right away, I have put together a goals worksheet for aspiring cheapskates. I have already given you the formula, but my experience is that most people do not follow up on great ideas unless they are made easier. This worksheet should make your goal-setting easier. The nature of your goals and the way you meet them is of critical importance in your planning process. The process of money planning is ongoing, so be prepared to review your goals every six months or so.

To review, ask yourself these important, simple questions:

➤ Where am I now financially?

➤ Where do I want to be in the future?

➤ How am I going to get there?

Keep these questions in mind as you set your goals and don't forget some other pointers to help you along:

➤ Be specific and set target dates.

➤ Quantify your goals. Use specific numbers.

➤ Visualize your goals. Picture yourself having already attained the goal to strengthen your resolve to succeed.

Frugality Footnote

Wrong: I want to live comfortably when I retire.

Better: I want to retire in fifteen years at age 60 and live in a luxury condominium in Phoenix, Arizona that has a pool and golf course in the backyard. My monthly net (after taxes) income will be $7,000.

Now, that is a powerful goal! When you word your goals in this manner, you can easily measure your success objectively on a monthly or annual basis and also vividly imagine them.

Goal-Setting Nitty-Gritty

Now that you have an idea of how to formulate money goals, get to work on this worksheet. If you need more space, use a separate sheet of paper or any blank pages in the book. Do it now!

Goal-Setting Worksheet

Short-term goals (write down specific 1-, 3-, and 5- year goals):
(Example: Pay off Chevy loan in 21 months and buy my next car with cash.)

Goal	Date
Pay off car loan	by December 2000

Long-term goals (write down specific 10-, 15-, and 20-year goals):
(Example: Retire in 20 years at age 65. I will own a home worth $200,000 over-looking a lake, and fish whenever I want.)

Goal	Date
Retire at 65 and own $200,000 lake home	20 Years

After you've listed your key goals, list the steps that will help you achieve the short- and long-term goals you listed in the preceding steps. (Example: Start a monthly savings plan.)

1._____

2._____

3._____

4._____

5._____

6._____

List obstacles that may impede the attainment of the short- and long-term goals you listed. Remember not to focus on them, though. Write them down just to be honest with yourself. (Example: Excessive monthly credit card debt.)

1._____

2._____

3._____

4._____

5._____

6._____

After you finish this exercise, copy the pages and tack them up in places where you'll see them regularly. Now you're taking charge of your finances and your life.

Down with Budget Drudgery

Cheapskates hate the word budget because they know that following a day-by-day budget is absolute hogwash unless you're an accountant. Budgeting conjures up images of deprivation and sacrifice, that is, of the negative idea of not spending, rather than the positive act of saving to produce a better future.

You may be shocked to read such harsh words about budgets from a cheapskate; the common wisdom is that making and following a budget is essential if you want to get control of your finances. Well, it's just not the case.

Cheap Shot

Budgeting doesn't produce riches; it only increases stress. Sticking to a strict budget and writing down what you spend every day is not the way to save money.

Example: I once heard a story about a church that was losing money and continually trying to find new ways to cut expenses. Every trustee meeting consisted of arguments about what should and shouldn't be cut from the budget until the head trustee got a brilliant idea. He suggested that they turn the problem around; stop thinking about how to cut spending and start looking at ways to make more money and save on things they were already buying. From that point on, the board began to focus on new programs and church functions to bring more money into their coffers and find cheapskate deals on supplies. The church is now not only in the black, it's been able to institute several new charity programs that had been a dream for years.

The moral: If your mindset is damage control, you're overlooking the many positive ways there are to produce more funds.

Frugality Footnote

Your objective is to increase the amount of your funds, not resign yourself to living with the tedium of daily budgets. Creating more money to invest for the long term is what cheapskates do best. They leave daily budgeting to the accountants of the world.

Of course, you have to think about how you're spending your money. Cheapskates regularly assess where they stand financially. You should do it too, with the income and expenses worksheet in this chapter. You'll quickly find out what you're spending so you can figure out what you can afford to save. But shopping for groceries with a pencil and paper to ensure you stay within a specified budget on pancake syrup is not my idea of inspiration.

Instead, you should focus on producing more money and saving more.

How to Stash More Cash

Pay yourself first. You've probably heard this advice over and over, and you'll probably hear it again. It means you must set aside some personal savings before you pay anyone else, even the landlord or mortgage company. If you can pay yourself even $10 from each paycheck, do it! It's about starting good cheapskate habits that will pave the road to tomorrow's financial security.

There's a simple and effective way to sock away money that doesn't demand much time or energy. Follow this method religiously, and you'll have hundreds, even thousands of dollars to save and invest every year.

1. To start, jog your memory for a half hour or so. Write down all the items you spend money on and total up what you pay out during the month (see worksheet in this chapter). If you have no clue as to what you spend, go to your checkbook and review the last couple of months; it's the easiest way to find the specifics.

2. After you have basic figures, review them to see if you're buying frivolous items that you could easily cut from the list.

3. Once you've calculated your spending, subtract it from your monthly income.

4. The result is what you can save every month. If the figure is negative, go back and recheck your expenses to see if there are more unnecessary items you know you can do without.

5. Go to the local office supply store and get a booklet of generic invoices for yourself— nothing fancy, the $1.98 variety does just fine. On the 20th of each month, write out an invoice to yourself for the amount of monthly savings you've decided upon. In the "from" section, write the name of the bank or financial institution to which the money will go.

Cheap Trick

An alternative way to keep up your monthly savings is to divide the amount you've set in half and write an invoice to yourself twice a month before each pay period. This often works better than plunking down the full amount in one payment.

You can also write in the "items" section exactly what account the money goes to (if you want to get cute). Put the invoice in an envelope and mail it to yourself so that it arrives with the rest of the bills around the first of the month. Before you pay any other bills, pay this bill, because it is by far the most important.

Of course, you don't need to go to the trouble of mailing the invoice to yourself if you don't want to, but it's not a bad way to reinforce your commitment to the process of saving.

Once you get into the routine of paying into your personal savings plan before you pay any other bills, you'll be forced to live on what's left. That makes saving and budgeting a crystal clear proposition. You won't find a better way to save, because, as long as you don't cheat, it's foolproof, and the emphasis is on saving money rather than on not spending it.

Frugality Footnote

A good start is to put your savings money in a bank savings account. If you prefer a higher return, a money market mutual fund is a good choice. When you've accrued the equivalent of at least three months' total household income, reserve it for any emergencies that may crop up. After that, you can start putting extra money into other investments (see Chapter 23).

As you save month after month and the money begins to compound in your investment accounts, you'll find new ways to free up more to save. Saving can get to be fun in addition to being rewarding. Check your plan every six months or so to make sure you're on track.

The Cheapskate's Budget-Buster

The following is a simple worksheet that will help you determine your income and expenses. The framework of this form follows the guidelines of the savings invoice method. You may feel as if you're doing some kind of budget, but remember that you're not going to be following this day by day. Your objective is to come up with a monthly savings figure to guide you in saving for the next several months. Subtract your expenses from your income and you'll have the amount that you can save comfortably every month.

Once you've done this a few times over a period of a year or so, you'll get an accurate monthly figure just by averaging out variable expenses and incomes from the last year.

Take about forty-five minutes to dig up the financial information you need to complete the worksheet, and do your best to stick with the saving commitment you come up with. Make sure that you're giving yourself enough leeway with your expenses. Don't strap yourself so much that you end up having to dip into your savings account if you fall short at the end of the month.

Budget–Buster Worksheet

Monthly Income	Amount
Salary (include take-home pay for you and your spouse)	_____
Self-Employment and Part-Time Income	_____
Investment Income	_____
Social Security	_____
Veteran's Benefits	_____
Pension	_____
Miscellaneous	_____
Other	_____
Total Monthly Income:	_____

Monthly Expenses	Amount
Fixed Expenses	_____
Mortgage/Rent	_____
Primary Residence	_____
Secondary Residence	_____
Car Payments	_____
Auto #1	_____
Auto #2	_____
Auto #3	_____
Insurance	_____
Auto	_____
Health	_____
Home (if not included in mortgage)	_____
Life	_____
Disability	_____
Taxes	_____
Real Estate	_____
Income (State, Local, Federal)	_____
Loans	_____
Student	_____
Personal	_____
Business	_____
Home Equity	_____
Alimony/Child Support	_____
Child Care	_____
Club/Association Dues	_____
Miscellaneous	_____
Other	_____
Total Monthly Fixed Expenses:	_____

Variable Expenses	Amount
Auto Care	_____
Cable TV	_____
Car Phone	_____
Cleaning/Maintenance (cleaning lady, lawn service, etc.)	_____
Clothes/Accessories	_____
Credit Cards	_____
Card #1	_____
Card #2	_____
Card #3	_____
Charitable Donations	_____
Dry Cleaning	_____
Electricity	_____
Entertainment	_____
Movies	_____
Dining Out	_____
Travel	_____
Other	_____
Food	_____
Gifts	_____
Medical	_____
Natural Gas/Heating Oil	_____
Personal Care	_____
Pet Care/Supplies	_____
Sports/Hobbies/Lessons	_____
Subscriptions	_____
Telephone	_____
Transportation	_____
Gas	_____
Bus/Train	_____
Tolls/Parking	_____
Water/Sewage/Trash	_____
Miscellaneous	_____
Other	_____
Total Monthly Variable Expenses:	_____
Total Expenses:	_____

Total Monthly Income: _____

–Total Monthly Expenses: _____

=**Total Monthly Savings Amount to Invest:** _____
(This is the only number you should focus on.)

The total monthly savings amount you come up
with should be the amount of money you put into
your favorite investment vehicle at the beginning
of each month. If you've calculated properly, you
should be able to live and pay your bills with what
you have left. Tap the monthly savings money only
in case of an emergency, or for a specified goal that
you and your family agree to in advance.

Review your worksheet every six months and
update any figures appropriately.

Cheap Shot

Oh, no, your monthly savings
amount is negative! Solution: You
need to do some work, so go back
and see where you can cut unnecessary expenses. This step may be
difficult, but you'll never get on the
road to financial independence
unless you make these hard choices.

The Least You Need to Know

➤ Spend some time thinking about what you really want out of life and how your
finances fit into the picture. If you're married, involve your spouse so that you can
plan and dream together. If you have children, there's no reason not to involve
them, too.

➤ Fill out the goal-setting worksheet completely. Be clear, concise, and specific
about the goals for your financial future.

➤ Copy the goal-setting pages and place them in highly visible areas around the
house and at work.

➤ If you currently have a written budget and are feeling more and more guilty for
not sticking to it, drop it into the trash. It's not worth the time and hassle to
concentrate on "not spending."

➤ Complete the "budget-buster" worksheet in this chapter and commit to salting
away your calculated savings amount every month. This figure should be at least
10 percent of your monthly gross (before taxes and expenses) pay.

➤ Finally, read Napoleon Hill's book *Think and Grow Rich* as soon as possible. It and
The Complete Idiot's Guide to Being a Cheapskate are all you'll need to be a
complete cheapskate and eventually live a life of unlimited abundance.

Chapter 4

The Cheapskate's Arch Enemy: The Debt Monster

> ### In This Chapter
>
> ➤ Are you drowning in debt?
>
> ➤ Negotiating lower credit card rates
>
> ➤ How to get out of debt fast
>
> ➤ The ten commandments of cheapskate credit
>
> ➤ Avoiding bankruptcy
>
> ➤ Cleaning up your credit mess

Credit can be like a bad drug. It provides instant gratification when you use it, but too much of it can make you do crazy things. It's only later that you realize what a tremendous price you paid for that high.

For the last several years, Americans have been overdosing on personal debt. According to the Bureau of Public Debt, Americans owe a staggering $400 billion on credit cards alone. But who can blame us? It's not as if the Government has set a good example!

It's remarkable how easy it is to get credit. Who hasn't gotten a pre-approved Visa card in the mail? Walk into a car dealership with suspect credit, plop down a few hundred dollars, and they'll "work it out." Debt was the "in" thing for a long time, until millions of people had to start living with the consequences. What's "in" now is cheapskating; that is, having control over the debt monster.

Are You Overextended?

If you have too much debt, you're at a disadvantage in two ways: Paying off your debts is a continual challenge, and you'll have nothing to put away for the future. Getting out of debt isn't easy, but it's well worth the effort in the long run. This chapter shows you exactly what to do if debt is a problem in your life. Even if you feel that having some debt is a necessity, and it's not really a concern, you can learn how to become a better borrower.

Cheap Shot

Be careful to use credit only when you absolutely must. A good example is if you have a family emergency that has to be taken care of fast. When you incur debt of any kind, you must exercise caution and use good judgement.

You may not have creditors pounding at your door every day, but you could be feeling a big squeeze coming. Check out the numbers: if your monthly payments on short-term and personal debts (car payments, credit cards, department store debts, student loans) exceed 20 percent of your net income after taxes, you may be in trouble. Don't include your mortgage; paying for your house is considered a living expense.

If the numbers tell you that you're in over your head, vow to make all your payments no matter what and get started right away on a debt pay-off strategy that works. Be prepared to free up from 2 to 5 percent of your income to start paying off your debts, and be strict about it, or your troubles will get a whole lot worse.

The two worst ways to use credit:

1. Absolutely the worst things to buy with credit are perishables such as food, gas, and meals because once they are consumed they instantly have no value. Buying such items on credit never crosses the cheapskate's mind.

2. Purchasing depreciable items that have only short-term value, such as cars, clothes, furniture, and electronics. They lose value fast, so buying them on credit means you're taking on an even bigger loss.

The two best ways to use credit:

1. To purchase appreciable investments such as stocks or mutual funds, or an interest in your own business. Getting a loan for such investments will at least give you a chance to profit from the interest rate risk.

2. To buy a home. This is the best use you can make of borrowed money. If you don't have the cash to purchase your own home (which is the case for the majority of Americans), taking out a loan is beneficial in the long run so you can avoid renting for long periods of time.

While you work on paying down the debts, quit buying on credit. Racking up more debt will make you feel like you're just spinning your wheels. If you're in serious trouble, you may need to curtail all discretionary spending for a few years. That's right cheapskates: no more new cars, trips, or stereo equipment for a while!

If you feel overwhelmed, seek dependable help. Contact the nonprofit Consumer Credit Counseling Service (800-388-2227). Their counselors can help you work with your creditors to design a reasonable repayment plan that's within your means. The advantage of using CCCS is that you need to make only one payment a month to this organization; they take the responsibility of making distributions to your creditors. CCCS charges about $10 a month for this excellent service.

Cheap Trick

If you can't make your debt payments on time, get in touch with your creditors and explain your financial situation. If they've dealt with you for a long time, they're much more likely to cut you some slack. The last thing to do is try to hide like a hibernating bear. If you're honest with your creditors, you can probably negotiate short-term relief based on your current budget.

Debt-Free and Loving It!

You may have heard or read that to have no debts is impossible and stupid. Typically, the reasoning behind this statement is that, if you were to pay off your mortgage, for instance, you would lose the only tax deduction you have left. That's a bunch of hogwash, and you'll learn why.

Ten Foolish Ways to Incur Debt

➤ Take a cash-advance on your credit card

➤ Get an equity line-of-credit against the equity in your home

➤ Charge expensive trips and luxury items on your credit card

➤ Not pay your bills on time. Once you're late, you increase your debt

➤ Use a credit card to buy excessive amounts of mail-order gadgets or clothes

➤ Opt for "buy now, pay later" deals at electronics or furniture stores

➤ Pay for meals with plastic

➤ Take out a loan for pleasure purchases, such as a boat or RV

➤ Borrow money from a friend or relative

➤ Make payment arrangements with creditors when you have the money in the bank to cover the bill

Cheap Talk

An *amortization schedule* is a printout your bank or finance company will give you that breaks down how much of each mortgage payment you make will go to interest and how much to paying down the mortgage principal. The amount that goes to principal will ultimately become part of your home's equity; that is, the amount of the home you really own after the mortgage balance is subtracted.

Cheapskates understand that whenever you borrow money from someone else, you give up your control over it. For example, at the end of an average $100,000, 30-year home mortgage, you will have paid the bank a total of $300,000, $200,000 of which is interest over time. That's TWICE what you paid for the house! If you're like most Americans, you're probably paying much more than that because you move into a different home every five to seven years. If you take a few minutes to study your amortization schedule, you'll see that about 95 to 98 percent of your monthly payments in the first years are for interest alone. That means that you're getting practically no equity buildup in your home. If you buy a new house five to seven years later, you start paying interest without building equity all over again. So, in essence, you're paying loan shark rates to borrow money to buy a home. If you don't know these cheapskate secrets you can get burned by your mortgage company.

Frugality Footnote

If you find that you must have a credit card for emergencies or travel, search for a bank that gives you a Mastercard or Visa debit card with your checking account. In most parts of the country, you can use a debit card to give you the convenience of a charge card. Just note that the funds come out of your account immediately as they do when you write a check.

Using an American Express card may also make sense because you are required to pay off the bill each month. However, the American Express card is a credit card.

A debit card is better because there is rarely an annual fee to pay. The important thing is to decrease the temptation to buy things on credit and accumulate debt.

You may be thinking that it would be nice to pay off all your debts, including your mortgage, and have lots of money to put into savings every month. Most people think this would be possible only if they got an inheritance or won the lottery. Actually, paying off all your debt *is* possible if you follow some simple steps that give you total financial control. Cheapskates know that true financial freedom is being debt-free and not having to grovel to some banker when you want to buy a car or house.

First, calculate how much you owe for your mortgage, auto loan, credit card companies, college loans, and any other debts. Don't include utilities, groceries, rent, and other basic expenses.

Then, determine the amount of extra money you can set aside to start your debt pay-off engine. It doesn't need to be much; even as little as $50 to $100 per month is a good starting point. It'll add up as the months go by, so don't think it's too little to make a difference. If you can, designate an amount that is the equivalent of about 10 percent of your total monthly debt payments. If your total on all debts is $1,000, then the initial amount to set aside would be $100.

Cheap Shot

Unless you haven't eaten for a few days, never take a cash advance on a credit card. Not only will you pay a ridiculously high finance charge on this money, you'll generally be charged a 2%–4% extra cash advance fee for the privilege.

If you think you may be tempted to continue charging, cut up and throw away all of your credit cards. (Years ago, I gave my credit cards the deep freeze by actually putting them in a bowl of water in the freezer; they were sealed in a block of ice. Talk about a symbolic gesture.)

Most people get nervous when you talk about trashing credit cards because they've been living by a "110 Ways to Use My Credit Card and Why I Can't Live Without It" philosophy. If you truly want to control your debt, get over this bad idea.

Follow this simple formula to get rid of your debts fast:

1. Gather all your debt bills together. Using the following "Get Out of Debt Worksheet," write down each account's total balance and its corresponding monthly payment. For your credit cards, write down double the minimum monthly payment as the total. The monthly minimum is usually only about 4 to 6 percent of your total balance, so don't think you can't afford to double this small payment.

2. Now, rank the payments in order, beginning with the lowest as number one, the next highest as number two, etc. Determine a ranking for each bill and write it down next to the monthly payment figures.

3. Begin to pay off your bills in the order in which you ranked them. Most likely, charge cards will be first, consumer and car loans next, and then your mortgage.

Cheap Trick

You can cut your credit card debts significantly with just one telephone call. If you feel the interest rate is a little too high, simply call the bank or institution that issued the card and tell them you'd like it lowered. So much competition exists among credit card issuers that they would much rather give you a lower rate than lose you as a customer.

4. Don't worry about which accounts have the highest interest rates. Focus on accelerating debt payoffs. Because you're going to pay off the debts fast, speed is more important than the amount of interest on the debt. What you'll be doing is taking the power of compound interest away from the bank and putting it to work in your favor as soon as possible. Keep that in mind as you pay off debt after debt, and a feeling of accomplishment should start to set in.

5. The small amount you determine, anything $50 or more, you'll use to help start your plan is the extra amount you should now add to bill number one. These two numbers added together will be your new payment for bill number one. Pay this every month until debt number one is paid off.

6. After you pay off this debt, take the total amount you were paying on bill number one and apply it to bill number two. Of course, you also continue to make the regular monthly payments you have always paid on bill number two.

7. Continue this process for every bill in the order in which it's ranked. By the time you get to your car and mortgage payments, the extra amount you're applying will be huge, and you'll be paying off these debts fast.

Cheap Shot

Be cautious about advertisements promising deferred payments for six months, or no payments until next year. They may require that you put a huge amount of money down to "hold" the item, or charge an outrageously high interest rate. The offers sound great, but you can end up paying more than if you'd saved for six months and paid cash.

Unless yours is an unusual situation, you should be able to eliminate all your small consumer debt, including car loans, within the first twelve to eighteen months of the plan. You'll then have an extra payment to apply to your mortgage that may be equal to or even greater than your normal mortgage payment.

Using this system, most people can become completely debt-free within five to seven years. That beats a 30-year mortgage by a mile! Use the following worksheet to calculate how long it will take you to become debt-free.

The main advantage of this plan is that you don't have to come up with a lot of extra money (or win the lottery) to pay off your debts. Just commit to these three small sacrifices and you'll eliminate all your debts and have 100 percent equity in your home in about seven years:

Get Out of Debt Worksheet

Debt Account	Rank	Total Balance	Monthly Payment	Extra Monthly Payoff Amount	Payoff Date
Visa	1	1,000	$40	$50 (Total $90)	01/01/00
1st Bank	2	5,000	$250	$90 (Total $340)	03/01/01

1. Stop adding to your debt.

2. Apply a small initial amount of extra money to pay down your debt.

3. Maintain your present overhead level for however many years it takes to get completely out of debt.

Cash Is the King of the Road

If you become a dedicated cheapskate, once you're debt-free, you can look forward to operating completely with cash; in essence, being your own banker. Just pay cash for consumer goods including clothes, groceries, dining out, movies, and miscellaneous products. Before you spend money on anything, you should have the cash in your wallet or the money in your checking account.

For instance, if you want to buy a new car, buy only what you can pay for in cash you have in hand. I'm not talking about a cash down payment, but actually purchasing a car outright. It's best to pay cash for most everything because, generally, things you buy with borrowed money won't make you any more money to help offset the finance charges. If you purchase a car with borrowed money, it depreciates in value every day. So, in essence, you're getting hammered twice, once with the lost value of the car and once with the interest you're paying to own it. The only exception would be if your old beat-up car is costing you a fortune in repair charges and you can't get your head above water to buy a better one with cash. In this situation, financing makes sense, as long as you pay off the loan as soon as possible.

Being a cheapskate means constantly resisting the temptation to pull out the plastic unless you're absolutely certain you'll be able to pay it off when the next bill comes. Going into debt makes sense only for something like a new home (I'll show you the best way to finance a home in Chapter 9) or other investments that will yield you interest.

Incurring debt on consumer goods can be the biggest detriment to your financial well being.

The Cheapskate's Ten Credit Commandments

Here are the ten basic credit tenets of the champion cheapskate:

1. Never pay for credit life insurance when you obtain a loan. You're better off purchasing cheap term insurance that will cover the debt in case you pass away. Credit life insurance is just overpriced term life insurance.

2. Always double your minimum payments on your credit cards. If you make only the minimum payment, it will take decades to payoff what you owe.

3. If you must make a major purchase and incur debt, always put at least 20 percent down; 30 percent would be better, and 50 percent better yet. Your objective should be to minimize the amount of interest you have to pay. By doing this, you have as much control over your money as possible.

4. Except when you buy a home, buy only things you can afford to pay for in cash. After you get the house paid off, you can buy your next house with cash, just the way you buy everything else (see Chapter 9).

5. Cheapskates carry only one credit or debit card, and use it only in emergencies. They generally use a Mastercard or Visa debit card that draws money directly out of their checking accounts.

Cheap Talk

Credit life insurance is life insurance attached to a loan. It is paid for by the consumer but protects the finance company or bank that is issuing the loan in case you pass away before the loan is paid off. *Term life insurance* is straight death protection for yourself and is generally much cheaper than credit life insurance (see Chapter 21).

Frugality Footnote

Look into trying to lower the interest rates on your payments, or consolidate where possible. If you haven't already done so, investigate refinancing your mortgage or getting a lower-rate home equity loan, or consolidate your high-interest credit cards with a lower-rate card. Many cards have introductory offers of 6% to 7% for a year to get you as a customer. Paying off debt with another debt is a good tool only if you've changed your spending habits, and you have the discipline not to use your new financial freedom to start buying on credit again.

6. On a monthly basis, keep track of the balances on all your debts. That will keep the extent of your debt in the forefront of your mind and give you the incentive to pay it off sooner.

Cheap Talk

A *simple interest loan* calculates interest compounded on a monthly basis rather than some loans that compound interest on a daily basis. A *balloon note* is one that has a large lump sum due at a specific time during the loan.

7. If real cheapskates have to borrow, they insist on loans that are calculated with simple interest. Never get any loan with attached balloon payments or one that compounds interest on a daily basis. Keep it simple.

8. Always pay your bills on time to avoid added interest and any credit difficulties.

9. Avoid leasing a car or any other item. Leasing is the worst way to finance because there are many ways a lease can be designed to deceive even the most savvy cheapskate (see Chapter 7).

10. If you must finance, always choose the shortest repayment period you can afford for any type of loan.

It's Not Uncle Sam's Job to Bail You Out

As dreadful as it seems, especially to the wise cheapskate, more and more people are looking at bankruptcy as a way to escape financial troubles. The number of individuals filing for bankruptcy protection is growing to alarming levels. In 1985, 298,000 individuals filed in the United States. By 1995, that number exploded to over 1.4 million! That's an 80 percent increase in just twelve years.

People file for many reasons: spending with no regard for the future, an investment that goes sour, job loss, massive medical expenses not covered by insurance, and frankly, because it's easy to file. Unfortunately, so many Americans are filing that bankruptcy has begun to lose the stigma it once had.

Consider filing for bankruptcy only if you're in dire circumstances. I've received letters from people who owe only $4,000 or $5,000 but feel that it's the only way to get out from under. Some of them may be depressed for other reasons, such as the loss of a job, but they're convinced that their debt is what's causing their depression. Typically, what they need is credit counseling, debt restructuring, and reassurance that things will get better. Bankruptcy definitely does not promote self-esteem, and it leaves a black mark on your credit record for up to ten years.

If you believe your debt load is insurmountable, or you think it will restrict you financially and emotionally for many years, then bankruptcy may be a reasonable alternative. Wiping the slate clean and starting over can give you a healthier outlook. Some firms readily extend credit to bankrupt people, operating under the theory that they can't claim bankruptcy again for seven years. Life is not over after bankruptcy, but you will have a new set of difficulties. For instance, declaring bankruptcy makes obtaining or refinancing a mortgage a real nightmare.

Frugality Footnote

There are two types of bankruptcy, Chapter 13 and Chapter 7. Chapter 13 consists of developing a plan to repay debts over a period of three to five years during which the court keeps a watchful eye. A household budget is formed, and creditors receive what is left after basic expenditures. You may be able to keep part or all of your assets. On the other hand, Chapter 7 filing is straight bankruptcy that liquidates most of your assets and frees you of all debts. You can generally keep the equity in your home, car, household goods, and jewelry.

If you must file for bankruptcy, see a qualified bankruptcy lawyer, especially if you have a complicated situation. Be sure the lawyer explains your options, and doesn't just push you into filing.

You do have options. You got yourself into this mess, and bankruptcy is not the only way you can get yourself out. Consider calling your creditors and honestly explaining your situation. They are likely to work out a payment plan with you rather than have to charge your debt off. If that doesn't work, contact the Consumer Credit Counseling Service in your area (800-388-2227). Even if you're determined to declare bankruptcy, at least let the dust settle for a few months. Given time, your finances could change dramatically.

Cheap Shot

Unless you haven't eaten for a few days, never take a cash advance on a credit card. Not only will you pay a higher finance charge on this money, but you will generally be charged a 2% to 4% extra fee for the privilege.

Get the Credit You Deserve

A cheapskate knows how important it is to establish a good credit standing early on. Without a good credit rating, you can have a hard time buying a home which, especially after you've paid it off, is the best investment you can make. Also, everyone has a few money crunches during their lifetimes, and you may need some cash fast. It may be for something positive like a great investment opportunity or for something not so positive, like an illness. Credit can be a lifesaver in an emergency, so it behooves you to keep your credit clean and be able to borrow fast if you need to.

To get the credit you deserve, there are really only two steps you have to take:

1. Buy a few things with credit or borrow money from a bank.
2. Pay off your debts in a timely manner.

To give you an example of how important timely payments can be, let me tell you a short story. I was just out of college and wanted to establish a good credit rating so I could borrow for a few investments. The first thing I did was go to a local banker I knew and ask for a $5,000 loan on a thirty-day note using my car as collateral. Twenty days later I repaid the loan plus interest and my banker was pleasantly surprised. Bankers love cheapskates who make early paybacks. He promptly raised my credit limit to $15,000 even though I only had about $7,000 of collateral in my car.

A month later I went back and borrowed the entire $15,000. The banker gave me the loan, this time with a year to pay it back. I paid the loan off early and again they upped my credit line. After I'd done this a few times, I established a credit line of over $40,000 and I was just 22 years old! I was out a little interest money, but I'd established a great credit rating and a $40,000 line of credit which I used several years later to purchase some investment property.

This was years ago, when it was almost impossible for someone out of college to establish credit. Today, credit lending policies at most banks and other financial institutions are much more lenient. It's easier to get a loan today, but the point is that only if you establish a good record will it be there for a rainy day.

Mop Up Messy Credit

Do your best to avoid the small mistakes that may put you on the books as a credit deadbeat. One common mistake is letting a small balance on a credit card carry over for another month because you don't want to write a check for so little. To credit raters, it's not the amount that matters, it's the fact you missed a payment. One thirty-day-late blemish on your record can ruin your chances to get any kind of credit in the future.

Sometimes you can get a blemish on your credit rating through no fault of your own. For instance, if you shop for a car and go to several different dealers, each one may do an inquiry into your credit. If several of those inquiries show up on your report in a short period of time, you could be denied the credit you want because it can look like you're seeking to borrow far more than your credit profile says you can pay back.

The consumer credit business is huge. Right now, credit reporting agencies are keeping tabs on over $1 trillion worth of consumer debt. The job of tracking all this credit falls to just a few agencies. For the most part, they do a pretty good job, but just a few errors turning up in your credit report can mean major problems. A recent study by Consolidated Information Services reported that as many as 50 million Americans have one or more errors on their credit report.

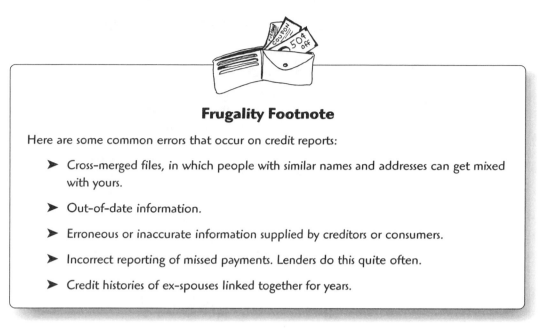

Frugality Footnote

Here are some common errors that occur on credit reports:

➤ Cross-merged files, in which people with similar names and addresses can get mixed with yours.

➤ Out-of-date information.

➤ Erroneous or inaccurate information supplied by creditors or consumers.

➤ Incorrect reporting of missed payments. Lenders do this quite often.

➤ Credit histories of ex-spouses linked together for years.

To check your credit rating and see if there are any errors in your report, contact the credit reporting bureaus below. If you have been denied credit within the last 30 days, they are required to send you a free report. If not, there is a small charge.

➤ Experian Information Services
Credit Reports
P.O. Box 2104
Allen, TX 75013
1-888-397-3742

➤ Trans Union Corporation
Consumer Disclosure Center
P.O. Box 390
Springfield, PA 19064
1-800-888-4213

➤ Equifax Information Services
P.O. Box 740241
Atlanta, GA 30374
1-800-997-2493

If you find errors on your report, notify the bureau immediately. Under the law, they must investigate and correct their mistakes. If they find the errors to be in your favor, they will send an updated report to you and the businesses that requested reports

Cheap Trick

The best way to guarantee a healthy credit rating is to maintain the cheapskate habit of always paying on time.

within the previous six months. If you have a special situation that may need to be explained to potential creditors, you have the right to attach a statement to your report.

Contrary to popular belief, there isn't a "credit rating" number in your file. Decisions on whether or not to accept you as a credit risk are up to the individual lenders. While one blemish on your credit report may not keep you from getting credit, a pattern of late payments may. Any delinquency you incur will stay in your file for up to seven years. If you do have some late payments or other credit problems, let the lender know what to expect when they look at your file, and give them an explanation. They will be more sympathetic if they know you are being honest with them.

The Least You Need to Know

➤ If you are up to your eyeballs in debt, create a plan to eliminate as much as possible in the coming years.

➤ Fill out the "Get Out of Debt Worksheet" to become totally debt-free in five to seven years.

➤ If you can't figure out how to get out of debt yourself, seek dependable help.

➤ Buy all your consumer goods with cash.

➤ Never declare bankruptcy unless you have explored all your other options and you have no choice.

➤ Order your credit report from the three major credit reporting agencies to see if there are any errors.

Part 2
Guerrilla Shopping Strategies

The motto of the American shopper is "Shop 'til you drop." Just hearing the word "sale" gives us a big adrenaline rush, but most people don't really know how to take advantage of one. Enter the savvy cheapskate, who is light years ahead of the average consumer. In these chapters, you'll learn how to be a better shopper using cheapskate strategies and tricks that leave average consumers in the dust.

Find out how to save bundles on shopping for groceries and household items by using a list, buying in bulk, staying away from name brands, and learning about supermarket schemes to get you to spend more than you have to. Chapter 6 will show you how to dress yourself and your family for success by staying away from fancy labels, shopping at outlets and thrift stores, and buying at the right times of the year. Don't forget one of your biggest purchases, cars. You'll learn why cheapskates never buy new cars in Chapter 7, how to negotiate the best deal possible if you do, used car traps to avoid, and how to maintain your chariot for less by finding the best deals on servicing. Finally, you'll see how cheapskates research everything, especially big ticket items, before they buy in Chapter 8. Find out how to shop from your armchair, and get great cheapskate guidance on the best places to buy just about everything.

Chapter 5

Markdown on Peas, Aisle 4... Markdown on Peas

In This Chapter

➤ Getting ready for grocery shopping on the cheap

➤ The wonderful world of coupons

➤ Supermarket secrets

➤ Cashing in on bargain brand bonanzas

➤ Finding the "real" price on products

➤ Making the most of the food you have

The truly savvy cheapskate knows that one of the best times to save money is while pushing a shopping cart down the grocery store aisles. There are lots of ways to save on groceries, not all of them obvious to the untrained eye.

If you shop right, you can slash your grocery bill in half without sacrificing the nutrition your family needs. By organizing your supermarket shopping sprees more carefully, you can save hundreds of dollars, and you won't have to live on Beanie Weenies or macaroni and cheese either.

Frugality Footnote

The typical American family spends about $10,000 to $15,000 per year on food...more money than it cost to buy a car or even a new house just a generation ago!

In other words, you can have your cake and eat it, too, only this time you'll do it in cheapskate fashion by spending a lot less than you do now. So, get ready to cruise the aisles with a new awareness and insight that will make you the envy of grocery shoppers everywhere.

List It, and You'll Resist It

A lot of people enter the grocery store, list in hand, thinking they have everything organized. Unfortunately, most of them end up filling their carts with items they had no intention of buying. Purchasing a few extra items you don't really need is understandable, but statistics show that the average shopper leaves the grocery store having bought about a dozen things they didn't plan to buy.

Cheap Shot

Most grocery stores are masters at marketing their products in sneaky ways. For instance, they stock the items they really want you to buy at eye level. They know you are more apt to buy if you don't have to bend over or get on your tiptoes to get a product off the shelves. Don't get taken in by end-of-the-aisle displays, either. Most of the time, they are only overstocked items at regular prices.

How does this compute in dollars and cents? No matter how carefully they plan their grocery shopping, most people will spend about $2,000 per year on impulse items!

Cheapskates, on the other hand, make a shopping list and stick to it. They spend an hour or so during the week clipping a few coupons, evaluating their food supply, and generally organizing their next grocery store visit. When it comes to actual shopping time, they know exactly what they need. Not only do lists make their shopping visit more cost efficient, but they also save them a great deal of time trying to decide what they need and don't need.

It's no coincidence that bread, milk, and other frequently purchased items are located on opposite ends of the market. Managers know this will make you walk across the entire store, improving the odds that you'll buy something you don't need. They also know that most shoppers are unorganized and wander through the aisles because their shopping lists are a hodgepodge of loosely organized items. To avoid this, and save a considerable amount of time, cheapskates group items on their lists: For instance, all fruits and veggies should be together, all baking goods together, and all meats together. If you group the things on your list, you'll be less likely to go back and forth through the store and be tempted by an impulse buy. You'll also save about fifteen minutes in shopping time and around $10 to $15 in unplanned purchases.

When you walk into any grocery store, look for store fliers that list current sales. You may even want to pick them up *before* you make out your shopping list. It's a good way to plan your food purchases and stock up on staples.

Frugality Footnote

Americans buy more Coke and Pepsi than any other single food product. An average of $140 is spent every year on these soft drinks per American family. More than cereal, meat, cheese, and milk. That's a lot of sugar to be pumping into our bodies and a lot of dollar bills to be wasting. Smart cheapskates keep their soft drink bill low, and only consume soda on special occasions.

The Great Coupon Bonanza

When most people think of saving at the grocery store, the first thing that comes to mind is using coupons. Coupons are the manufacturers' way of getting consumers to buy their products. Because most manufacturers build the cost of coupons into their products, you're technically paying *too much* if you don't use a coupon. No doubt coupons can save you money, but there are some major drawbacks to using them. The cheapskate uses coupons but knows when to hold 'em and when to fold 'em.

For one thing, cheapskates know they could spend endless hours clipping and organizing their coupons, which is not an activity that ranks high on their priority list. For another, coupons—and the idea of getting a bargain—make it easy to buy products you don't want or regularly use. If you don't watch out, you can end up spending much more than necessary.

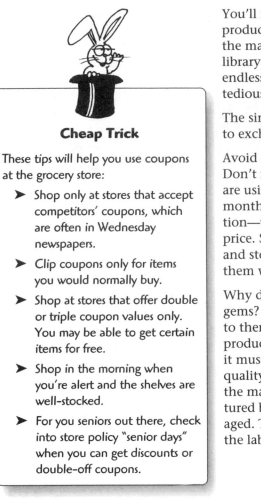

You'll find coupons in magazines, newspapers, on product packages—and sometimes they even come in the mail. Coupon exchanges in stores or at your local library are another good source, but searching through endless piles and checking expiration dates can be tedious.

The simplest way to get the coupons you really want is to exchange them with friends and relatives.

Avoid a common mistake often made with coupons: Don't redeem them too soon. Wait until the item you are using a coupon for is on sale, generally about a month or two after the coupon appears in a publication—that way you get the cents-off on top of the sale price. So the best strategy is to get a small accordion file and stockpile your favorite coupons so you can use them when the sales start.

Why do so many people overlook generic supermarket gems? I think it's because people prefer what is familiar to them. Most people get their information on food products from television—they think that if it's on TV, it must be good. They believe they are getting better quality, but they've been sold a bill of goods. The fact is the majority of generic and house brands are manufactured by the name-brand companies and just repackaged. The only difference between the two are the how the labels look.

Cheap Trick

These tips will help you use coupons at the grocery store:

➤ Shop only at stores that accept competitors' coupons, which are often in Wednesday newspapers.

➤ Clip coupons only for items you would normally buy.

➤ Shop at stores that offer double or triple coupon values only. You may be able to get certain items for free.

➤ Shop in the morning when you're alert and the shelves are well-stocked.

➤ For you seniors out there, check into store policy "senior days" when you can get discounts or double-off coupons.

Frugality Footnote

Here's a great example of a typical savings: A brand-name cereal costing $3.99 offered a coupon for 75¢ off in the Sunday paper. About a month later, after a local grocery store had overstocked the cereal due to this coupon advertisement, they put the cereal on sale for $1.99. Taking advantage of the sale and the coupon offer you would have saved about 70%. If you'd used the coupon immediately you would have saved only 20%.

If you use coupons frequently, like most cheapskates, find a local store that has double- or triple-coupon days (the store credits your bill with double or triple the face value of the coupon). These offers can *really* save you a bundle. Some stores limit the allowable deduction per coupon to one dollar. Even so, you can still easily save $10 to $15 per grocery store visit if you take advantage of the special days. If you combine these savings with other strategies, you may even be able to get many items for free!

Above all, don't be swayed by the marketing hype behind coupons—sometimes you really have to look closely at the savings they offer and compare them to the deal you can get buying store brands or generic products. Many times the generic product is a better buy than the name-brand product, even if you buy the name brand with a coupon. It's important to look at coupons as a part of your entire cheapskate plan and not the only means saving at the grocery store.

Cheap Talk

Store-brand and *generic* products on the grocery store shelves are often just repackaged name-brand products. If they are not the exact same product, they are likely to have been manufactured at the same factory as the name brand and have similar product traits.

I Like the Colorful Package!

Cheapskates aren't influenced by pretty packaging. They know that one of the ways grocery stores and manufacturers get you to buy their products is through creating the illusion of better quality. Cereal is a great example. They put flashy advertising on television, make the packaging look great, and then mark the price up 50 percent and make you pay for all the pomp and circumstance. Why should you subsidize *their* promotion costs? Unfortunately, many unenlightened consumers believe that if the packaging looks so good, the product inside must be top quality. But that's not always so. Most of the time, you are just paying for a fancy label, not better quality food.

Champion cheapskates pay special attention to generic and store-brand items when they want to save a bundle. You may not see colorful labels on the package or even have heard of the name, but if you are looking for savings, try them out. You'll get a much better deal, about 25 percent on average, on generic and house brands.

Cheap Shot

Cereal is one of the biggest rip-offs out there. When you see some cereals selling for $4.99, you have to wonder if there are flakes or gold nuggets in these boxes! Never buy cereal in a slick marketed box unless you have a $1 off or better coupon. Buy generic or store-brand cereal or the name brands in plastic bags. You'll save significantly on your breakfast costs by doing this. Also consider buying plain oatmeal or Malt-o-Meal as an alternative to packaged cereals.

Most people have different preferences about what they may or may not like in off-brand products. Here are just a few things you can buy at savings of up to 50% that are almost always the same quality as the name brands:

Flour	Sugar
Trash bags	Tin foil
Ammonia	Bleach
Salt	Pepper
Vinegar	Light bulbs
Baking soda	Beans
Paper towels	Popcorn
Rice	Cat litter
Dog food	Tea
Butter	Ice cream
All spices	Oils
Lemonade	Orange juice
Tuna	And more!

Keep your eyes peeled for others. You may need to test a few products to see which ones suit you the best.

Bulky Buys

Buying in bulk is the cheapskate's idea of a great way to save money and needless trips to the grocery store. By joining a wholesale merchandising club, such as Sam's Club or Costco, you can realize substantial savings on products you purchase in large quantities. If you compare the prices on the exact same products to national supermarket chains, clubs win hands down. On average, the smart cheapskate will save about 20 to 30 percent a year, and all for a measly $30–$40 a year membership fee.

Beware of getting overenthusiastic about the idea of buying in bulk. When you feel you're getting unbelievable prices, the impulse buying urge goes into hyperdrive. This is one of the things wholesale merchandising

Cheap Trick

Use some cheapskate discipline. Don't strap your budget trying to buy everything in bulk. You don't want to put off your rent payment because you spent your paycheck on a 10-year supply of cornmeal. And make sure you'll use all the product you purchased. Don't buy more than you know you'll use before the product goes stale.

clubs thrive on, just like regular grocery stores do. They want to get you into the store, get you pumped up, and then sell you everything but the kitchen sink. If you want to be a champion cheapskate, it's up to you to be savvy enough to buy only those items you truly need. The goal is to beat them at their own game. Armed with solid cheapskate knowledge, it's easy to do.

Reading the Fine Print Adds Up to Crisp Bills

When you're shopping, pay special attention to unit pricing. This lets you compare different products according to how the units in ounces, servings, or pounds are priced. Many stores will boldly display the price of a packaged product, and put the unit price in small print. Remember that the unit price is the true price.

When you look at a product, do you naturally assume that the larger size is a better buy? This is not always the case. The only way you can really tell is by checking the unit price below or next to the retail price. It is almost always there, and just not as prominent. If you take a moment to compare the unit prices of different-sized products, you can save quite a bit.

Cheapskates know it doesn't hurt to do some price comparisons. Shopping for green beans, you can save over $1.00 per pound buying a store brand. On corn flakes, you can save over $2.00 per pound on one of the name brands by buying a family sized 18-ounce box rather than purchasing individual packs. Here's how unit pricing helps you shop:

Cheap Shot

Watch out for product downsizing. Manufacturers are stepping up the practice of keeping the price the same but giving you less product. Just because some coffee manufacturers sell coffee in the same size cans doesn't mean they have the same amount of coffee in them. Look for downsizing in condensed milk, canned tuna, paper towels, baby food, and hundreds of other products. Compare unit pricing and you can avoid being tricked, and save as much as 50%.

Saving with Store Brands and Using Unit Pricing

Item	Price ($)	Unit Price ($)
Store-brand frozen green beans in 10-ounce package	.68	1.09 per pound
Name-brand frozen green beans in 10-ounce package	1.19	2.12 per pound
Name-brand corn flakes in 18-ounce box	1.49	1.32 per pound
Name-brand corn flakes in individual .75 ounce packs	1.35	3.60 per pound

When you compare the unit pricing of the same products you'll usually find that they're cheaper at a wholesale club than at a grocery store. However, if you are trying to save by buying in larger quantities at the supermarket, it is often hard to pinpoint the best deals.

The Meat of the Savings

Unless you're a vegetarian, the single biggest expense in your food budget is meat and poultry. One of every three dollars you spend goes to buying steaks, ground beef, chicken, pork and other meaty delights. If you happen to be one of the estimated 250 million meateaters in this county, you are probably spending over $2,500 per year in this area, but you don't have to become a vegetarian to cut your meat bills.

You can beef up your savings to over $500 per year just by following a few strategies of cheapskate carnivores.

Don't overlook the fact that meat prices fluctuate by the season, just like vegetables. During the summer picnic and grilling season, steaks and ground beef are generally higher, and roast cuts go down in price because they're more popular as winter meals. If you have an extra freezer, you can save as much as 20 percent on meat by buying in bulk just before or after a season.

Example: Stockpile steaks and ground beef in April before the peak summer months hit. In August, stock up on winter meats, such as pork chops, roasts, and steaks. If you don't have storage room for bulk purchases, save by going against the grain and buying and cooking off-season cuts.

Frugality Footnote

It's usually better to buy a more expensive cut of meat that has little or no fat or other waste. On average you pay only about 10% more, but you get about 20% to 30% more to eat.

One way cheapskates save a bundle on meat is to buy larger cuts and do their own slicing. For example, if you buy a complete piece of meat—say a side or a quarter—rather than individual cuts, you will generally save about 30 percent per pound. At home, simply cut it into individual steaks, briskets, or whatever, and freeze them in meal-sized packages.

Don't overlook this technique for poultry. Buy whole chickens and cut them up if you want to save even more. You can pay up to $4 a pound for boneless and skinless breasts, but you can get a whole chicken for as little as 80¢ a pound.

Consider buying your meats in family-pack sizes. Larger quantities mean higher savings. Again, freeze what you don't use immediately, and take advantage of the savings at a later date. Some cheapskates even go to cattle auctions where you can get full side of beef for a quarter of what grocery stores charge. Usually, an outside company will freeze and store the meat for you for up to a year. If you live near cattle country, this is the cheapest route of all.

If you are a vegetarian or health food nut, you can save, too. You may *want* to buy many of your groceries at a local health food store, but you'll usually find pretty high prices. To keep your costs down, look for a health food store that is large and sells in quantity. If you shop smart, you can get many healthy items from your regular grocery store in special healthy and organic produce sections.

Eat What You Got

One way cheapskates save on their grocery bills every year is to cut down on the amount of food they throw away. Of course, you can't always avoid the green fuzzy stuff growing in your refrigerator or the can of beans that's been in the pantry for three years. But with proper planning you can reduce or even completely eliminate wasting food.

With these cheapskate guidelines you can reduce the amount of food you waste by about 5 percent:

Cheap Trick

Air trapped in plastic bags shortens the life of food being preserved. To get rid of excess air from a storage bag try a couple of cheapskate tricks: First, if the bag is sealed using a twist tie, simply bunch up the top of the bag and suck the air out and then tie the bag immediately. You will see the bag surround the food before your eyes. Second, if you are using a zipper-lock bag, fold the top of the bag over the food and then lock.

➤ Always shop at grocery stores that take good care of their food. You never want to take home food that has been damaged or improperly stored. Chances are that some of it will quickly become inedible. Don't buy refrigerated items that are lukewarm, canned goods with dents and bulges, crushed boxes, or frozen goods that aren't frozen solid. If you are shopping at a store that seems to have a lot of damaged goods, shop somewhere else.

➤ Never buy more food than you can use in a reasonable amount of time. If you are buying in bulk, be smart about coordinating expiration dates with your eating habits. Nothing is worse than having frozen food that gets freezer burn after just a few months. That type of mistake can blow your grocery budget for the whole year.

➤ When you cook, make enough food for two meals. The reason: Leftovers are much cheaper than buying for entire new meals. You'll also save yourself preparation time. Store leftovers in good quality containers, and they'll last three or four days. Then pull them out and add one new dish for a little variety. If you want to wait a while before you eat the same dish again, freeze the leftovers in the smallest containers that will hold them to ensure freshness.

➤ It's best to thaw food in the refrigerator, especially if you're planning leftovers—if you leave perishable food thawing for more than a couple hours, it can easily become contaminated.

Cheap Shot

Never, ever refreeze food that has been previously frozen and thawed. If you do, you run the risk of contaminating the food.

➤ Clean and organize your refrigerator, pantry, and cabinets regularly. A good cleaning can reveal items you don't use often and probably shouldn't purchase again. You should also organize by grouping products by type—for example, milk and orange juice can go in the refrigerator door, butter and mayonnaise on the top shelf, fruits and veggies on the second shelf, and so on, so they aren't overlooked and left to deteriorate.

Cheap Thrills on Groceries

➤ Don't know how much you really spend on food each month? Simply designate an envelope for all your grocery receipts in and then go back and analyze them at the end of the month. Separate what you may have spent on toothpaste, soap, etc. What's left is your food budget.

➤ Never buy toiletries at the grocery store. The prices are generally marked-up about 25 percent. The best place to purchase these products are the discount drug stores, such as CVS, Revco, or even general discount stores, such as Walmart and Target.

➤ Why do convenience stores have great deals on coffee and drinks? Because they know most people who go in for these beverages usually buy one or two additional items at 50 to 100 percent more than regular grocery stores charge. Don't ever purchase anything but coffee and soft drinks at a convenience store, or you might just as well take dollar bills and burn them one by one. Smart cheapskates don't carry matches.

➤ Limit your major grocery shopping to once every two weeks. It's a good way to check your impulse-buying tendencies and also save a lot of time. You can pick up items such as milk, eggs, and perishable meats when you need them. Just remember: Don't buy them at a convenience store.

➤ Avoid shopping for groceries on an empty stomach, or you'll probably spend 10 to 15 percent more. Again, make a list and stick to it. This practice will curb any impulse-buying desires you may have. Also, if you can avoid it, don't go shopping with your spouse or kids. A cheapskate's grocery shopping is hard enough without having the temptations of several others to deal with.

➤ You'll pay 15 to 60 percent more for products that include added sugar, seasonings, and other extras you can easily mix yourself at a lower cost. Pre-sweetened cereals are probably the best example. You typically pay about 50 percent more for a box of frosted corn flakes compared to regular corn flakes. The only difference in quality is the sugar coating. You are better off if you buy the regular corn flakes and pour a cup of sugar into each bowl. Yuck, can you believe we eat this stuff? Also, beware of frozen vegetables. A bag that includes its own sauce or seasoning costs about 60 percent more than the same size bag without the sauce. Plain versions also have less fat.

Cheap Trick

Always check the "reduced" section of the grocery store. This is where they put packaged goods that are day-old bakery items, and other slightly askew products. If there is something you need in this section, check it carefully to make sure it passes your quality test.

➤ Look for meat, fish, and poultry that have reached the "last day of sale" marked on their packaging. If you eat them within a day, you will generally realize savings of as much as 50 percent.

➤ For top quality produce, shop at a nearby farmers' market. Since the general quality of most store-bought fruits and vegetables has been declining steadily over the last several decades, farmers' markets are a smart stop. Most allow you to haggle a little bit and take home food that will increase your family's nutritional well being.

➤ One of the easiest ways to blow a food budget is to buy expensive snacks. Here are just a few cheap alternatives to the chips, candies, and desserts so many people buy at the grocery store: Popcorn, pretzels (fat-free, too), graham crackers, celery, carrots, Popsicles made from fruit juice, and pound cake. If you are a candy nut, buy candy in bulk after Halloween, Valentine's Day, and Easter.

➤ If you make casseroles often, consider buying economy brands for the ingredients. Often, they make no difference in the taste of the dish because it's all mixed together anyway.

➤ Consider using potatoes more often with your meals. They are inexpensive and offer a great deal of nutrition. A potato with some healthy toppings can be a meal in itself.

➤ Buy orange juice in frozen concentrated form rather than in the carton. A cheapskate is willing to do a little mixing in order to save about 60 percent.

➤ Create your own garden in the backyard to provide inexpensive and nutritious vegetables and herbs. If you have a green thumb, this beats buying at the store hands down. To see if a garden is the thing for you, try planting just a few tomatoes and then work up from there.

The Least You Need to Know

➤ Always grocery shop with a list and avoid impulse buying by understanding the tricks of the product manufacturers and supermarkets.

➤ Use manufacturer coupons only on products you normally use or when you can save more overall.

➤ Pay special attention to store brand and generic products. They will save you a bundle.

➤ Buy in bulk, but check the unit pricing to make sure you are really saving. Also, buy only what you can use in a reasonable amount of time.

➤ Organize your kitchen to avoid as much food waste as possible.

➤ To save on meat and poultry, buy in quantity, be your own butcher, and freeze what you want to use later.

Chapter 6

Rags to Riches for the Smart Clothes Shopper

In This Chapter

➤ Cheapskate secrets to always getting the best clothes deals

➤ Mixing and matching to produce an ever-expanding wardrobe

➤ A guide to cheap but stylish outfits for men, women, and children

➤ Foil fat-cat designers' plans to put you in the poorhouse

➤ Know each season's biggest bargains

Unfortunately we live in a society that is very image conscious. Let's face it, many people judge a person by their appearance, especially in business situations. Likewise, the way we dress can affect our image of ourselves. Champion cheapskates do a great job of presenting a stylish and savvy image, but they can do it on a sensible budget.

Most people are suckered in by Madison Avenue designers and go overboard on looking good. But running out to buy the latest designer clothing to impress others is the surest way to break your bank account. Once you've bankrupted your budget, you could find yourself all dressed up with nowhere to go. Cheapskates always look put together no matter what they wear, because they know how to look smart on a budget that fits their wallets.

If you really understand what you like and need in clothes, you can build a flattering wardrobe that's also practical, and you don't have to spend a fortune to do it. Basically, you have two choices: You can spend 10 to 15 percent of your household budget on having the latest and greatest designer stuff, or you can spend about 5 percent on clothes and still look great. It's up to you.

Dressed to Kill Without Killing Your Piggy Bank

The first step in buying clothing the cheapskate way is the same as for buying anything else: Do your homework first. Begin your wardrobe planning by taking a look in your closets and drawers and assessing your needs. Review what you have a few times a year, then throw out the old, mend the torn, and decide what you really need to purchase. At the end of this process, you may even realize that you don't need anything new at all!

Frugality Footnote

The smart cheapskate often buys clothes that can be used year-round. For example, by rolling up the sleeves on long-sleeved shirts, you can wear them in summer as well as winter. Jeans can be worn throughout the year, and a coat with a zip-out lining can be used for both fall and winter.

"Mix and match" when you can. Buy different separates that work as several different outfits for half the cost. For instance, for women, just seven pieces of clothing—a navy blue skirt, blue blazer, gray tweed skirt, a white blouse, a light blue blouse, a pair of navy slacks, and a sweater vest—can make as many as fifteen different outfits! Simply base your wardrobe on some of your favorite colors and fabrics, and make sure your new purchases fit into your basic mix-and-match pieces.

Whenever possible, add style to your look with inexpensive jewelry, belts, ties, scarves, and shoes. These items can expand your wardrobe significantly without costing a fortune. You can change the look of a suit with a new tie, shoes, or suspenders, while a simple navy dress can go from casual to sophisticated by adding a strand of pearls or a classy scarf. Always buy your accessories at discount stores and outlets and choose classic styles that will stand the test of time. Make sure that whatever you buy is of good enough quality to last for years.

But whatever you do, avoid getting caught up in fads. Cheapskates know that fads in clothing come and go as fast as the seasons change. If you wear fashion classics, such as the navy blue suit, white silk blouse, knitted vest, neutral overcoat, and the like, you will save a tremendous amount of money and never get caught in what are obviously last year's fashions. By devoting most of your wardrobe dollar to the classics, you may even have enough left over to splurge on that funky fad outfit without jeopardizing your cheapskate status.

Women Had BETTER Bargain Hunt

We've talked about some basics when buying clothes. Now it's time to get down to the nitty-gritty. In general, women's clothes cost more than men's—even for similar types of garments. This doesn't seem fair, and it *isn't*. But manufacturers know that women shop more for clothes than men do, and they are willing to pay higher prices. Still, with a few good techniques and some shopping ingenuity, women can level the playing field to get around this unfair price structure.

First, be prepared to set up—and stick to—a strict budget (but do set aside a few extra dollars for that must-have dress or pair of slacks. This will make your budget realistic, and won't throw everything off-kilter if you decide to buy one or two extra items a year.). When you do buy, always think about what's in your closet and how the item you are buying will coordinate. A new blazer is not a bargain if you have to buy a new blouse and skirt to go with it because it doesn't match anything else you have.

In general, the simpler your outfits, the easier to add complementary pieces to mix and match with them. Don't buy clothes with decorations all over them. Beads, fur, and other trim increases the cost of items and makes them harder to coordinate with your wardrobe. It's a much better idea to buy plain outfits and dress them up in your own style using jewelry, belts, and scarves.

If you are one of those "I must have the latest fashions" women, don't buy any apparel the minute it hits the stores. Wait for three or four months. By then, most new fashions have come down in price and also been copied by several other manufacturers. Buying at the end of the season will save you a bundle. In general, avoid buying very much in the larger stores; women's departments are the most overpriced. For items like casual clothes, socks, and T-shirts, shop in the men's or boy's departments.

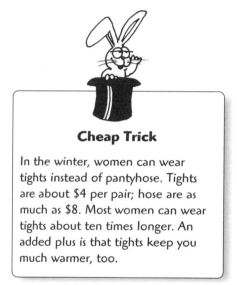

Cheap Trick

In the winter, women can wear tights instead of pantyhose. Tights are about $4 per pair; hose are as much as $8. Most women can wear tights about ten times longer. An added plus is that tights keep you much warmer, too.

How to Spot Quality and Value in Women's Clothes

One of the most important things to consider when buying women's clothes is the balance of quality and value. The following tips should help you make the right buying decisions:

➤ Pleats in skirts should be smooth along the hips—they should never gap open.

➤ When you try on a coat or jacket, bend your arms. The sleeves should come to your wrists.

Cheap Shot

Whatever you buy, make sure that comfort is your first priority. Don't buy that great-looking outfit that you can't sit down or walk easily in. It may look great in the dress shop, but once the newness wears off, you will be left with an outfit that gathers dust in the closet.

➤ When trying on a new coat, make sure you wear the bulkiest garment you intend to wear under it. You should have plenty of room to move your arms.

➤ When you buy a suit jacket, check to make sure the shoulder pads stay in place. Take the jacket on and off several times. If the pads need constant adjusting, you are dealing with a poorly constructed garment.

➤ Jacket lapels that are flattened or even stiff are a good sign that you'd better stay away. Lapels should be soft and rounded and should keep their shape even if you crumple them.

➤ Sit down when you try on a skirt. There should be enough room in it to avoid creases across the front from sitting.

➤ The waistbands for most skirts should fit snugly, with no indication that they will roll over.

➤ Any hems on a garment should fall smoothly without any unevenness or rippling, and the stitching should be invisible to the naked eye. However, if you find a garment that is otherwise a good buy, except for hemline problems, go ahead and buy it—you can always fix the hem (or have it done).

➤ Zippers should lay flat and be totally covered on any garment.

➤ Buttons should be functional and, if intended, match the look of the garment.

The Man Wants to Stay in the Cave

On the whole, men tend to shy away from shopping for clothes, which gives them a few distinct advantages when they *do* venture out to the clothing stores. Shopping for men can be much easier, in part because they don't face the huge variety that women do—not to mention that the pricing structure for men's clothes is much more favorable. And while women's fashions change from one season to the next, men's clothing styles stay in fashion for much longer.

For men, as with women, it's best to stick with a classic look in expensive clothes and complement with inexpensive accessories. Since most men's stores are simply designed, it's easy for men to shop at the best discount store and not make too many mistakes. If you find an unbelievable deal on suits, shirts, or slacks, it's a good idea to stock up. Often, men's clothes will be marked down 70 percent or more.

For a very small investment, you can be formal, businesslike, or casual—all with the same suit. How? Use the power of ties. On the holidays you can be festive with a special occasion tie, and during the summer months, add a little zing at the office with a splashy floral tie. You can pick up a top quality silk tie for as little as $10 at some outlet stores.

And ties aren't the only way to spice up your wardrobe. For a new look, try some patterned socks, or buy a new pair of shoes. When they need new shoes, cheapskates don't skimp. If you buy a top-quality pair of shoes and take good care of them, they will last for ten years or more and be much less expensive in the long run.

Cheap Trick

Join a club or go to a store that rewards you for frequent under garment purchases. If you call various clothing stores in your area, you will find one that has rewards such as free hosiery and underwear when you purchase several items. However, it's important their clothing is a good value to begin with.

How to Spot Quality and Value in Men's Clothes

One of the most important things to consider when buying men's clothes is the balance of quality and value. The following tips should help you make the right buying decisions:

➤ Make sure there is felt backing stitched into the collar of any shirt or jacket.

➤ Zippers should be sewn in straight and lay flat.

➤ A well-made shirt should have two rows of stitching under the sleeves and along the sides.

➤ Extra fabric in suits is a sign of good quality and value. Make sure there is a minimum of one inch extra fabric in pant seams and jacket sleeves.

➤ On a good suit, stitching should be tight and not pull too much when you tug on it. If you see a seam that looks like it will unravel easily, don't buy it.

➤ Buttonholes should have several rows of stitching around them to avoid any tearing. The buttons should also be reinforced with extra stitching, and there should be extra buttons sewn to the bottom of any shirt.

➤ In better quality suits, look for lining in the upper part of the pants. This adds years of wear and also comfort.

➤ Squeeze jacket lapels. If they don't spring back to their original shape, don't buy the jacket or suit.

➤ All good pants have a second button inside the fly on the left. This keeps pressure off the waistband.

➤ If a jacket doesn't lay flat on your shoulders, put it back. There is no way it can be altered to look and fit right.

Wow! Look at the Label in This One!

Cheapskates know that a designer label doesn't always mean better quality, but they *are* always accompanied by a price tag that's 20 to 30 percent higher than the store-label equivalent. Although a top designer may have designed and made the dress or suit you buy, other items carrying the designer's name are almost always made by another manufacturer. Shoes, coats, hats, purses, and bathing suits are commonly "farmed out" to other companies that may not have the same quality standards as the designer. Sometimes an item is worth the extra price, but more often you are just paying for the name. Scrutinize these items just as you would any other purchase.

Cheap Talk

Private-label garments and goods are purchased directly from the manufacturer and then have store labels sewn into them. Because stores buy directly from the factory and cut out the middleman, private-label merchandise is much cheaper.

The best route for any cheapskate is private-label merchandise. Many stores position their private-label garments to be competitive with a designer label, but then greatly reduce the price to attract buyers. Most of this merchandise will be sold "on sale." Very few designer labels are sold at discounted prices except during seasonal clearances.

The bottom line: Never buy private-label clothes and accessories at the list price. They should always be bought at a significant discount, preferably 50 to 60 percent. Don't get caught up in the "sale" game, because an item "on sale" doesn't always mean it's a good deal. A private label dress may normally sell for $100 and be discounted 40 percent. You pay $60 and think you just got the deal of the century. Actually, the wholesale cost of the dress was probably about $25 to $30. Does $60 still sound like a good deal?

If you absolutely *must* have the $60 dress, go ahead and buy it, but be aware if you wait a little longer, the store will eventually mark it down 20 percent more. The store needs to make a profit, but even at 60 percent off they still come out ahead of the game. If you consistently overpay the store, you will be headed for the Cheapskate Hall of Shame.

Dressing Junior

Children's clothing can be very expensive, especially if you are prone to making your kids look like the latest Polo poster child. Children outgrow and wear out their clothes in what seems like no time, so buying expensive outfits for them isn't worth the money. Instead, look for sales on clothes that are durable and may be a few sizes too big. With the kids' fashions of today, they'll probably love things a few sizes too big. There are also many alternative sources for children's clothing, such as Goodwill and the Salvation Army. Also, scouting out neighborhood garage sales can yield barely worn clothing at great prices.

Kids' clothing can be handed down and around, and acquired from friends and relatives. This can be an especially good way to save if you have several kids. Borrowing is big, too. For instance, you can always borrow a boy's suit from a friend or relative for the rare times Junior needs to look spiffy. The same goes for your young princess that must look ravishing at her school dance.

'Tis the Season

One of the ways cheapskates save big bucks on clothes is buying at the right time of the year. For instance, right after Christmas is one of the best times to buy. Retailers want to unload overstocked merchandise that didn't sell during the holidays to make room for the new spring clothing line that will hit the stores soon.

Cheap Shot

Resist the temptation to buy kids fancy shoes at inflated prices. Since they often grow out of them in two to three months it is important to be cautious. Buy inexpensive, well-made sneakers or medium quality formal shoes.

It is not uncommon to find 60-percent-off sales practically everywhere you go. You can get some of the year's best deals all through the month of January. January is also a good time to buy gifts for next Christmas. Or consider buying gift certificates for those on your list and explain to them that they can get a whole lot more gift by shopping in January.

Clothes prices take a nosedive when Rudolph's nose isn't shining anymore. Here is how prices compare during the Christmas season with the deals you can get at department and discount stores just a month later in January:

The Cheapskate's "True" Christmas

Merchandise	Xmas Cost	January Cost	Savings
For Women			
Coat	$410.00	$195.00	52%
Suit	$169.00	$89.00	48%
Jeans	$39.99	$19.99	43%
Sweater	$54.00	$18.00	67%
Blouse	$19.95	$9.95	50%
For Men			
Suit	$495.00	$249.00	50%
Sport Coat	$185.00	$74.00	60%
Tie	$19.95	$8.95	55%

January isn't the only time to realize great cheapskate values. You can also buy summer clothes in mid-summer and get hot deals of up to 50 percent off. Most people may think the best time to shop is in September. In reality, July and August are the best times for grabbing summer bargains. With all the outdoor activities people do in the summer, this is traditionally the slowest time of the year for retailers.

Don't overlook the big sale holidays when department and discount stores go crazy. These are traditionally Columbus Day, Labor Day, Presidents Day, and Memorial Day. If you are willing to put up with crowds, you can get some great cheapskate deals.

Most smart cheapskates can cut their clothing bill in half just by shopping at the right times of the year. For the average family, this could be reflected in over $1,000 in savings per year.

Care for the Clothes on Your Back

One of the best habits of any champion cheapskate is the proper care and maintenance of anything they buy. This is especially true when it comes to clothes. By properly cleaning and storing clothes, you can add months, even years to their useful life. In the long run, a little time and effort spent in taking care of them will save you hundreds of dollars.

Cheap Trick

A great way to store seasonal clothing is to use inexpensive, clean garbage cans. Simply put your clothing in plastic bags, then the garbage can, and close tight. The moisture- and mildew-resistant, bug-proof cans will help your clothes last years longer.

One of the first rules of clothing care is to repair damage as soon as it occurs. If a hem comes loose, don't wait months until it's turned into an unraveling nightmare. It's also especially important to pay attention to stains, because the longer they set, the harder they are to get out.

Many people have their suits cleaned and pressed on a monthly basis. Don't dry clean your clothes unless you absolutely have to. The harsh chemicals used in dry cleaning weaken and fade the fabric. Cheapskates who have wrinkles in clothes that aren't really soiled break out the iron and put the dry cleaner off for several months longer. For men, a great trick is to wear dry-cleaned shirts two or three times and simply touch them up with a little ironing between wears. Don't iron in the armpits, necks, or cuffs, though—you will set perspiration stains into the fabric.

Always read the care label on a garment and decide for yourself whether it makes sense to you. Silks, for example, usually have care labels that recommend that they be dry cleaned, but you can generally hand-wash silk in Woolite or a similar mild product, line or flat-dry, and then press if needed. The savings can be significant. As a bonus, your blouse will last about twice as long, since it hasn't been subjected to cleaning chemicals.

When you wash and dry clothes, use lower temperatures when possible. Cold water works well for most clothes as long as you use a quality detergent. If you have clothes with stains, use a stain stick to get the spot out rather than opting for hot water. Likewise, using a lower temperature when drying clothes will help them last much longer. If you take them out of the dryer immediately, you will save time and money by not having to iron. Still, the best way to dry clothes is to put them on a clothesline.

To protect your clothes from unnecessary soiling, wear an apron when cooking, and put on old grubbies when you are working in the yard or doing maintenance around the house. Also, be prepared for bad weather with a raincoat, umbrella, and galoshes.

If you have leather shoes or jackets, you need to be very careful if you want them to stand the test of time. Treat all your leather goods once every six months with a waterproofing spray that protects against all kinds of stains. Polish leather shoes regularly, and buy cedar shoe trees to absorb moisture and help shoes keep their like-new shape. Leather jackets tend to fade and soil around the collar due to your body oils, so wearing a scarf is a good idea.

One of the first things to go on a pair of jeans are the knees, especially when the jeans are on kids. To avoid holes and tears, use iron-on patches on the inside of the knees where they would normally wear. If your kids like bright colors, you can also buy an assortment of patches and iron them right onto the outside of any other heavily worn piece of clothing.

Cheap Shot

When you plan your clothes budget, be realistic about any tendency you have to gain or lose weight. A wardrobe of classic clothing is useful only if it fits properly. Changing sizes, whether you gain or lose weight, means buying new clothes. Don't purchase clothes the size you're hoping to be. I don't think any studies have been done on laboratory mice with this clothing dilemma, but my hunch is that you'll end up with lots of unused clothes taking up space.

Cheap Thrills with Clothes

➤ If you buy heavy coats with buttons that will be under a lot of stress, reinforce the stitching around them with dental floss. Dental floss is much stronger than any thread you can use and will last forever.

➤ Resist the temptation to buy expensive, hyped-up running shoes. Manufacturers around the world pay only about $5 to $7 to produce even the so-called "best" ones. Nike, for instance, has to mark their shoes up considerably just to pay for advertising costs and endorsement fees. The fact is that running shoes are not all that different in quality, unless you buy the under $10 variety. You can get a perfectly good pair of tennis shoes for around $20 if you find a good sale. Let me tell you, being a smart cheapskate is a heck of a lot more hip than having the Nike swoosh on your shoe.

➤ Men, if you wear ties often and tend to use them as a bib, buy a can of inexpensive tie spray to protect them. Silk ties are especially hard to clean once they have been soiled. Tie spray will help repel both food and drink, which means you won't even have to dry clean them, much less throw them away.

➤ Off-price stores such as TJ Maxx, Filene's Basement, and Marshalls are great places to find seconds and irregular garments for a fraction of the cost of perfect ones. These stores give you the prices of outlet stores, but generally have better selections. You may not always find what you want at an off-price store, but you may find a pleasant surprise or two. It's a good idea to put them on your places-to-shop list, and at least stop by.

➤ Learn to make your own clothing or find a family member that enjoys sewing. You can save a tremendous amount of money just by making a few dresses every year instead of buying them at a store. You can find pattern kits at most major discount stores and easily put together your own garments. Also, if you learn how to sew, you will be able to easily mend damaged clothes immediately and extend their lives.

➤ Swap clothing with relatives and neighbors. This is a great tactic, especially for kids clothes. Why pay for brand-new clothes every time a new kid comes along when you can get them free? You can even organize "swapping" parties in your neighborhood.

Cheap Trick

You don't always need to pay full price for an item that has an imperfection. If you see a garment with an open seam or missing button, for example, don't hesitate to ask for a discount or a similar item that is unflawed. If you shop frequently at local stores, get to know the managers and ask them to contact you when they are having a sale, or get on their mailing lists. In small stores, it's not uncommon for owners to give regular customers discounts.

➤ Do you cringe when you think of going into a thrift store or Goodwill shop? If you do, you may be losing out on great shopping opportunities. Not too long ago, I dropped into the local thrift store to see if I could find a good buy. Most of the stuff seemed pretty junky, but I was able to find two pairs of almost-new khaki pants for only $3. With $15 worth of alterations, I saved about $60 on comparable pants at the retail cost. Some people do all of their suit shopping at thrift stores. Often, you can find a fashionable outfit that just needs a little tailoring and dry cleaning to make it like new.

➤ If you live in a part of the country where the seasons don't change dramatically, buy medium weight clothes you can wear year-round. By doing this you will avoid the cost of having to have two or four different wardrobes for the different seasons of the year.

➤ Find a good local shoemaker and think about fixing your old shoes rather than buying new ones. There are several tricks you can use to make your shoes last longer and a quality shoemaker can tell you what they are.

➤ Always rent formal wear instead of buying it. Unless you happen to be some Hollywood movie star or the President, it's not necessary to buy a tuxedo or a formal dress. There are plenty of places that rent formal wear and will do it cheap. So next time you get invited to that once-every-five-years posh party, just open up the Yellow Pages and let your fingers do the walking to the local rental shop.

Frugality Footnote

What to do with those old clothes? Put them in plastic bags and take them down to the nearest Goodwill or Salvation Army store. Your donation will not only help the charity, but is also a tax deduction. If some clothes are particularly worn, use them for dust rags. If your donation is over $250, you must get a written letter from the charity to document your deduction to the IRS.

The Least You Need to Know

➤ Always buy clothes that fit into a pre-planned wardrobe and accessorize around the wardrobe.

➤ Never buy designer-label clothes unless you think you'll die if you don't (no one I know has died yet). Purchase private store–labeled or just plain generic clothing only. Be sure to check quality.

➤ Do your major clothes shopping during the month of January if you want to save the most. You can also get some great deals during the months of July and August and on the major holiday sale days.

➤ Buy used clothing or swap clothes with friends to save the most on your clothing needs.

➤ Learn to take care of your clothes, and add years to their wear. Dry clean your clothes as little as possible and fix them immediately when you see a hole, tear, or stain.

Chapter 7

Driving a Hard Bargain

In This Chapter

➤ Why buying a new car can be a big mistake

➤ Buying a used car the cheapskate way

➤ Car-buying traps for the cheapskate to avoid

➤ How to finance your next car like a pro

➤ Becoming your own used-car salesperson

➤ Keeping your wheels in tip-top shape

The average American goes through about fifteen cars in a lifetime.

What amazes me is that some people can become experts on saving pennies on clothes and groceries, but think nothing of blowing all their savings on an overpriced car. The average new car costs about $19,000, so you can understand why car manufacturers are eager for you to buy the latest and greatest model. They are betting that if they can put you in their car, you'll be back, year after year, for the latest model at the latest outlandish price.

If your cheapskate potential is high, you can save thousands of dollars on buying and maintaining that monstrosity in your driveway. If you're *car-savvy,* you can beat the car sharks at their own game, and save up to 30 percent on new cars and even more on used ones. You can also significantly reduce the cost of maintaining these wallet-draining hunks of junk.

New Car Jinx

You may have heard the cliché, "You are what you drive." Could that be sporty, fun, practical, adventurous, serious, or conservative? If you buy a new car, the salesman that sold it to you can tell you exactly what you are: generally, a sucker.

Buying a new car is like few other purchases because, when you negotiate the price, you are always at a disadvantage. Car dealers hide the true value of the car by creating high sticker prices, including overpriced add-ons, and hypnotizing you with slick sales tactics. This is all an attempt to get you to plunk down your hard-earned cash without too much of a fight. Everytime a person in America does this, they lose money, big time.

Cheap Trick

There are good times and bad times to buy a new car. Always avoid buying a new model in November, when it first comes out. That's when its market value is greatest. Instead, you can get last year's models, which are actually still the current year's, at a reduced cost. Also, buy during a prolonged period of dismal weather when showrooms are deserted. Another slow time for the dealers is at the end of the month when they are usually looking to meet quotas and move cars out of the dealership, regardless of their profit margin.

Of course there's Bob, your neighbor, who thinks he's a world-class cheapskate and has told his friends and family countless stories about how he's out-cheapskated car dealers. Bob pulls into his driveway one Saturday with his brand-new Mazda RX-7 and, of course, you go and check out the new wheels. He tells you about the great deal he got: He talked them down over $2,000 and also twisted their arms to give him the $1,000 manufacturer's rebate. Plus, they threw in rust protector, and Scotchguarded the seats for free. Wow!

Little did Bob know that the car was priced $4,000 over invoice anyway, and those extras they threw in cost the dealership about $10. The dealership actually netted about $2,000 on the car, but Bob walked away thinking he got the deal of the decade. Another thing Bob didn't know was that when he drove the car off the lot, it instantly lost about 18 percent of its value. That is, if he tried to sell it the next day, the most he could get for himself would be about 18 percent less than he'd paid! This doesn't even include the sales tax, finance charges, or any special dealer charges he paid. The fact is that Bob got suckered, as do most people who buy a new car.

I don't know what it is, but there's something about a car's shiny finish that attracts even the cheapest of cheapskates. Maybe the "something" is nothing more than the slick advertising that has conditioned our buying habits. Champion cheapskates may be tempted, but they know that the best way to save money is to buy a used car. If you want to break the rules and are dead set on buying shiny and new, it's important that you negotiate the best deal possible and plan to drive the car until it dies. That's the way to avoid a huge loss on resale and get your money's worth out of your investment.

If you insist on buying new, the first place to start your car negotiating is at the library or on the Internet. I know it sounds crazy, but that's where you can research the real cost of the car you want. Many sites on the Internet will give you this information. Just type in keys words "new car costs." One of the best Web addresses is http://www.carprice.com.

Pick up a copy of *Consumers Digest* or *Consumer Reports*. These publications tell you exactly what the car you want costs the dealership. *Consumer Reports* also has a telephone pricing service.

Armed with this knowledge, go into the dealership at the optimum time of the year/month and start negotiating. If you work hard enough and the dealership really wants to move the car, you can often swing a deal for less than the invoice cost. This approach works best at high-volume dealerships—you know, the ones that run TV ads with goofy car dealers running around in funny hats. Don't worry, though, dealers still make money because the manufacturers pay them incentive bonuses for moving the cars. With the dealer's cost in hand, when they swear to you that the car cost them X dollars, and you know that it was hundreds less, you can negotiate confidently. If you have to, pull out a copy of the magazine or price sheet that lists the costs.

A Little Use Cuts Down Pocketbook Abuse

A common misconception is that if you buy a used car you are buying someone else's headaches. Well that may be true for some, but if you're a smart cheapskate you know how to avoid this. There are good used cars and bad used cars. The key is to make sure the car is mechanically and structurally sound before you buy.

Cheap Talk

The *invoice cost* of a car is the amount the dealership paid for the car to the manufacturer. They then mark-up the price of the car and resell it. Anything they get between the invoice cost and sales price, they get to pocket.

Cheap Trick

Quite often, demonstration cars from the local dealership are still virtually new. If you buy one, insist on a new car warranty to be included in the deal that protects you if the car turns out to be a lemon. You may also want to consider buying a car from a rental agency; look for one with the lowest mileage. Have an independent mechanic check out the car thoroughly before you buy so you know you aren't purchasing a car that has been abused.

On average, new cars depreciate about 20 percent once the car leaves the dealership lot. By the second year of ownership, they depreciate another 15 to 20 percent. This is roughly a 30 to 40 percent drop in value in just two years. Cheapskates take advantage of this drop and buy cars that are about two years old. If you do some homework, you can find a well-maintained two-year-old car with an active life of 100,000 miles or more left; it may also have some of the factory warranty remaining.

Never take the seller's word for the car's condition. Take it to a qualified mechanic for inspection and get a detailed opinion. The few extra dollars you'll pay can help you make a good decision. Even if the car is in good overall shape, you may be able to negotiate the price even lower if the mechanic finds any problems.

Frugality Footnote

A used car dealer is likely to charge you about 20% for the "privilege" of buying off the fancy lot. They are not always trying to sucker you, but, to pay the huge amounts of overhead typical in their business, they have to make as much as they can on any car deal. Buying privately from an owner usually allows you to get honest answers to your questions without high-pressure sales tactics. About the only downside to buying from an individual is that you won't get the 1-year warranty most dealers provide. Have a mechanic inspect the car you buy from an individual just as you would if it were from a dealer. Even if you end up buying your dream used car from a dealership, insist on talking to the previous owner about the car's condition.

Ten Used Car Traps to Avoid

1. Interior rust. Exterior rust is a sign of what's to come; interior rust is a sign of what is. Check between doors and seams and underneath the trunk. If rust eventually eats through the trunk, exhaust fumes can enter the car and cause health problems.

2. Fluid leaks of any kind. Stop and look for another car.

3. Brakes that don't operate smoothly.

4. A noisy engine, or clicking noises. Listen for rattles, sputters, and squeaks.

5. Strong smoke that could mean major engine damage. Some exhaust smoke is normal; look for drastic, billowing white or black smoke.

6. A strong musty smell inside the car, which could mean that the car was in some sort of flood or has a leaky roof. Repairs will be costly.

7. A car that has been seriously wrecked.

8. Annoying rattles throughout the car. This could be a sign that it has structural problems. The rattles will only get worse as the years wear on.

9. A verbal agreement. Always get everything in writing.

10. Buying the car without having it inspected.

How Do I Pay for My Wheels?

The champion cheapskate tries never to borrow money to buy a car. When you borrow, the car actually costs a lot more because of the tremendous amount of money you pay in interest over time. The more you borrow, the more you'll pay in interest, and the longer the loan repayment period, the higher the interest rate.

If you're thinking of financing your next car purchase, think again. The following is a break-down of how much money it costs to finance a $10,000 car loan over four years (which is, unfortunately, the average length of a car loan today). This is money down the drain:

Cheap Trick

If you can't avoid borrowing, opt for the shortest term loan you can manage. If you are a true cheapskate and are concerned about your payments, here are the ways to buy a car in order of best to worst:

➤ All cash

➤ Big down payment and short-term loan

➤ Smaller down payment and short-term loan

➤ Big down payment and long-term loan with high interest rate

Costs of the Borrowing Bug

Rate	Monthly Payment	Total Interest Paid
8%	$244.13	$1,718.24
8.5%	$246.50	$1,832.00
9%	$248.90	$1,947.20
9.5%	$251.30	$2,062.40
10%	$253.70	$2,177.60
10.5%	$256.10	$2,292.80
11%	$258.45	$2,405.60
11.5%	$329.76	$2,522.73

If you must finance your next car, one thing you want to avoid is the ever-popular lease. If you listen to the salesperson's pitch, you may wonder why you ever thought about buying. A lease sounds sooo good! You have no down payment, the payments are lower, and you can deduct the amount you pay. These are the "facts" the dealer gives you. Actually, trying to read a lease agreement is like trying to decipher Egyptian hieroglyphics.

Leases are extremely complex documents for average folks like you and me. Remember, too, that leases generally require you to have the greatest possible car insurance protection because the finance company wants to protect its investment. This insurance can cost hundreds over the lease term. Never buy *credit life* or disability insurance coverage because these policies are inflated by 50 percent over what you would pay for regular coverage. Also, decline extended warranties that will make the finance and insurance company richer and you poorer.

Frugality Footnote

The smart cheapskate isn't a big fan of car leases because you can be zapped in about 10 different ways. Leases are just too complex. Buying is much smarter because the deal is simpler and you own the car when you are finished making payments. You also can get a better deal on the car when you buy it outright.

Five Myths About Car Leases

Myth #1: Leases don't have down payments. Wrong. What's the difference between putting $1,000 down on a car you are buying outright, and coughing up $250 for a security deposit and $375 for the first and last month's payments on a lease? Maybe the difference is that this amount is not called a *down payment*. It's obviously a much better deal for you if you buy outright and just ask to have the first month's payment deferred for two months. Most finance companies don't have a problem with this arrangement. If they do, find another financing source.

Myth #2: The payments are less on a lease. Not so. You are paying for the difference between the price of the car now and the car's expected value in the future, usually in two to five years. In many cases, this future value figure can be trumped up depending on the resale value of a particular model. How does anyone really know what the car will be worth at that future time? Bottom line: You won't have a car at the end of the payments unless you pay that "future value figure" in a lump sum. Because you are paying a lump sum at the end of the lease, you can understand why the lease payments are lower.

Myth #3: Leases are tax-deductible. Yes, you can deduct a lease payment, but only if you use the car solely for business purposes. Many a car salesperson has led an unsuspecting customer into believing all leases are deductible, seizing on the fact that most people associate leases with tax deductions. Never fall for this line.

Myth #4: You don't pay any interest when you lease a car. When you ask about the interest rate (APR) on the lease, you're often told, "Leases don't really have interest rates; it's just how the lease is set up." Baloney! Leases have what is commonly called the *implicit percentage rate* or *yield.* Just ask for the yield if you get embroiled in heated negotiations. Dealers are required by law to quote you this rate.

Cheap Talk

The *implicit percentage rate* or *yield* on a lease is the actual percentage rate charged annually. It is calculated using a complex formula that is too lengthy to explain. Just make sure you ask for the annual yield if you are dead set on leasing a car.

Most people get burned by paying way too much in interest. Some finance companies have been known to charge over a 20 percent yield without the customers having any inkling of what is going on. State regulators are beginning to crack down on the practice of hiding this rate.

Myth #5: What is the real cost of the car? You must find out the real cost—the price you would pay for the car if you bought it rather than leased it. In the leasing biz, this price is called the *capitalized cost.* Ask the dealer to show you the capitalized cost in writing on the lease agreement. If the dealer refuses, walk away from the deal.

Sell It Yourself: All You Need Is a Leisure Suit

How would you like an extra $1,500 in cash the next time you decide to get rid of your used car? Put a little time and effort into fixing up your car, and you can keep the cash you normally sacrifice when you trade in your car to a dealer.

A cheapskate fact of life is that dealerships almost always give you a terrible price for your trade-in, even if your car is in good shape, so they can make a tidy profit when they resell it. If the dealer decides to sell it at auction, you'll get about $1,000 less than the auction price. This all spells "bad deal" for the cheapskate.

Car salesmen can use the value of your trade-in to manipulate the deal in their favor. For example, if you think the trade-in price is fair, the dealer generally tells you that the car is great and in demand. If you don't know your car's true value, the dealer can then inflate the price of the new car. If you object to the trade-in price quoted, the dealer often tells you that your car is not worth very much and isn't in demand. Follow the Cheapskate Creed: Never trade in your used car!

How can you sell the old clunker privately for the maximum value? First, you can't be in a hurry, and you'll have to be able to invest some time in it. Start by determining the true value of your used vehicle. Call your local banker and ask for the National

Cheap Trick

Before you sell, clean your car to perfection. Detail the inside, wax the finish, and clean the engine at a local pressure–wash facility. If you don't want to clean the car yourself, or you just don't have the time, hire a service. For about $100, someone else can make it look like new. You will recover the $100 several times over when you sell it. Also, fix any minor mechanical or noticeable surface problems. The important thing is to get your car in shape so it makes a good first impression.

Automobile Dealers Association (NADA) retail value of your automobile. The retail value is the price at which a used car lot might sell it. But don't expect to get this amount unless you are the world's greatest salesperson. You should settle for somewhere between the trade-in value of the car and the retail price. Remember that the trade-in price in the NADA book is not the arbitrary price that a dealership might place on your car. NADA lists the car's true trade-in value for loan purposes. You can also go onto the Internet, search keywords "used car prices," and find several sites that will help you determine the value.

The next step is to advertise your vehicle. Advertise in the most popular local paper and also in a car shopper newspaper or on the Internet. Two great Web addresses for free advertisements are http://www.autos.yahoo.com and http://www.carshopper.com. Of course, weekends are the best time to advertise, but don't ignore special week-long advertising deals. Take a look at some current ads in the paper for ideas on what you should include in your ad. Something catchy always helps. Make sure you put your asking price in the ad to encourage only serious inquiries. Your asking price should be $300 to $500 more than you really want.

Frugality Footnote

Cheapskates set up just one appointment for all potential buyers to view their car. This adds perceived value to it because everyone will wonder why so many other people are looking. Nothing sells a car faster than getting the buyer worried about whether they will "miss out." To avoid no-shows at your viewing, get potential buyers' names and phone numbers when they call so they feel they are obligated to show up.

Have a dollar figure in mind that is absolutely the lowest amount you will take for your car, and stick to it. When you're not wishy-washy about the price, the buyer is aware that you know what the car is worth. If the buyer quibbles at your price, take out a copy of the NADA book with the listing for your car. When the deal is done, accept only a cashier's check as form of payment. Never take a personal check. Be prepared with paperwork and details about signing over the title. The more you know about the rules and laws, the faster you can get the car sold.

Maintaining Your Hunk of Metal

Where is the best place to have your car maintained and repaired? The dealer, a local mechanic, or a national chain? I don't recommend that you take it to a dealer. If you call around town to the different car dealers, you'll find that they are very expensive for even the most minor repairs. Dealers usually charge about 30 percent more than independent mechanics.

Many car owners are suckered into taking their cars to the dealer, thinking that the dealer provides better service or is the only one who can do the repairs properly. In reality, many independent mechanics can do just as good a job and charge much less. Car dealerships are slick marketers and get the majority of their customers from new car sales. Customers often get used to taking the car in for warranty checks and then continue to take it to the dealership year after year.

Cheapskates know that it's best to have their cars maintained and repaired at a reputable local shop rather than a car dealership. Check your area to find the best independent mechanics. Auto parts stores often can recommend experienced and honest mechanics. Ask friends and relatives whether they have found a reliable local repair shop. Before leaving your car at the shop, ask for references and talk to regular customers. If people come back to the shop year after year, it's probably well-run and provides good customer service. If you're lucky, you can find a shop that has great prices as well.

Cheap Shot

Beware of repair shops that overcharge for maintenance. The best way to avoid getting taken is to shop around before you get any repairs done on your car. If you know what the going rate is for a certain repair, you will be armed with the knowledge you need to negotiate a fair price. It may take you a while, but if you check out prices at enough repair shops in your neighborhood, eventually, you will be able to settle on a shop where you know you'll have few cost disputes.

If you hire someone to change your oil, go to a franchised oil-change center rather than the dealership. Change your oil every 4,000 miles, not every 2,000 to 3,000 miles as recommended by many new car dealers. Dealers want you to bring your car in for costly "maintenance checkups" that quite often turn into overpriced oil changes anyway. If you take your car to the local oil-change center, you'll save up to 50 percent on routine service. Also, these centers do several other checks on your car without charging extra for this service. You can often get coupons from your local paper or through the mail to save even more. But if you want to be a true cheapskate, learn how to change the oil yourself.

Squeezing Every Penny Out of a Gallon

Shell Oil did a study on specially designed cars that were able to get 400 miles per gallon! This feat was accomplished by minimizing resistance and drag, creating new engine designs, and using clever tricks to increase fuel economy. Of course, you cannot get this mileage in your ordinary car, but you can increase fuel efficiency in many other ways. Follow these simple rules and you will find yourself rolling down the highway for a lot longer:

1. Keep your engine in good shape by having regular oil changes, once every 4,000 miles. Get a tune-up every year and a half to ensure that your engine is running at peak performance. Spark plugs and air filters are the number one cause of lost engine efficiency, so replace them when needed. You can lose as much as two miles per gallon if the air filter or spark plugs are clogged or dirty. Think this is peanuts? You will save as much as $75 per year.

2. When you're looking to buy a car, pay special attention to the Environmental Protection Agency (EPA) average miles per gallon. A car that gets just a few more miles to the gallon can save you several hundred dollars over its lifetime. Some of the most fuel-efficient cars on the road such as the Geo Metro can get 50 miles to the gallon. The average for all cars is 28.1. Hopefully you can find a car that gets results at least this good.

3. Don't use high-octane gas in your car unless your owner's manual specifies it. Studies show that higher octane gasoline does not increase mileage efficiency. Your car will run just fine with the cheaper stuff. Also, pump your own gas and pay cash when you can get discounts. You have no reason to charge your gas with an oil charge card that features an outrageously high interest rate.

4. Never drive your car without first warming it up for about three minutes. A cold engine uses about 10 percent more gas. Also, if possible, avoid driving your car very short distances, such as to the neighbor's house or the mailbox down the street. Over time, turning your car off and on for short periods puts undue wear and tear on your engine and your exhaust system.

5. Some people like to use their trunks as storage space. You pay to have extra weight back there. Take out all the tools and sports equipment and store them elsewhere. When you go on a trip, though, pack the trunk and other areas of the car as fully as you can so you don't need to put a luggage carrier on top of the car. These carriers can decrease fuel economy significantly by creating a drag.

Cheap Thrills with Cars

➤ To save big, just slow down. Driving at the speed limit will save you money in a number of ways. First, it improves your gas mileage and reduces maintenance costs. Second, you'll avoid speeding tickets. Finally, it's a whole lot safer and could save you money in undue accident repair costs.

➤ The color you choose for your car when you purchase it can mean more money in your pocket when you resell. Red and beige are the safest colors because they have the best resale values. Medium and dark blues also sell well. You may not consciously realize it, but the color of your car is of importance if you want to get the most money when you get rid of it.

Frugality Footnote

What about oil additives that claim to extend your engine life, increase horsepower, and increase gas mileage? Products like Slick 50 or DuraLube are great when they are new, but over time their viscosity becomes like glue on the inside of your engine's pistons. Some mechanics claim to have found a quarter inch or more of sticky dirt build-up inside the engine, years after an additive was used.

➤ If you live in a big city, owning a car can be an outrageous expense. Unless you need the car to get to work, consider not owning one and just renting when you absolutely need to have one. If you rent a car for only two or three days a month, you come out way ahead of what you would pay for a car loan, gas, insurance, parking, and maintenance. Use public transportation or ride your bike or moped to work. Any of these options can save you as much as $6,000 per year!

➤ When you're driving at speeds above 50 miles per hour and need fresh air, turn on the air conditioner and don't roll down the windows. It does cost to run the air conditioner, but today's cars are designed to run best when they can maximize airflow and reduce drag on the car. If you roll down any windows, the wind resistance significantly reduces fuel economy and will cost you more in the long run than just running the air conditioning.

➤ *Automobiles* Nationwide Auto Brokers can send you a form ($9.95) showing you all the optional equipment available on the car of your choice and then arrange local delivery with your dealer. You automatically save between $500 and $4,000 just by letting Nationwide negotiate a dealer-to-dealer price break that eliminates the need for a commission. Address: 17517 W. 10 Mole Road, Southfield, MI 48075; 800-521-7257.

➤ The days of the full-service gas station are over, so it's up to you to check the pressure in your car tires regularly. Why? When your tire pressure is low, you lose

2 percent in gas mileage efficiency. Also, the Department of Energy estimates that you can save about 3 percent of your total gas bill over one year just by keeping your tires properly inflated. Check your tires at least once a month. You also save by prolonging the life of your tires and ultimately your engine. Also, have your tires rotated once a year to prevent improper wear.

➤ When you buy a car, make sure it has plenty of safety features. Not only will the car be safer to drive, but features such as air bags, auto seat belts, and a theft device will significantly reduce your auto insurance premiums.

➤ An auto club can save you money if you have a slightly older car. Not only do you have coverage for towing, but most clubs now have other services. Trip planning, hotel discounts, and free maps are just a few. Call 1-800-JOIN-AAA to become a member of the most well-known, AAA. Allstate Motor Club, 1-800-347-8880, or Amoco Motor Club, 1-800-334-3300, are two other good choices. Compare clubs to see which is best for you.

The Least You Need to Know

➤ If you are thinking about purchasing a used car like a good cheapskate should, go to the local library or get on the Internet and research the invoice cost through one of the consumer magazines. This way you can negotiate the best deal possible.

➤ When you sell your used car, get it in tip-top shape by meticulously cleaning it inside and out and having it checked out mechanically. If there is anything wrong, have it fixed before you sell the car.

➤ If it has been more than 4,000 miles since your last oil change, have it changed immediately and get on a regular 4,000-mile oil change schedule.

➤ To squeeze every mile out of a gallon of gas, be aware of gas mileage claims when you buy a car, and keep it in excellent shape by doing regular maintenance and watching how you drive.

➤ If you are thinking of financing your next car, consider your options. Champion cheapskates always pay cash for their cars. If they only have $1,000, then they get a $1,000 car. Unless you're having major problems with your car, consider making due for several months with what you have, and save $200 or $300 a month until you have enough cash to purchase a decent used car.

➤ If you want to maximize your profit, if you're able, always personally sell your car to an individual buyer. If you have maintained the engine well and there are only minor exterior problems, you'll get top dollar for it.

Chapter 8

Where to Go to Grab the Dough

In This Chapter

➤ The best places for cheapskate bargains

➤ Salvage dollars at your local thrift shops

➤ Cash in on garage sales

➤ Bare-bones shopping establishments

➤ The factory outlet phenomenon

➤ Mail-order madness

➤ Grab your share of government giveaways

Everybody wants a bargain, but all too often that bargain turns into something that needs to be repaired or replaced sooner than we think. Part of the cheapskate's shopping savvy comes from knowing where to get a bargain without sacrificing quality. Whether you are buying a car or next year's wardrobe, when you plunk down your dough, you need to feel confident that you are shopping at the right place. These carefully chosen places to shop will save you big bucks and determine the size of your bank account, and also your eventual lifestyle.

Just three decades ago, there were only a few bargain stores in the whole country, most of them for wholesalers only. Today, there are so many discount shopping choices that hardly anyone pays retail anymore. The champion cheapskate is not just anybody, though. Cheapskates take advantage of many ways to save big dollars that are not known to the average shopper. They can be found at garage sales, thrift stores, flea markets, and many outlet malls. They know where to go to shop and also know enough not to buy junk.

Nifty and Thrifty

Smart cheapskates check out local thrift stores in their neighborhood. Stores run by the Salvation Army, Goodwill, and other charitable organizations generally carry a lot of junk, but if you look hard enough you will find some real deals. Some stores receive good quality merchandise on a regular basis. It's up to you to research which stores are best in your local area.

The best thrift stores are usually run by churches and synagogues in affluent areas. Have patience, though, because you can spend a lot of time and effort going through other people's junk just to find that one gem. Keep your eye out for special charity sales. The American Cancer Society, for instance, often sponsors weekend rummage sales with great merchandise donated by its members.

Some people cringe when they think of going into a thrift store or Goodwill shop. If you do, you may be losing out on great shopping opportunities a champion cheapskate would take advantage of.

If you find the right thrift stores to shop at you can really get some great deals. Just check out some I've gotten in the last few years:

Cheap Trick

If you want to find out what your thrift store shopping options are, set aside a Saturday to do some bargain hunting. The first place to start is your local Yellow Pages. Under the thrift stores and charities sections you will generally find several shops you can visit. Call them and ask what kind of items they stock and where they are located. Make a list of the stores you want to see and then start driving. Generally, you will be able to find a store or two that suit your taste.

Thrift Saving Examples

Item	Thrift Store Price	Alterations	Retail Cost	Savings
Two pair almost-new khaki pants	$3.00	$15.00	$60.00	$42.00
Navy shirt with stain	$5.00	$3.00	$40.00	$32.00 (dry cleaning)
Kid's bicycle	$7.00	$0	$75.00	$68.00
Set of kitchenware	$6.00	$0	$50.00	$44.00
Men's designer suit	$25.00	$25.00	$250.00	$200.00
4 porcelain figurines	$40.00	$0	$300.00	$260.00
Total Savings				**$646.00**

Your Neighborhood Has a Bargain

'Tis always the season to be rummaging—through the closets, that is. Spring and fall may be the best times for garage sales, since the cool air tends to make money flow more easily from neighbors' pocketbooks. Since you've been putting it off for years, why not do it now? A garage sale is a great way to get rid of some of the clutter in your life and also add to your cheapskate bank account. If you don't do it, I'm sure your neighbors will, so you might as well beat them to the punch. You may also want to keep up to date on the garage sales in your neighborhood to get some bargains for yourself.

Unless you live in Beverly Hills, there is no use in trying to get big bucks for your used items. Sell everything at what you might think is about 70 percent off retail unless you know that they should be classified as antiques or collectibles. You might want to get those appraised before selling.

A simple pricing system is to mark everything in round numbers like 50¢, $1, $2, etc. This makes figuring much easier. None of this 99¢ stuff. Again, you're not a retail store, you're just trying to get rid of some junk and make a few bucks in the process. Get a bunch of different colored stickers and use them to denote prices, then put up a color-coded sign so that people will know what things cost. Most cheapskates think this is a clever system. For more expensive or unique items, just mark the price right on the merchandise.

Frugality Footnote

When tromping through the attic and other storage areas in your house, look for some of these "hot" items: old books, desks, tables and chairs, toys, big band records, pictures (people like frames), gardening tools, and sporting goods. These items sell like lemonade at a summer little league game. Forget selling clothes; it's a real pain trying to sort and price them all. Save them for Goodwill or the Salvation Army and take a tax deduction at the end of the year.

To make a garage sale successful, you have to advertise. Put an ad in the most popular paper around your area and also some more localized shopper papers. The best days to have your sale are Thursday through Sunday, with the weekends obviously being the highest volume days. Your ad should be eye-catching with a lead line such as "The

Mother of All Sales" (a little exaggerating never hurts). In the ad, mention your top two or three items. You'll also need to post neon-colored signs all around the neighborhood. Also, make a family project of passing out 100 or so flyers around the block. You will be surprised at how many neighbors show up.

When the day arrives for the big sale, have a couple of bargain tables with very low prices on them and a sign saying something like "Everything's a Quarter." This works great for small items you want to go fast. Anything left over from your sale can go to Goodwill or the Salvation Army. Another cheapskate tax deduction.

Cement Floors and No Ceilings?

Cheap Shot

People who aren't savvy cheapskates tend to buy much more than they can use. These warehouses rely on impulse buying that comes from the soaring excitement people experience when they see the lower prices. Finally, watch out for a lack of selection in warehouses. If they have only one brand of a product, you may be paying more than if you shopped at a store with a range of selections.

One of the most popular shopping choices today is the discount warehouse club. These clubs such as Sam's Club and Costco generally offer bare bones surroundings in exchange for discount prices. The membership fee you pay for the "privilege" of shopping at the club will generally pay for itself if you shop wisely.

Some people wonder how discount warehouses make money. It seems like the deals are so good they couldn't possibly make much. The fact is that you can still get taken even in these low-cost havens. First, you buy everything in bulk. Because of this, the warehouse is guaranteed a profit on every bulk package they sell. It is important to maximize your membership in a warehouse club by using it often and only purchasing items you need and will use. Then it's a great way to save as much as 25 percent off your regular grocery bill. They also carry general merchandise on which you can save even more. Most cheapskates belong to a warehouse club where they shop regularly.

Drive a Little, Save a Lot

A long time ago, the word "outlet" meant the thing on the wall that you plugged your vacuum cleaner into. Times have changed. Now the outlet means a great way for cheapskates to shop. Outlet malls are cropping up just about everywhere in the country.

Frugality Footnote

Outlet malls are usually located in smaller towns off highways. The reason for this is that the land they are on is much cheaper. If you can't keep yourself from buying designer clothes and name-brand merchandise, an outlet mall is the place to go.

You can save as much as 75 percent off regular retail prices. Most outlets sell clothing, but many also include general merchandise such as china, linens, and cookware. Ralph Lauren, Van Heusen, Nike, Lenox, and Liz Claiborne are among the leading outlet stores.

If you have never visited a large factory outlet mall, be prepared to be overwhelmed by the great number of stores and the huge selection of merchandise. If there's an outlet mall nearby, you may want to devote all of your first trip to familiarize yourself with what's there, and go back at a later date to do your shopping.

The stock in the stores changes on a regular basis. For instance, if you bought a great pair of jeans at the Liz Claiborne outlet last year, you may not be able to get the same pair this year. It used to be that outlet stores sold only overstock or irregular items that couldn't be sold retail. Now, since times have become tough for many name-brand companies (mainly due to us great cheapskates), they are beginning to stock newer designs in their discount outlets. If this trend continues, manufacturers will be looking at outlet stores as their chief source of income.

Cheap Shot

Cheapskates need to be aware of a few things if they want to get the best deals at outlet malls. First, just because it is in an outlet store doesn't necessarily mean that all the deals are great. As outlet stores have become more popular, unfortunately, the prices have gone up. It's a good idea to check local department stores to see what the going retail price is for certain designer products before you buy at an outlet. Also, you may be purchasing an irregular or damaged item without even knowing it. Make sure you check a product thoroughly before you buy.

The merchandise in outlets is generally top quality, although some may be marked seconds or irregular. Overall, outlet mall shopping is a very pleasant and rewarding experience for the champion cheapskate. If you drive a little bit, you can truly save a lot.

Frugality Footnote

Many outlet malls are located in vacation destinations, so you might want to know where they are before you plan your next trip. You can order a helpful book that will give you the location of over 250 of America's best ones. Just send $4.95 to The Joy of Outlet Shopping, Box 7867, St. Petersburg, FL 33734. It will also tell you what stores are in each outlet and what kind of discounts you can expect. If you want to shop the outlets from home, hook up to the Internet and go to http://www.factorymall.com.

Shopping from Your Armchair

Why settle for the best deal in town when you can be shopping all over the country just by picking up the phone? You can save tremendous amounts of money by shopping with the various discount mail-order and price-quote companies throughout the country. You can save on appliances, furniture, household gadgets, and electronics just by calling these companies and asking for catalogs. You also can find items like clothes, art supplies, and sporting goods. Here's a sampling of some of the best price companies carrying different products:

➤ *Furniture*   Cedar Rock Furniture carries all major brands of furniture at up to 50 percent off retail. Address: Box 515, Hudson, NC 28638; 704-396-2361.

➤ *Appliances* EBA   Wholesale offers dozens of products from more than 50 name-brand manufacturers including Admiral, Kitchen Aide, Panasonic, Westinghouse, and GE at savings of up to 60 percent. Address: 2361 Nostrand Avenue, Brooklyn, NY 11210; 718-252-3400.

➤ *Computers*   CMO offers name-brand computers like IBM, Apple, and Hewlett Packard as well as other systems and software for about 40 percent off retail. Address: 2400 Reach Road, Williamsport, PA 11701; 800-233-8950.

➤ *Fitness Equipment*   Better Health and Fitness can get you what you need to complete a home gym for up to 25 percent off retail. Address: 5302 New Utrecht Avenue, Brooklyn, NY 11219; 718-436-4801.

➤ *Anything you can think of*   The Internet has become one of the cheapskate's great hangouts. Whether you are searching for a new car, a new computer, or anything else, you can usually find some of the best deals in the country simply by browsing the net. The reason: Online marketers have very little overhead costs on the

Internet, so they can pass the savings on to us. All you need to tap into these savings is either a computer (see Chapter 12 for suggestions) or an inexpensive Web TV hookup.

If you're looking to buy smaller items, there are hundreds and hundreds of fabulous catalogs you'll never know about unless you scour newspapers and magazines to find their ads. You may also hear about the catalogs through word of mouth. These catalogs offer you the opportunity to buy your favorite products at discounts, and you don't need to waste time trekking through busy shopping malls. You can find catalogs for just about anything from the mundane to the exotic. Here are some less-known but great catalogs for the picky consumer:

➤ *Art Supplies*   Cheap Joe's Art Stuff sells paint, canvas, matte cutters, and art books at 30 percent less than retail. Address: 300A Industrial Park Road, Boone, NC 28607; 800-227-2788.

➤ *Fragrances*   Essential Products Company can save you up to 80 percent if you don't mind wearing good-quality imitations of designer fragrances. Address: 90 Water Street, New York, NY 10005; 800-217-7249.

➤ *Bed and Bath*   Harris Levy can help you save as much as 50 percent on Wamsutta, J.P. Stevens, Springmaid, and other manufacturers. Address: 278 Grand Street, New York, NY 10002; 212-226-3102.

➤ *Quilts and Collectibles*   You can save as much as 30 percent on antique quilts when you buy from Quilts Unlimited. Address: 440-A Duke of Gloucester Street, Williamsburg, VA 23185; 800-358-5899.

➤ *Boating Supplies*   Goldberg's Marine Distributors can save you up to 60 percent on boating equipment and nautical clothing. The company delivers your shipment in three to five days. Address: 201 Meadow Road, Edison, NJ 08818; 800-BOATING.

Cheap Talk

Web TV is a special service that allows you to hook up to the internet and also have worldwide e-mail for about $300–$500. You then pay a small monthly fee for your internet access. There are several companies that sell systems such as Philips and RCA. Check your local electronics store or better yet, get on the internet at a nearby library and search for a deal.

Cheap Shot

Buying clubs, which are different from warehouse clubs, are becoming popular throughout the country. A buying club is a service that offers you deals on travel, long distance, and shopping all rolled into one package. I have found that most clubs do not offer a tremendous amount of benefits, however. Quite often, clubs mail out slick brochures and fancy letters that make it look like you get the world by joining. But after you sign up, you may find the discounts they offer are no better than those you could have gotten yourself by doing some homework.

➤ *Vitamins*   Puritan's Pride offers all natural vitamins at wholesale prices. Often they have two for one sales and have even had buy two and get three free! Address: 1233 Montauk Highway, Oakdale, NY 11769; 800-645-1030

➤ *General Merchandise*   If you are looking for a great general catalog that has all sorts of items from toasters to toys, browse through Damark International. You can receive substantial savings on a variety of name-brand products; in some cases prices are as much as 70 percent off retail. Address: 7401 Winnetka Ave. N., Minneapolis, MN 55440; 800-729-9000.

Whether you call for price quotes or a mail-order company, be sure you ask about the return policy. Sometimes you pay a substantial charge for returns. Use a credit card to further protect yourself, and make sure you keep a record of your order and all receipts.

Barter: The Ultimate Money Saver

Consider bartering services and exchanging products with business associates, friends and neighbors. How does bartering and exchanging work? Next time you are thinking about buying something to make your life easier, consider exchanging a service or product you have for someone else's services or products. Both parties generally come out ahead in the long run. Sometimes you don't come out even, but if you barter often, the results seem to work out well for everyone. In addition, you build much stronger relationships with people when you barter. Centuries ago, bartering was the only way man did business in the world. Money has simply replaced what was once a much more personal way to trade.

Cheap Talk

Bartering simply means trading–out an item or service with another person. You give them something, they give something back. The best thing is that no money changes hands! Don't forget to claim the goods or services received on your tax return if their value is over $500.

If you don't run a business, you can also barter with friends and relatives. For example, if you are a good cook and your neighbor is a good gardener, you may want to exchange a meal or two for the planting of some tomatoes. If one of your kids has grown out of baby clothes, you can exchange those old clothes for your next door neighbor's older kids' clothing. You can be very creative with bartering because anything you don't particularly like to do or want to keep can usually be bartered out.

The Great Government Giveaway

Nobody gives you a better bargain than the government. Well, maybe Uncle Sam takes a lot from us to start, but if you are a smart cheapskate, you can get a little of that back. Whether it's property taken from criminals or packages left for lost in the post office, our government is anxious to sell stuff cheap. Fortunately, when government sells an item, by law we are the first ones that get a crack at it. Through various auctions the government unloads billions of dollars worth of merchandise every year. If you go to one of these auctions, inspect the item or items you want to bid on carefully, and have cash or a cashiers check with you to pay for what you buy; the government doesn't take credit cards.

There are a lot of government auctions each year. The goods for sale include everything from used office furniture to luxury cars and boats. If you do your bidding properly, you can generally purchase merchandise for pennies on the dollar. The key to getting these great bargains is to know about them. Here are several auctions and how to find them:

1. The General Services Administration (GSA) is the government's general housekeeper. It buys and sells all sorts of government property and therefore is the best place to pick up surplus goods. Most of the goods are office equipment and supplies. Some of the equipment is in good shape, but most of it is junk. For information on sales in your area, ask the GSA to put your name on a mailing list and request a Surplus Personal Property sheet. This form allows you to select the kinds of property you are interested in and your geographical location. Just contact the regional office closest to you, listed in the blue pages of the phone book.

2. The U.S. Marshal's Service is responsible for any property seized from the commission of a felony. They confiscate boats, houses, and cars from thousands of criminals every year. They have some of the most desirable merchandise the government has to sell. Most of the merchandise they sell at local auctions is in excellent shape and of superior quality. The best place to find out about these sales is your local newspaper's classified section. For further information, write to the U.S. Marshals Service, U.S. Dept. of Justice, 600 Army-Navy Drive, Arlington, VA 22202.

Cheap Shot

Too many people are being taken in by the lure of home-shopping channels, such as QVC and The Home Shopping Channel. Although some of the products they sell are of good quality and may be priced right, most are overpriced. The companies that run these networks rely heavily on bored consumers many of whom shouldn't be spending *any* money at all. Don't get drawn in by the personalities who are doing the selling, and buy things you don't need and can't afford.

3. The U.S. Postal Service is also a good source of government deals. They have hundreds of undeliverable shipments piling up every week, and damaged goods for which they have paid insurance claims. All of it is put on sale. For information on the five nationwide auctions, write the U.S. Post Office, Superintendent of Claims at the address closest to you:

➤ J.A. Farley Building, 380 West 33rd Street, New York, NY 10199

➤ 2970 Market Street, Room 531A, Philadelphia, PA 19104

➤ 443 E. Fillmore Avenue, St. Paul, MN 55107

➤ 730 Great SW Parkway SW, Atlanta, GA 30336

➤ P.O. Box 7837, San Francisco, CA 94120

4. The Internal Revenue Service (IRS) has plenty of property seized from taxpayers that haven't paid up. This could include anything: houses, cars, boats, furniture, or whatever else they can think of seizing. IRS sales usually have a mixed bag of merchandise. Since there are so many different types of items, prices are extremely low. Notices of sale are usually posted in major newspapers' classified sections, so keep your eyes open.

Cheap Thrills in Shopping

➤ It's a good idea to think about buying gifts whenever you shop. If you see items on sale that would make great gifts later in the year, buy them and store them in a special gift closet at home. Have Christmas, Hanukkah, birthday, and anniversary gifts on hand so you don't have to rush to the store a day or two before the big event. If you see the right things on sale, you can save a tremendous amount of money by not having to pay last minute prices.

➤ Army-Navy Stores can be great places to grab cheapskate deals. Inventory is somewhat limited but you can get a lot of casual wear for pennies on the dollar. You can also pick up camping supplies on the cheap.

➤ Buy pet food and supplies at a discount pet supply store. Many cities now have pet supply warehouses where you can save as much as 40 percent on selected products. If Fifi or Fido gets the best in food, then these stores can save you a lot, because they mark down high-quality products tremendously. If you are feeding your pet "designer" food, scale down your extravagance a little; your cat or dog isn't going to notice the difference. These discount stores also carry a wide range of pet care products below retail. Check your local Yellow Pages for the discount pet store closest to you.

➤ It never hurts to ask for a further discount at an outlet store. Often, if the manager is available, it's not uncommon to be given an additional 10 to 20 percent off the already low prices, especially on overstocked items.

➤ Consignment clothing shops can serve a couple of purposes. They allow you to purchase decent quality clothes and also allow you to sell clothing you no longer wear. Most of them pay you half of what the garment will sell for. They also have many designer fashions for much less than you would pay at a department store.

Frugality Footnote

Cheapskates never shop at the last minute. They realize that this is the time when impulse buying is at its peak. Cheapskates play by the rule: The more expensive the product, the longer the planning period for the purchase. For instance, if it's a car, they might start planning six months in advance so they'll buy what they really want at the right time of year to get the best bargain.

The Least You Need to Know

➤ When you know you have to do a lot of shopping, don't head immediately for the major mall. On a Saturday, check out some of the local thrift stores and visit a few garage sales. You'll save plenty of money and probably find a lot of the things you need.

➤ For grocery shopping, consider getting a membership to a local warehouse club. You will save about 25 percent over regular supermarkets even after you pay your membership dues.

➤ If you are considering a major purchase, call one of the discount mail-order companies mentioned in this chapter or log onto the Internet. You'll save a lot of money and a lot of time racing around town trying to find the best deal.

➤ If you have never tried bartering before, experiment by putting together a simple bartering situation between yourself and a relative or business associate. Always try to make it a win-win proposition for both parties.

➤ Find a local factory outlet in your area and take a day trip to see if you can find any bargains. You don't have to buy anything, but you may be tempted when you see some of the great deals.

➤ Send away for some information on the government auction that is most appealing to you. Then follow up with a visit to the actual auction. Don't plan on purchasing the first time out. Just watch and see how everything works. The next time you will be ready to bid.

Part 3
Save Cash All Over Your Place

It's the American dream—buying a home of your own and living happily ever after. But if you're a first-time homeowner, your dream can easily become a nightmare. Learn what cheapskates know and most real estate agents won't tell you about the tremendous responsibility that goes along with home ownership in Chapter 9. In Chapter 10, find out what to do when the pipes burst in your basement, how to handle difficult neighbors, where to get the best mortgage, and ways to save by avoiding maintenance problems. How can you keep your utility costs to a minimum? Read about it in Chapter 11, and find out how to save lots of cash on the big ticket stuff you need to fill the house up, like appliances and furniture.

Take the Home Ownership Plunge— Not a Dunk!

It doesn't matter if your dream home is a ranch style, Victorian or even a little shanty. Buying and selling your humble abode can be a stressful and frustrating experience. As if the cost of a home weren't enough, you also have to contend with real estate agents' fees, inspections, points, interest rates, title searches, and mortgage companies. All this increases the difficulties of buying a home and, of course, the price tag.

Then there are the lifestyle considerations: Does the area you're moving to have good schools? Is the neighborhood safe? How close is it to work? Are shopping and entertainment convenient? These are all things you have to evaluate carefully if you want to make the right decisions. If you're selling your home you have similar frustrations to deal with, such as people tromping through, and real estate commissions to pay that sometimes resemble the national debt.

Cheap Talk

The money you pay to buy-down your interest rate on a mortgage are often called points. They simply represent a percentage of the loan amount, and one point is equal to 1% of the loan. So if you had to pay 2 points on a $100,000 loan, you would pay $2,000 to buy-down the interest rate on the loan. The IRS treats seller-paid points as a tax deduction.

Cheap Shot

If you're renting a house and thinking about buying it, beware of lease/option plans and equity-sharing. Under many plans, it can cost you much more to buy if the property increases in value during the lease or equity-sharing period. For example, if you sign an equity-sharing agreement to buy a house in two years, and the property value goes up by $15,000, you'll have to pay $7,500 more to buy the house.

But fret not, because one of the hallmarks of being a cheapskate is the ability to make owning a home gratifying as well as financially rewarding. Cheapskates know how to maximize a housing investment by making it in the right place at the right time.

To Own or Not to Own

The first thing cheapskates need to evaluate is whether they're good candidates for home ownership. What does this mean? Even though home ownership is the American dream, many people should not buy. Before you start looking, you need to consider several factors.

First, you need to be relatively sure about the length of time you will live in a new home. If you know you'll be living in it for at least seven years, I think it's a great idea to buy. Unfortunately, these days it's not uncommon for a family to move into a new house and buy again after only two years because of a job transfer or simply because they want a bigger and better house. If you know you'll stay planted for at least seven years, set a time frame for when you want to get the house paid off. You can do it in under ten years if you use the painless cheapskate techniques outlined later in this chapter.

Because the costs of purchasing a home are so high, it is very difficult to recoup your initial investment if you live there for only two or three years. Closing costs, real estate commissions, furnishing, redecorating, repairs, and landscaping are all costs that can be incurred with a home purchase. Unless you get lucky and pick an area where housing is appreciating at unprecedented levels, it is almost impossible to come out ahead in just a few years. You may lose thousands if you choose this route.

In addition, you have almost no equity build-up in your home during those first years because practically all of your early mortgage payments go for interest. Real estate is no different from many other types of investments: It is difficult to get a return on your investment in the early years, but you will see results later.

Sit down and thoroughly evaluate your future plans. If there's a chance you'll be moving out of your new home in the first few years, look into the possibility of renting until you're in a position to stay in a home for at least five years; seven is better. If you rent, you may be paying more per month and not getting any equity build-up, but you won't have to come up with thousands of dollars for closing costs, down payments and repairs. You wouldn't be getting much equity build-up in a new home during this short period anyway. Use the time you spend renting to save and prepare further for your future home purchase.

Finding the Right Loan

The first step in house hunting is getting pre-qualified for the right loan. Getting the wrong type of mortgage or overpaying on fees could end up costing you thousands. Here are a few things cheapskates watch for when they talk to the local mortgage banker.

1. Adjustable rate mortgages. Lenders have been playing around with them for some time. They usually give you ten different options, confuse you, and then hit you with recommendations that are rarely in your best interest. Never fall for a ridiculously low rate without looking at what it will cost you down the road. The lender generally wants to find out what you can afford before quoting you an interest rate. You should do research, too. Call around to several different lenders in your area and ask for current rates. When you choose a lender, hold them to the quoted rate. On the day that you sign the contracts, get your lender to show you the daily rate card so you know that the rate you're paying is the one you committed to.

2. Annual percentage rates. Don't be misled about the APR. Lenders may follow different guidelines on how to calculate it. Always ask for a detailed, itemized list of estimated closing costs when you hand in your loan application. It's required by law. On closing day, look carefully at the figure called "amount financed" on your settlement papers. If it doesn't equal the principal you are borrowing minus any points or interest paid up front, ask the lender why. Some fees may have been added in, which means that you'll pay more interest.

3. Rate lock-ins. Be careful of this option. Lenders have been known to stretch out the application period if it means they'll get a higher rate than they may have gotten if they'd locked you in immediately. Only accept this option when you are confident that rates are going up and you know your transaction will be processed within the lock-in period.

Cheap Trick

If you can put at least 20% down on your home, do it. If you don't, most lenders will require that you purchase Private Mortgage Insurance (PMI), which is expensive and often non-cancelable. If you have no choice, make sure that there's a clause in your mortgage that allows you to cancel the premiums after you've built up at least 20% equity in your home.

4. Closing fees. Ask plenty of questions about these fees. If any fee looks unusually high, point it out. It's not uncommon for lenders to make mistakes and over-charge their customers. Don't accept the lender's word that a "quickie" qualification has pre-qualified you. If anything (such as a flaw in your credit history or incorrect information on your application) comes up between the time of your pre-qualification and your closing, the mortgage company can reject your application. Make sure you go to a lender that does extensive pre-qualifying so that there are no surprises in the process.

5. Prepayment of mortgage principal. Lots of cheapskates pay down their mortgage principal every month to save thousands in interest charges over the long haul. The problem is that most lenders can't figure out how to credit this money to your principal. It sounds crazy but the bank computer systems aren't designed to deal with prepayments. If you want to prepay, ask your lender if it is acceptable and what procedure to follow to do it. Generally you need to send a separate check marked "principal only" for the bank to credit the amount correctly; otherwise, the extra money is put into an escrow account and you won't save yourself a dime. Making extra principal payments is an easy way to get your mortgage paid off sooner. A simpler method is to figure out what you can afford to pay in extra principal every month, and religiously send in this amount towards paying off the principal. If you send in an extra $100 per month, you'll knock off about thirteen years on a 30-year, $100,000 mortgage and save a whopping $47,000 in interest!

Cheap Talk

The annual percentage rate on any loan is the actual annual interest rate you pay on the money you borrow. This rate is usually higher than the "rate" you are quoted because it includes all the fees for the loan in addition to the principal amount.

6. Lender liquidity. Finally, make sure the lender you go through has an excellent reputation and is in sound financial shape. There are lenders going out of business every day and it is up to you to check the stability of the firms you are considering. Simply ask them for the recent financial statements sent to their shareholders. This information will tell you all you need to know about the company's liquidity. Remember you are much more likely to have a good experience with a lender that has been recommended or has done thousands of loans than if you go to one you know nothing about.

The Cheapskate's Best Mortgage

If the idea of paying thousands of dollars in interest on your mortgage makes you ill, you can find cheapskate ways to cut those finance charges down to size.

The best and easiest way to accomplish this is to switch your mortgage over to a biweekly plan. By making half your normal monthly payments every two weeks you pay one extra payment a year—and cut as much as ten years off your mortgage! On a $100,000 mortgage, you'll save about $75,000 in interest, making your mortgage payment a minor item in your budget. Not all mortgage companies will let you do this, but you have a good shot at convincing them if you use the following cheapskate strategies for going on a biweekly plan:

Cheap Trick

If you go on a biweekly pay plan to pay down your mortgage, make sure your payments get made every two weeks by having them automatically deducted from your checking account. Some employers also allow automatic payroll deductions that send the money directly from the company you work for to your mortgage company. This way, you don't have any paperwork hassles either.

➤ Write a formal letter to your mortgage company asking them to amend your mortgage agreement (enclose a copy) to include biweekly payments as an option. Explain that you would like those payments credited to your account immediately upon their receipt, and any overpayments credited to principal only. Tell them that you will assume they've agreed to the payment plan if they do not notify you to the contrary within one month.

➤ If your bank or mortgage company refuses to comply, be persistent. If you put enough pressure on them, they may just accept your proposal to get rid of a good cheapskate like you. Also, a short letter from a lawyer friend might just be the ticket to put the lender over the edge.

➤ If your lender is being stubborn, and all else fails, you can still make extra principal payments to help reduce your mortgage. Have your banker or mortgage company run you an amortization schedule that tells you how much of each payment is principal and how much is interest. Every month, make your regular payment, and also write a separate check for the next month's principal amount. Write on the check that it is for "principal only."

Paying down your principal every month can cut your finance charges by thousands over the years.

Frugality Footnote

Maximize your cheapskate strategy and get your 30-year mortgage paid off in under ten years. Simply combine a biweekly plan with making extra principal payments every month.

Divide and Pay Down

Still another way is to divide your monthly payment by 12 and send this amount every month to pay down your principal. For instance, if your monthly mortgage payment is $800, you would send an extra $66 each month to pay down your principal.

However, the best plan is to make biweekly mortgage payments, because once you begin paying you don't really notice the extra money going out of your budget. But you must be disciplined and make two payments a month. It's worth the time and energy because you'll own your home that much sooner. Another advantage to a biweekly plan is that it will be much less of a bite out of your budget than if you make the entire payment on the 1st of the month.

How to Calculate Your Mortgage Payments

The following table shows you an easy way to calculate what your monthly mortgage payments will be for every $1,000 you borrow, not including insurance or taxes. For example, if you were to borrow $100,000 at 7.5 percent on a 30-year note, your monthly payment would be approximately $700.00 (100 x $7). You can quickly figure the cost difference between a 15-year note and 30-year note using this chart:

Monthly Payment Per $1,000

Interest Rate	15-Year	30-Year
5.00%	$7.91	$5.37
5.25%	$8.04	$5.52
5.50%	$8.17	$5.68
5.75%	$8.30	$5.84
6.00%	$8.44	$6.00
6.25%	$8.57	$6.16

Interest Rate	15-Year	30-Year
6.50%	$8.71	$6.32
6.75%	$8.85	$6.49
7.00%	$8.99	$6.66
7.25%	$9.13	$6.83
7.50%	$9.28	$7.00
7.75%	$9.42	$7.17
8.00%	$9.56	$7.34
8.25%	$9.71	$7.52
8.50%	$9.85	$7.69
8.75%	$10.00	$7.87
9.00%	$10.15	$8.05
9.25%	$10.30	$8.23
9.50%	$10.45	$8.41
9.75%	$10.60	$8.60
10.00%	$10.75	$8.78

The Ideal Down Payment

What's the ideal amount to put down on a home you are purchasing? It's hard to give a specific figure because there are so many variables involved, but most cheapskates follow a few good rules.

➤ If you have to trade up to the highest-priced house you can buy, or if it's your first home, then you should put as little down as possible. In other words, take the most you can from the bank, assuming you have the cash flow to support it. In the 1980s, it was not uncommon to see a lot of "nothing down" deals. In the current environment, 15 to 20 percent down is average.

➤ If you have enough cash in savings to put more down on your mortgage, the amount of the down payment should be determined by the investment return you can get elsewhere. Compare the interest cost on your mortgage to the expected return on another investment. If the investment is taxable, take this into account: If your mortgage is at 8 percent, for example, then you should be getting 3 to 4 percentage points more on your investment to make a smaller mortgage worth it. Try to

Cheap Shot

Cheapskates always prepay their mortgage, regardless of the fact that they may be reducing their interest tax deduction. You receive a tax deduction on the interest portion of your mortgage payment only, but only up to your tax bracket. If your tax bracket is 28%, you will save taxes on only 28% of the interest you pay. Also, your tax deduction withers away as you pay off the interest.

look at investments from an after-tax perspective. You may find, for example, that the after-tax return on a tax-free municipal bond exceeds the after-tax cost of the mortgage. Don't forget to look at all fees associated with your loan, and add in your investment fees, such as brokerage costs.

➤ You should also consider that the money you put into your home ties that money up, so you're losing liquidity and flexibility. If you lose that liquidity, you could be squeezed financially if an emergency crops up or you come across an outstanding investment opportunity. Many cheapskates feel as if their net worth is down when they don't have funds or cash to invest. If all your money is tied up in a home, it's hard to gauge exactly how much you really have.

Frugality Footnote

There are some cheapskates who can afford the luxury of buying a home with all cash. This can be a good idea if it doesn't deplete your entire savings and you have a significant monthly cash flow that is reliable. The cash flow can help replenish your lost savings.

In general, it's best to focus on the big picture. If you were to purchase a home and deplete all your investment savings, then you could put yourself in a very tight spot. Putting 20 percent down on a home is a good starting point, but it shouldn't make you "house-poor." If you feel you can handle more than the required amount down, look at different scenarios, starting with 5 percent increments. For instance, see how it would impact your financial picture if you put 25 percent down, or 30 percent, etc.

Don't ever buy a home if:

➤ There is extensive water damage, especially to structural beams.

➤ The house is not hooked up to the city sewer system, or it needs a new cesspool.

➤ A new roof is needed and the seller won't pay for it.

➤ The building is structurally unsound due to poor workmanship or poor materials and has hazardous materials such as asbestos or lead paint.

➤ There is evidence of termite infestation.

➤ The house is built on a cliff.

All these things could require extensive and expensive repairs. Nothing is worse than falling in love with a house that is unsound and thinking that you can "fix it up." Go on to the next house—the one without any major problems.

Building a New Home

If you're planning to build a house, shop around for the best builder. Estimates for the same house can differ by as much as 15 percent. On a $150,000 home, that's a difference of $20,000!

Price is a big factor, but not the only one. Check the builder's quality of workmanship by visiting homes they've constructed. Ask for ten or more references, and ask them tons of questions. Ask the builder for an approximate cost per square foot. If you are evaluating several different builders, this is a good way to gauge whether the added cost per foot is worth the gain in quality.

Cheap Shot

To avoid inflated estimates on new homes, it's best to stay with one of the builder's stock designs. They've probably built several, so costs will be lower. A custom-built house always costs more than you expected it to, and it may not turn out quite the way you envisioned it.

If you decide to build a new home, ask the builder if you can do the post-construction cleanup yourself. Not only will this save you money, but you and a few of your family members can probably do a better job. Contractors often hire inefficient and costly cleaners who may not clean up paint splatters, dust in corners, and so forth. Depending on the size of the job, you may save several hundred dollars.

Taxes Are Killing Me!

Like many Americans, you may be faced with enormous property taxes this year. When you get the bill, you may react with disgust and pay it along with all the other bills. If you think there's nothing else you can do because it's a tax, you're wrong!

Many counties make mistakes when it comes to calculating property tax levies. Often the dimensions of the land are inaccurate, skewing calculations. The descriptions of the land or the buildings on it might also be wrong. Improvements can be calculated incorrectly. There are many things that can go wrong in evaluating properties. Call a reputable attorney and find out your rights. Many cheapskates have been pleasantly surprised when they've pushed the assessor's office up against the wall and won their case for lower taxes.

A Second Home Is a Second Hassle

Boy, it sure would be nice to have a vacation home. It sure would be dumb, too. Vacation homes are rarely a good investment, despite what vacation area Realtors might tell you. These homes or condominiums usually cost a ton of money to buy and maintain, and that giant sucking sound (as Ross Perot would put it) continues on, year after year. Only in a few cases does the rental income received help to "pay for" the investment. There's also a risk factor that you must take into consideration: If a recession hits, vacation properties are likely to be the first investments to drop in value.

113

A better plan is to search for the best vacation deals you can make on a yearly basis. (See Chapter 13 for vacation values.) If you're dead set on a certain area, find the best and cheapest place to stay and go back every year. You'll save a lot of money in the long run.

If you just can't live without a second home, make sure you spread the risk considerably by inviting four or five other families to split the cost. This is better than going it alone, but it's still not a terrific investment.

Cheap Thrills in Homes

➤ Your monthly mortgage payment for a new home should be no more than 25 to 30 percent of your gross family income. Simply put, this means you should not buy a home with a price that exceeds two to three times your gross income.

➤ When you buy a home, don't automatically think that it's your responsibility to pay for all closing costs. Just like everything else in the cheapskate's world, closing costs are negotiable and may even be paid completely by the seller.

Cheap Trick

Never make fancy improvements to your home to make it the best one in the neighborhood. Likewise, never purchase the best home in the neighborhood. In any neighborhood, increases in property value are greater for more modest homes than for costlier ones. Buy a house that is about mid-level in price if you want the best investment.

➤ What's up with the American way of life? We save for years to buy a beautiful home and then a year later we're thinking about a bigger and better home. Resist the temptation to trade up to another house for as long as you can. Even when you feel like you just have to move, make do with what you've got for several more years. If you don't, you'll just get deeper into debt.

➤ If you've got the time, consider selling your home yourself. There's some work and aggravation involved, but it's well worth it when you get to pocket the real estate commission you'll save. If it becomes too difficult for you to sell it yourself, you can always hire a real estate agent.

➤ If interest rates drop about 2 percent below what you're paying on your current mortgage, you can save a lot of money by refinancing. But refinance only if you're planning to be in the home for several more years. You'll need that time to recoup your refinancing costs.

➤ Even though, granted, buying a house is partly about a lifestyle change, it's important not to get too emotionally involved in your choices. Remember that, above all, you're making an investment. Cheapskates always keep a level head when negotiating, and make sure that all the numbers are in their best interest before they buy.

Frugality Footnote

You won't find many smart cheapskates living in the city. Generally, housing costs get lower the further you move from urban areas. You may want to live in the suburbs, or even in the country, where you can get lots of land for practically nothing. The commute will be farther and an added cost, but you'll save on housing in Green Acres and may enjoy the quieter lifestyle.

➤ If you're antsy to get out of the house you're currently in, before you spend the money to buy a new one, consider making some home improvements. Often, an updated kitchen, bath, or added room can make your home much more comfortable and costs considerably less than buying a new house. Just make sure that the major improvements you undertake will add value to your home.

The Least You Need to Know

➤ When you evaluate your housing needs, if you aren't going to stay put for a long time, consider renting. Buy a home only if you're going to live in it for at least five years, preferably seven.

➤ When you search for a home mortgage, call several different companies and ask lots of questions. Make sure the lender thoroughly pre-qualifies you before you proceed with the loan.

➤ Once you get a loan, make extra principal payments every month to pay off your mortgage a lot sooner.

➤ Put the maximum possible amount down on a mortgage. Shoot for at least 20 percent to avoid having to pay for overpriced private mortgage insurance.

➤ If you're building a new home, shop around to find the best builder with the best prices.

➤ Resist the temptation to buy a second home. A second home is nothing but a second hassle and a bank account drain.

Housekeeping 101

In This Chapter

➤ Fix it yourself and save

➤ Some paint on your shirt isn't gonna hurt

➤ Zap the pests and save the rest

➤ Keep it spic 'n' span with the cheapskate plan

➤ Home improvements that pay off

➤ Maintaining your yard doesn't have to be hard

So, you're wondering how a cheapskate can possibly save money housekeeping? The expenses associated with keeping the house clean and well maintained may seem minor compared with what it costs to maintain your car or shop for electronics. But if you're not doing it cheapskate style, you can spend some big money. Detergents, paper towels, trash bags, tools for repairs, and cleaning supplies can take a big bite out of your budget. With preventive maintenance, you can avoid many major housekeeping chores, but that means there are things that have to be done every week.

There's really no end to housekeeping. As soon as we finish one chore, there's another waiting in the wings. Then, when that one's done, it's time to get back to chore number one. Whew! Well, maybe you can't cut down on the number of chores you have to do, but you sure can make them easier and less expensive. So let this cheapskate take you on a tour of your home, and you may be amazed at how many ways you'll find to save time and money on housekeeping.

Break Out the Tools

Even if you're one of those picky types who pays meticulous attention to maintaining your home, there will always be things that need repair. Cheapskates save a lot of money around the house by doing simple maintenance themselves. Buy a home repair manual at the local discount home warehouse, or get a book from the library, and you can learn how to do your own repairs, too. A little time invested in education will save you a lot of time and money later.

Frugality Footnote

Time/Life Books has a great home repair book series. It covers everything from building a deck to basic plumbing. If you're wondering if the books may be too complex, forget it; the electrical book even tells you how to change a light bulb! Now that's my kind of repair book! Buy books individually as projects come up, or just check them out at the library.

If you learn how to repair simple things around the house, you'll save hundreds of dollars a year in professional repair costs. For example, you should learn the basics of your heating and air-conditioning systems. Where are the pilot lights on your furnace (and gas range, too)? How do you change the air filter? Where are the power boxes, and how do you turn them off and on? All these things are simple to learn about, and are common trouble spots for homeowners. When the pilot light gets snuffed out, if you know how to relight it, do it yourself, and save the $50 an hour it would have cost if you'd called a repair person.

By doing regular maintenance yourself instead of calling a professional you can save as much as 75%, because you'll have material costs only. But let's not jump too soon. There are trickier projects that should be tackled only by pros. Here's a guide to what a good cheapskate should and should not do.

When Should You Call In the Pros?

Job	Do It Yourself	Call in the Pros
Paint Interior	✔	
Paint Exterior	✔	
Install a window		✔
Fix broken window	✔	

Job	Do It Yourself	Call in the Pros
Install carpeting		✔
Install Tile	✔	
Replace damaged pipes		✔
Install new furnace		✔
Wallpaper	✔	
Insulate attic	✔	
Refinish wood floor	✔	
Install dimmer switches		✔
New electrical wiring		✔
Build a deck	✔	
Install paneling	✔	
Install kitchen cabinets		✔
Install exterior siding		✔

A Little Sloppy Savings

Doing your own painting can save you a heap of cash because hiring a paint contractor can be costly. With a little planning, you can tackle walls, ceilings, woodwork, and even the exterior of your home without getting too sloppy.

The first thing you need to know to get started is that you must have adequate equipment. Nothing can make a job go slower and come out worse than poor equipment. Go to a reputable paint supplier and spend a little money on good-quality scrapers, brushes, rollers, and ladders. Don't skimp. It pays to spend a little more for equipment that you'll be able to use over and over for years to come. And remember that you're saving a lot by not hiring a professional painter.

Cheap Shot

If you can't handle a home project yourself and need to hire a contractor, be careful. Always check on their licensing, talk with previous clients, and insist on everything in writing. Never pay the full amount up front; pay in thirds. Beware of standard contracts from office supply stores; they usually protect the contractor legally, not you.

Latex is generally the best type of paint to use on most jobs and is much easier to work with than oil-based paint, which will soon be banned by the government anyway. Until the ban takes effect, oil-based paint still has its uses for exterior priming and for interior woodwork.

The painting is the easy and fun part. The most important part of any paint job is how you prepare the surface for painting. A great preparation job will ensure the paint's adhesion.

Frugality Footnote

The exterior of your home may not need painting at all. Check the surface by putting a little water on an area that looks bad, and then rubbing it. If dirt comes off, not paint, you can probably make the house look brand-new again simply by cleaning it. For about $40, you can rent a power washer and clean the whole house in about half a day.

1. Scrape any loose or peeling paint and repair any holes or cracks in the surfaces with spackling or caulk.

2. Sand any areas that look shabby or seem like they may not hold the paint well.

Cheap Trick

The cost of paint is escalating rapidly, and it's now not uncommon to pay $30 for a gallon. Too rich for a cheapskate's blood. Call around to different paint stores and suppliers to find the best price. You don't want to go too cheap, though. Inferior paint will not last as long, so make sure that what you're putting on will stay on. Go to your local home improvement warehouse and ask the experts in the paint section to give you some advice.

3. Prime any bare wood with an oil-based primer. Unlike latex paint, oil-based paint soaks into bare wood, allowing the latex paint to bond properly. After the preparation work, make sure the surface is clean.

4. Conserve paint and make less of a mess by pouring it into a pail with a handle rather than trying to paint from the can.

5. Indoors, paint one wall at a time. First fill in the corners with your brush, and then roll the paint on to the rest of the wall. Rolling over wet brush edges immediately will ensure an even look.

6. On the exterior of your house, start by filling in the corners of the entire house and then applying paint with a roller as in indoor painting.

7. If you choose to do the painting yourself, make sure you have plenty of touch-up paint left over for the years to come. Label the touch-up containers, and check the entire house once a year for areas that need touching up. If you keep up this annual maintenance, your paint job will last years longer.

If you decide to hire a professional painter because you think you just can't handle the job or don't have time, go with a reputable firm that has insurance and plenty of references. Most painters will negotiate on price if you feel the cost is too high. You may try swapping out some of the work that you'll do yourself for a lower price on the bid. Just make sure the contract specifies exactly what you'll be doing.

Don't Pay to Keep the Critters at Bay

Yazooks! More bugs in the cupboard! How are you going to get rid of them without paying an exterminator hundreds of dollars? Well, cheapskates always have an inexpensive solution.

Most exterminators use a product called Dursban® to get rid of almost all household insects. It's a milky-like chemical that just mixes with water. If you make a trip to the local hardware or discount home supply store you can pick up a bottle for about $5. Also purchase a regular garden sprayer if you don't already have one.

Mix according to directions and spray all along the outside of your house and in your basement, once in the spring and once in the fall. You can also use this spray indoors, but do so sparingly. To make sure you kill every kind of bug, also get two or three bottles of insect fogger and set them off twice a year in your entire home.

If you spray with Dursban® and use a fogger twice a year, you'll do just as good a job as the exterminator for about a quarter of the cost. If you're unfortunate enough to have fleas, you may need to repeat this process for several weeks in a row. Keep an eye out for any major problems like carpenter ants or termites. If you do find these nasty critters, or a hive of bees or wasps, call in the pros.

Cheap Shot

Be very careful when you work with any extermination chemicals. Always follow the safety procedures. Wear a particle mask over your mouth and nose when spraying, and avoid getting any of the chemicals on your hands by wearing gloves. If you spray or fog indoors, stay out of the house for an afternoon and wash all dishes afterwards. If you play it safe, you'll have no problems.

Spic 'n' Span with the Cheapskate Plan

Good cheapskates aren't above getting on their hands and knees to do some scrubbing. There are a number of condensed organic cleaners on the market that can make cleaning easier and less expensive such as Simple Green. These cleaners usually come in gallon jugs—you have to take the time to dilute them appropriately for each cleaning job—but in the cheapskate scheme of things, that's time well spent.

The best products have a citrus base, and you simply mix them with water in the right proportion for the particular job. I recommend buying four or five professional squirt bottles, labeling them, and mixing them for different cleaning jobs. One gallon of cleaner can last a year or two and can handle any job around the house, including windows. Wouldn't it be nice to be able to throw away those twenty bottles of brand-name cleaners you never use? Check your local warehouse club or discount store for the kinds of condensed cleaners available.

If you have a dishwasher, use just a tablespoon of dishwashing detergent rather than the cup or more the machine holds. You'll find that your dishes get just as clean, and you'll save in the long run.

When you're washing clothes, use the same trick. I think you'll find that you can get the same job done with a lot less than is recommended by manufacturers of many cleaning products. Why? It's common sense that the more we use, the more they sell.

Some liquid cleaners are so potent that you can dilute them 50 percent with water and they will still do what they're supposed to. Try using smaller amounts of household products such as glass cleaner, dishwashing liquid, and furniture polish, too.

If you need cleaning supplies and are a little low on cash or run out of a certain type of cleaner, try some of these inexpensive alternatives:

Cheap Trick

Remodeling can help you lower your taxes. When you sell, you can deduct the cost of your improvements and the original cost of your home from the new selling price. The amount left over is the total capital gain for tax purposes. Hey, Einstein? It doesn't take a lot of improvements to lower your taxes considerably.

Cleaning Alternatives

Product	Use For:
Shampoo	Removing ring around the collar
Vinegar/lemon juice	Cutting grease and cleaning glass. And, when added to hot water, unclogging drains.
Crumpled newspaper	Cleaning mirrors and windows
Hair spray	Getting out ink stains on shirts
Hydrogen peroxide	Works well on blood stains
Baking soda	Good scouring powder
Cornstarch	Removing grease stains from clothes and carpet

Smart Home Improvements

Cheapskates often choose to do major remodeling jobs on their current homes rather than move to a new one. The reason? If the remodeling is done correctly, it's much more cost effective to add an addition, say, than to pay for a whole new house. For instance, if you add an extra bedroom in your basement, it may cost about $3,000 if you do some of it yourself and contract out the more difficult jobs. If you wanted an additional room in a larger house, it could cost you as much as $10,000 just for the room, plus there are closing costs to consider. Also, looking for a larger home will tempt you to purchase something that's a lot more than you need.

When you make home improvements it's easy to spend foolishly. In the past, cheap-skates who wanted to add a new kitchen or bath to their home would take out a personal loan and just deduct the interest. Now, because deductibility of personal loan interest has been done away with, they use home equity loans to accomplish the same thing. But is it really necessary to get a loan to make improvements? Often, if you plan it right, you can pay cash for even a major job such as a new kitchen.

How to Remodel the Kitchen Without a Loan

Project	How to Handle It	Cost
Cabinet facelift	Just replace the doors and hardware yourself	$700
Countertops	Hire a pro to put in good quality materials	$1,600
Sink Tiles	Get a kit from the home supply store	$100
Floors	Hire a pro to lay quality vinyl	$800
Sink	Hire a pro to install a new sink and disposal	$500
Major appliances	Buy inexpensive floor models	$1,400
Walls	Paint or wallpaper yourself	$200
Total:		**$5,300**

As you can see from the table, you can accomplish a complete kitchen remodeling for about half the cost of contracting it all out. You don't necessarily need to take out a loan to do it if you save and plan for it to happen.

Frugality Footnote

Cheapskates always think about how long they'll live in their home before they remodel. In general, the longer you stay in your home after a project is completed the more money you'll get back when you sell. Many improvements, such as adding more insulation or installing energy-efficient windows, take years before they pay off in savings.

If you want to get the most out of your remodeling, you have to be very careful about what choices you make. For instance, if you remodel a kitchen or bath, or add a room to your home, eventually you'll get top dollar from those improvements. When you go to sell your home, you'll most likely recoup the cost of the additions. If you spend money on other jobs such as adding a game room or sun room, it's very difficult to get your money back.

To make sure you aren't going overboard with your improvements, look at what other homeowners in the neighborhood are doing. You never want to do more than your neighbor, because having the fanciest house on the block will not make it any more valuable; in fact, you'll just lose your extra investment when you sell. Stick with the basics and you can't go wrong.

Rake in the Cash

Now it's time to turn your attention outdoors. There are a lot of things you can do around the yard to save yourself plenty of dough. All you have to do is be willing to get your hands a little dirty.

1. First, make a special effort to learn how to be your own gardener. Go to the local library and pick up a book or two on gardening and landscaping to make sure you do the job right. You can plant flowers, start a vegetable garden, mow the lawn, rake the leaves, and seed the lawn all by your lonesome. If you live in an area that has snowy winters, shovel the snow yourself. If you paid someone to do all these things around the yard, you would probably end up broke at the end of the year.

> **Cheap Trick**
>
> If you have a deck, clean it off every two years with a deck renewer and protect it with a quality wood preservative. You can get both of these products at a discount home warehouse. They'll prolong the life of the deck by many years.

2. Take time this spring to clean that grimy old patio furniture. You should really do this twice a year to keep it in good shape and prevent corroding. Use a strong cleaner; the dirt build-up on patio furniture is usually tough to get off. It's a good idea to put the furniture indoors for the winter if you have the space to store it.

Cheap Thrills When Keeping House

➤ To prevent bacteria in your kitchen on counters, stoves, and in the refrigerator, use different sponges and towels for different duties (such as wiping counters, cleaning dishes, and drying dishes). Buy a value pack of sponges and use new ones every month or so. Clean your can opener every time you use it so you don't get rotten food build-up on the blade. Be careful not to use the same knives and cutting boards for vegetables and meats. Thaw frozen food in the refrigerator or in the microwave. Thawing food on the counter all day can be risky. Last, don't overcrowd your refrigerator, because it will cost more to operate. Clean it out every couple of months.

➤ To avoid unnecessary wood rot and leaks, clean your gutters once a year. If you're afraid of heights and don't want to handle the job, it's worth it to hire someone to come in and do it. To avoid endless cleanings, install plastic strips of mesh along the tops of all the guttering. You can get this mesh very cheaply at any home supply store, and it will reduce the need to clean your gutters dramatically.

➤ Do you have an extra room in the house, or perhaps a finished basement that no one ever uses? Consider taking in a boarder to help defray your housing costs. They can also help you with housekeeping. Post notices at local colleges or companies. An ad in the newspaper is good, but be prepared to interview a lot of people before you can find one who seems appropriate. If you can, install separate eating and bathing facilities for the tenant. If you don't want them getting in your way, the extra expense can be well worth it.

➤ I was in the bookstore a while back and spotted a book about the hundreds of ways that you can use duct tape to fix things around the house. It first struck me as a cute book about impractical ways to use it. Then I opened it up and realized how many very good uses there are for this amazing glue-like stuff. I also remembered that there are probably three or four things in my house that are held together by this miracle tape. Some ideas: Repair a leaky hose, mend broken wires, repair a slight leak in a pipe, clamp items down for gluing, fix punctures in air mattresses, seal leaks in rubber boots, and of course, mend an air duct (how ingenious). There are hundreds of inventive ways it can be used. One note of caution: Always buy good-quality duct tape for added durability. You'll notice that the good stuff has a lot of thread mesh.

Frugality Footnote

Cheapskates have several tasks they perform on a twice-a-year basis: turning mattresses, major house cleaning, beating rugs, rotating car tires, and inspecting appliances. The best way to remember to do these things is to coordinate them with the change from standard time to daylight savings, and then back again.

➤ Buy a six-pack of soda water and use it to clean spots or pet stains out of your carpet or upholstery. The reason for a six-pack? The soda works best when it has plenty of fizz. So be prepared to open a new bottle if you have to. Soda water works better than any other cleaner on carpets and upholstery and is a fraction of the cost of name-brand cleaners. If you can keep on top of the stains, you'll save big bucks on costly professional steam cleaners, too.

➤ How do you know if the carpet you're installing in your home is good quality? First, check the density. Closely packed yarns and tight backing make for carpets that wear a long time. Simply bend the carpet backward and see if a lot of backing is visible through the pile. If it is, it's probably not good quality. It's not a good idea to buy plush carpeting for high-traffic areas, since it has a tendency to mat down. Always buy good padding to go under the carpet; it provides more comfort and helps the carpet last longer. If cost is a problem, don't skimp on quality. You'd be better off buying less carpet or putting lower quality carpeting in high-traffic areas.

➤ Unless you live on a football field, it's really not necessary to have a gas-guzzling, smoke-producing lawnmower. Consider buying a clean and quiet non-power push mower. Your neighbors may think you're batty, but it's environmentally sound, and not bad exercise either. You can cut your annual lawn maintenance costs by as much as 500 percent just by making this simple change.

The Least You Need to Know

➤ Consider doing repairs and routine maintenance yourself, and more often. If you are stumped by a project, before you dial the nearest pro, consider getting a book or manual on the project and trying your hand at it. It may be difficult, but next time it will be that much easier.

➤ Doing your own painting and wallpapering can be one of the easiest projects and biggest money-savers there is. If you're considering hiring a pro to do the job, try it yourself first.

➤ Get rid of household insects and your exterminator, too. All you have to do is prepare a simple formula and spray away all the creepy invaders yourself.

➤ Use inexpensive and environmentally safe cleaners instead of the name-brand products. You'll save a bunch and do a much better cleaning job.

➤ Before you run out and buy a new house because "you've grown out of the old one," consider remodeling to add needed space.

➤ Do all yard work around your home yourself, and enlist the help of the rest of the family, too. You'll save hundreds of dollars per year on landscapers and lawn professionals.

COSTS

POWER

Chapter 11

Power-Up, But Keep Costs Down

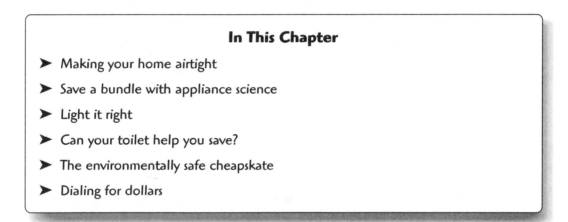

In This Chapter

➤ Making your home airtight

➤ Save a bundle with appliance science

➤ Light it right

➤ Can your toilet help you save?

➤ The environmentally safe cheapskate

➤ Dialing for dollars

Most people spend almost as much on keeping their house or apartment running as they do for the mortgage or rent. In the old days, utility and energy costs didn't amount to much; today it's a different story. According to government statistics, the average American will spend about $1,500 per year just to heat and cool their humble abode. Not us cheapskates!

As with any cost-cutting effort, reducing your utility bills and energy costs means paying attention to details. You need to make small adjustments here, clean a filter there, replace an outdated appliance with an energy efficient one—then, at year's end, you'll see how much you've saved. Everyone needs to become more energy conscious. It's good for our community, our planet, and, of course, the cheapskate's pocketbook—what's not to like? Read on for great ways to cut your energy bills without sacrificing your creature comforts.

Seal It Tight

Test your home at least once a year for any air leakage problems. Air leaks in the typical American home account for at least 30 to 40 percent of all heating and cooling bills. No matter how you heat or cool your home, you can save a lot of money with a relatively small investment in insulation, caulking, and weather-stripping.

Check around windows and doors, and also look for cracks that may allow energy to escape. Locate joints where window frames do not meet the wall, and cracked or chipping putty around window panes. To test an outside door, open and close it quickly. If there is resistance (a vacuum effect), the door is properly insulated. If it opens too easily, you may need to add weather-stripping around one or more sides. Another way to test for leaks is to walk around windows and doors with a lighted candle. If the flame wavers, you probably have a leak.

Once you find the leaks, here are some tips to fix them:

1. Caulk both the interior and exterior surfaces that are causing problems. Fill spaces around doors and window frames, sink and toilet pipes, and where cables enter your home. After you caulk these areas, you may find that new leaks have developed because drafts have shifted, so check again.

2. Weather-stripping can be applied in very thin layers around doors and windows.

3. Invest in quality storm doors and storm windows to fully protect your house from leaks. An added benefit of quality storm windows is that they'll help cut down on window maintenance costs.

4. Often, door or windowsill drafts can be taken care of with a draft guard. These are long, circular tubes filled with sand. You can make one yourself by sewing together old tube socks and filling them with sand.

5. In the winter, cover your air conditioner to keep wind from entering it and going into the duct system of your house. Also, install glass fireplace doors to prevent heat from escaping up the chimney.

Cheap Shot

Be sure to have adequate insulation in your ground floor, attic, and along interior walls exposed to the outside. Select quality insulation that has the right "R–value," for heating and cooling in your area of the country. Your local home discount warehouse will have what you need.

Cheap Trick

Check with your local electric or gas company to see if they will do a free energy audit of your home. Many larger utility companies are starting to do this to improve their customer service image. If they won't do it free, it's worth paying them a $40–$50 fee. An audit will save you much more than that in the long run.

Mother Nature's Heating and Cooling

Use nature's own heating and cooling system to your advantage.

➤ In most parts of the country, nights are cool about nine months out of the year. If you want to cool the house, open the windows at night and let the cool, fresh air circulate. Add an attic fan to this equation and you'll dramatically increase air flow.

➤ To help Mother Nature along during the hotter months, in the morning and afternoon, close the curtains and shades on the sunny side of your home. Keep the windows on the "dark side" open for air circulation.

➤ If it's cold outside and you want to keep the house warm, keep your windows, curtains, blinds, and shades shut until the sun comes out, and then open them to let the sun warm the house. When the sun sets, shut them again to keep the house warm.

If you just pay a little more attention to nature's ways, you can save substantially. How do you think the cheapskates of old survived when there was no heating or air conditioning?

Save a Heap with Appliance Science

We've become a society dependent on modern conveniences, so it's best to use the most efficient appliances possible and keep them in good shape.

➤ Once a year, check the seals around refrigerator and freezer doors. Cracked or broken seals mean your refrigerator has to work a lot harder.

➤ Keep the dust bag in your vacuum clean. If it's full, the vacuum loses its suction and is less efficient.

➤ Don't forget to change the furnace filter every three to six months. It can get clogged fast.

➤ Keep the drains in your dishwasher clear; clogged drains can cause your machine to malfunction or overflow.

All these easy maintenance procedures can save you a lot of money over the years.

You can really save a bundle with many of the new energy-efficient appliances on the market. The following is information from the Council for an Energy-Efficient Economy. It gives average annual savings figures if you use regular appliances as opposed to energy-efficient models.

Frugality Footnote

Annual heating and cooling checkups save money in the long run. Although an inspection costs about $40, you'll lose even more if your system is malfunctioning or the airflow in your home is improper. Call a reputable heating and cooling company to inspect your systems at least once a year. You'll be more comfortable in your home, and your equipment will last many more years.

Appliance Annual Operating Costs

	Average Appliance	Energy-Efficient Appliance	Annual Savings
Central air conditioner	$300	$150	$150
Window air conditioner	60	40	20
Electric clothes dryer	70	55	15
Gas clothes dryer	30	25	5
Clothes washer	90	45	45
Dishwasher	70	45	25
Frost-free freezer	135	75	60
Manual-defrost freezer	75	40	35
Household light fixtures	75	50	25
Frost-free refrigerator	120	70	50
Manual-defrost refrigerator	45	30	15
Electric stove	60	50	10
Gas stove	45	35	10
Television	25	10	15
Electric water heater	300	150	150
Gas water heater	160	130	30
Total Annual Savings:			**$660**

Turn Off Those Darn Lights! #@*&+!, Did You Hear Me?

Few of us can forget those fond childhood memories of Dad yelling at the top of his lungs for us to turn off one of the ten lights we had on. Truth is, Dad was only trying his best to be a good cheapskate. He always had good intentions, but what Dad didn't know was that just turning off the lights wasn't the answer.

Most people tend think it's sensible to turn the lights off in a room when you leave. The truth is that turning a regular incandescent light off and on shortens the life of the bulb. If you're leaving the room for only a while, and are an obsessive light switch flipper, think twice about flipping that switch. You'll be better off leaving the light on for the few minutes that you'll be gone.

Think those long-life light bulbs are a lifesaver? Think again. Avoid long-life bulbs except for hard-to-reach places. They cost more and are less energy efficient than normal light bulbs. Buy generic bulbs at the supermarket or discount home supply store, and buy special energy efficient bulbs when they're on sale.

Turn off decorative outside gas or electric lamps when you can, unless they're used for safety purposes. A couple of gas lights that burn year-round can use up enough gas to heat an entire house for a winter! Depending on the part of the country you live in, it can cost as much as $5 a month to keep that flame aglow. If you have to have outdoor lighting, buy an inexpensive timer or photocell that will turn the lights on and off automatically.

Cheap Trick

Use fluorescent bulbs when you can because they're the most efficient of all lighting sources. You can leave a room for several hours with the lights still on, come back, and they will have consumed an infinitesimal amount of energy. Fluorescent bulbs are also less prone to burning out from switch flipping. They're used in office buildings because of their lower cost and durability.

Can Your Toilet Help You Save?

Does a good cheapskate really have to talk about toilets? You bet. Strange as it may seem, toilet flushing accounts for the greatest demand on the country's water supply—about 38 percent of all the water consumed! For decades, the normal toilet used 5 gallons per flush. In the late 1970s, manufacturers introduced the so-called water-conserving toilet that used 3.5 gallons per flush—not a big difference. The newest toilets, introduced over a decade ago, use only 1.5 gallons of water per flush and are inexpensively priced. They also have excellent performance records.

Water and sewer rates vary widely from city to city, but it's probably safe to say that you could easily save $50 a year per toilet by using low-flow toilets in your home. That may not seem like much; however, you must remember that you are also conserving water that could be vital to your community. If you replace old toilets with new ones, they should pay for themselves within three to four years. If your toilets are more than 20 years old, they're less efficient, so think about replacing them.

Wash Up Without Washing Out

Showers consume more than one-fifth of all the water used indoors, and more hot water than any other fixture or appliance. Installing a low-flow showerhead is a simple and inexpensive way to cut down on water consumption. For approximately $10 per shower, you can install a new showerhead and save your family about 10,000 gallons of water per year. You also save the energy it takes to heat part of that water, which can run about $30 to $60 per year. Of course, savings will depend on how often your family uses the shower, what kind of showerheads you currently own, and how much you pay for heating your water.

Cheap Shot

Fix water drips and leaks fast. A running toilet can use as much as 2,000 gallons of water a year. If it runs on for just a week, it could double your monthly bill. Avoid watering the lawn during the day when the sun is out; do it at dusk. Tell your family not to let the water run while shaving, brushing teeth, washing dishes or hand-washing clothes.

Installing a new showerhead is simple: Just unscrew the old shower head with large pliers or an adjustable wrench. If it's stuck, steady the pipe with a pipe wrench while you turn the head. Then simply screw the new head into place.

It used to be that showerheads delivered about five to eight gallons of water per minute. Manufacturers have recently done a good job of cutting back the flow rates and not lowering the quality of the shower. Showerheads designed for low water flow usually have a smaller spray area and might also mix air with the flow to provide more pressure. Most new showerheads deliver about three gallons of water per minute. Quite an improvement.

Being Kind to Your Cheapskate Environment

We can keep the environment healthy and save money at the same time. The key to accomplishing both is to reuse as many items in your household as possible. Instead of throwing things out, find new and creative ways to use them. When you've stretched the life of a product for as long as you could, dispose of it in an environmentally sound way.

➤ When possible, choose products that have long life spans. Disposable products, such as razors, cameras, cups, plates, lighters, and diapers, all end up in the same place—your local landfill. As an example, in the United States, 500 million lighters are tossed out every year. From a cheapskate's point of view, it's a bad idea to smoke, but if you must, buy a permanent lighter to save money and decrease waste.

Frugality Footnote

Buy whatever you can in bulk and pay special attention to the kind of packaging a product uses. Some estimates point to the fact that 60% of American waste is just product packaging.

➤ Use recycled paper products when you can. They are usually cheaper than other products and quite often provide the same quality as the name-brand stuff. You can find facial tissue, toilet paper, napkins, paper plates, paper cups, and other products that have been recycled.

➤ If you change the oil in your car or lawnmower, take it to a local recycling center. Studies show that 2.1 million gallons of oil seeps into our rivers and streams in a year's time. A quart of motor oil can contaminate over 250,000 gallons of drinking water! Call local gas stations or your energy board to find out the best places to recycle used motor oil.

➤ The U.S. Postal Service estimates that every family in America receives over 300 pieces of junk mail a year. When you order anything through the mail, include a note that that you not be included on any mailing lists that they may rent out. Most companies will oblige. This will dramatically cut down on your junk mail. To get off junk mail lists, call or write The Direct Marketing Association, 1120 Avenue of the Americas, New York, NY 10036; 212-768-7277. Or you can hop on the Internet and go to http://www.junkbusters.com to get off the lists fast.

➤ Use only biodegradable detergents and soaps. You can use less of these products than is recommended by the manufacturer. They usually tell you to use more than is needed (for obvious reasons).

➤ Plastic is one of the biggest polluters in our environment. Try to buy as little plastic as possible. Not only does it not decompose, but most things that are made from it can break easily and end up in the trash pile quickly. Toys are a good example. Opt for more heavy-duty toys such as blocks, wooden cars and trucks, and handcrafted items. These will be in the family for a long time.

➤ Of course, the most practical items to recycle are paper products. Have a special box or container around the house for newspaper, junk mail, and other paper items. Have a container for aluminum cans, too.

Reach Out and Touch Someone with "Real" Savings

Cheapskates know that they can save big bucks when they use the phone. Following are several tips to keep from dialing and losing at the same time.

Research Rates and Check Charges

Everyone knows that long-distance rates vary depending on the day of the week and the time of day. It's important that you know the rules of the long-distance company you use, and the guidelines for your local phone company. Some local companies around the country charge access fees during the most active time of the day. If you don't know your company's rules, call and find out. It can save you quite a bit of money if you know the cheapest times to call, and try to make your long-distance calls in those windows. If you find it extremely hard to control your long distance calls, you may want to check into pre-paid phone cards. Just limit yourself to a certain amount on the card each month and don't buy anymore.

When you get the details on your plan, you may think it's way overpriced for today's market. The best way to find a plan that works better for you is to search the Internet. Type in keywords "cheap long distance," and you'll find lots of different companies offering some great deals. Your best route is to pick a company that you feel will provide good quality fiber optic service at a flat rate per minute.

Anything at 10¢ or less a minute at any time of the day or night is a good rate. Also consider going with a company that gives you a flat rate on a calling card, somewhere around 20¢ per minute, with no surcharges. Make sure that they charge in 6-second increments and don't round up to the nearest minute. The key is to always check the fine print, because many companies can hide fees to make up for revenue lost in their per-minute charges. Charges and fees for phony services is a growing scam.

Cheap Trick

If you find yourself on perpetual hold with electronic push-button-operated answering systems (like the kind your credit card company has), try a new strategy to talk to a live person fast. When the computer asks to press 1 if you have a touch-tone phone, don't. Hold the line until customer service answers. Companies usually have special attendants to quickly handle "rotary phone" calls.

Cheap Distance Assistance

Does it annoy you that, to get a number for someone in another state, you have to call directory assistance to get the area code, then make another long-distance call to get the number? Here's the solution: Call 1-800-CALL-INFO to get around this hassle and expense. You can get the number of anyone in the country with just their name and the city they live in, plus they can automatically connect you. It costs about 75¢ per call. This is a savings when you consider that you'll probably be charged for your local directory assistance and long-distance if you go the conventional route. I figure you could probably save as much as 50¢ per call, and a lot of time.

Different Strokes

Hey, is your hand broken? You would think so if you consider how even some good cheapskates use long distance. How about an alternative? Next time you want to make a long-distance phone call, write a note instead. People love to receive letters in the mail, so it's much more special. If you're lucky, you'll get a reply back. If you want to be creative, send video or audio tapes with instructions to have the other party tape over them and send the tape back. Have everyone in the family pitch in their two cents worth. If you are online, use e-mail to have a "conversation." These alternative ways of communicating are can be a refreshing change, and they cost a lot less than a long distance phone call.

Cheap Shot

If you have a cellular phone, beware of the latest scam. Criminals are tapping into radio frequencies and eavesdropping on phone calls. If they listen long enough they can get credit card information, business information, and bank account numbers. Be careful about what you talk about on cellulars, because they are not as secure as your phone at home.

Own Your Phone

Finally, don't ever lease a telephone from the local telephone company. Telephone companies make oodles of money from residential lease programs. Buy your phones instead of renting them. The initial purchase of the equipment may cost you, but you'll spend much less in the long run, since you won't be paying for the phone for years. When the lease is up on your rented phone, you walk away with nothing, whereas if you'd bought it, you'd have something to show for it.

Buy good quality phones so you won't have to be concerned about their breaking. If you check in the phone book, you should be able to find a store in your area that sells reconditioned phones at about half off retail. Most of the time, the phone company will lease you reconditioned equipment anyway.

Cheap Thrills in Energy-Saving

➤ Cleaning the condenser coils on your older refrigerator can save you a lot of money in the long run. They're hard to get at behind the refrigerator, but if you clean them once a year, air will flow more easily and you'll avoid overheating problems. Simply move your refrigerator out from the wall and vacuum the coils. Your refrigerator will run longer and more efficiently, and you'll save what you would have spent on service calls.

➤ If you have a fireplace and burn wood often in the winter, consider a new twist. During the summer months, roll your used newspapers into tight logs and tie them with cord. For best results, wet the paper before you begin rolling. Let the logs sit for a few months, and when winter rolls around, you have recycled logs! You'll appreciate the news all over again as you sit by your politically correct fire. Al Gore will love ya!

➤ Keep your clothes dryer exhaust vent clean and clear of debris to help it run as efficiently as possible. If your vent is clogged, it can reduce the ability of your dryer to dry clothes properly. It's similar to having a clogged lint screen. Check the vent at least once every six months to make sure it's clear.

Cheap Trick

Invest in a programmable thermostat for your home. Department of Energy studies have proven that a homeowner can save as much as 25% on home heating and cooling just by having the thermostat a few degrees higher or lower for a portion of every day. You can purchase a good one on sale at a discount home supply store for as little as $35.

➤ Have you had the Freon in your air conditioner checked lately? If the hot summer months are approaching, it may be a good time to have a qualified professional check it out. If it's low, your air conditioner could work twice as hard to cool your home. We all know how much electricity air conditioners can use. This is one of the tasks that I don't recommend you do yourself because of the dangers associated with Freon. Call in an expert if it's been several years since you've had your air conditioner checked.

➤ If at all possible, try to locate your refrigerator away from the dishwasher and stove. They both radiate heat that can cause your refrigerator to run harder. If it must be next to one of these appliances, put a sheet of foam insulation between them.

Frugality Footnote

If you want to save time and money at home and on the phone, set up a home message center. Get a small bulletin board and plenty of thumbtacks, and put it next to the main phone. Then, everyone's notes, messages, and lists will be in one place, not strewn all over the house.

➤ Is your refrigerator or freezer door's gasket tight? To check, simply put a 150-watt outdoor flood light inside and aim it at each side. With the kitchen light off, close the door and look for light coming out. A poor gasket seal can often be fixed simply by adjusting the leveling legs on the bottom of the refrigerator. If this doesn't work, then you'll need to replace the gasket seals. If this all sounds too complicated, consider having a professional do it. Having a tight seal can save on your energy bills.

➤ After you barbecue on a charcoal grill, close or cover all vents in the grill, both on the top and bottom. This will cause the remaining charcoal to burn out quickly. For the next grilling, shake the grill a bit to loosen the ash from the charcoal, add a few more briquettes, then light as usual. A bag of charcoal lasts about three times longer than if you let it burn itself out.

The Least You Need to Know

➤ Check your home for any problems associated with air leakage. Check around windows, doors and siding. Immediately caulk or weather-strip leaky areas.

➤ If you have out-of-date or faulty appliances, consider replacing them with newer energy efficient models.

➤ To save money and also help save the environment, consider recycling as a way of life. Buy recycled products when possible and be conscious of recycling your plastics and paper products.

➤ Fix any water leaks around your home right away. Also, consider installing low-flush toilets to replace old, less efficient ones.

➤ Change long distance carriers if you are with a company that doesn't charge a flat rate per minute. 10¢ per minute is a good rate to shoot for.

Chapter 12

Big-Ticket Stuff That Makes You Cringe

In This Chapter

➤ Cheap appliances and electronics

➤ The best places to buy furniture

➤ Computer gobbledygook

➤ Deck the walls

➤ Rings on your fingers

➤ Moving made easy and cheap

➤ For better and cheaper

The cheapskate call to arms is to avoid ever paying out lots of money, but the fact is, cheapskates have to buy the big stuff just like anybody else, unless they want to live on the street. Everyone has to buy appliances, electronics, furniture, and other expensive items at some time in their lives. The problem is that the price tags on this stuff can strike terror in the bravest cheapskate's heart.

Smart cheapskates know how to find the bargains on these big ticket items. For example, they may buy them used instead of new at full price, or at a time of year when the product is cheaper. Whatever you do, first learn the tricks to saving on major expenditures, so your wallet won't look like a school of piranhas got at it. Here's how you can avoid a feeding frenzy.

Cheap Shot

Avoid purchasing extended warranties. Manufacturers' warranties are all consumers really need for most modern appliances and electronics. Besides, extended warranties are overpriced and rarely used. The only exceptions: big ticket items that have a tendency to break, such as gas range ovens, large screen TVs, and camcorders. Make sure you read the fine print for any provisions you may have missed in any warranty before you pay for it.

Cheap Trick

A great strategy is to shop at stores that advertise "can't beat this." These stores guarantee the lowest prices anywhere. If you find the same product elsewhere for less (which is unusual), they'll match the price, and sometimes beat it.

Appliance Reliance

Appliances are designed to make our lives easier, but it can be painful to read those zeros on the price tags and utility bills. Most people would say that you have to pay a lot for conveniences like refrigerators, washing machines, dishwashers, dryers, and TVs, but they all tend to agree that it's well worth it. The fact is that you can enjoy the best of today's technology without having to pay through the nose for it.

Have you ever noticed that big ticket appliances and electronics vary in price from store to store? That's because there are no set retail prices for items like TVs and dishwashers, even when they're exactly the same. Most stores mark up these products the way car dealers mark up their cars; there's always room to haggle. For instance, that refrigerator you have your eye on for $600 may be priced at 100 percent over what the store paid. You would never think of paying full price for a car or a home, so why should you pay full price for an appliance or TV?

The first thing to do is check the Sunday paper for deals around town. Once you've decided where you want to buy, simply ask them for a discount. They'll often discount 10 to 15 percent from the already advertised cost; so it pays to ask. You may want to visit a few other stores to compare prices before you buy. If you find a better price elsewhere, tell your store of choice about it; they may meet it to keep you as a customer.

Out-of-date models figure prominently in the cheapskate buying scheme. These are last year's versions, usually discounted up to 30 percent. Doesn't this sound very similar to cars? The difference with appliances is that their resale value doesn't take a big drop in the first year. Even if it did, resale value is not a factor if you're a cheapskate buying for the long haul.

Savings from Last Year

Last year's models generally cost a lot less than those that are fresh from the factory. The features are usually the same, but the price sure isn't.

Appliance	Last Year's Model	Current Model	Savings
TV	$489	$625	$136
Dishwasher	$599	$699	$100
Stove	$649	$789	$140
Refrigerator	$760	$890	$130

You can also save by buying appliances and electronics off the floor. An older model that has been used for display may have some nicks and dings that don't affect its efficiency; and if you can live with a few cosmetic flaws, you can save as much as 50 percent. Actually, flaws can work to your advantage in negotiating the best deal possible. I've bought several straight-from-the-factory products that had scratches and dings when they came out of the box. That's how I learned that buying new doesn't necessarily mean buying perfect anyway.

Finding a Seat

Goldilocks had it pretty easy; she just had to choose between three chairs. Today's cheapskate has a much harder task trying to choose among hundreds of stores to shop at with prices ranging from downright cheap to a king's ransom. Unfortunately, most prices are in the royalty range, since the average markup on furniture is around 200 percent. Many pieces are sold for an unbelievable 700 percent of what retailers pay for them! Of course, as with many other big ticket items, it pays to negotiate. Since the furniture market is so competitive, many retailers are willing to cut 30 to 40 percent off their already inflated prices.

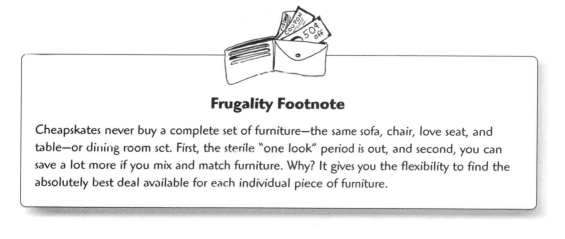

Frugality Footnote

Cheapskates never buy a complete set of furniture—the same sofa, chair, love seat, and table—or dining room set. First, the sterile "one look" period is out, and second, you can save a lot more if you mix and match furniture. Why? It gives you the flexibility to find the absolutely best deal available for each individual piece of furniture.

Be a Mail Order Miser

One of the surest ways to save on furniture is to buy directly from the manufacturer or wholesaler. North Carolina is the furniture discount capital of the world and has hundreds of stores to choose from. If you don't live nearby, you can always have the furniture shipped. Of course you have to pay for shipping yourself, but the better stores generally have special shipping rates to some of the major cities on the East Coast, such as Atlanta and Washington. It can still pay to have your purchase shipped to other cities, too.

If you buy by mail order from one of these furniture dealers, you can save a bunch with their discount prices, even after shipping costs:

➤ Blackwelder's Industries, 1-800-438-0201

➤ James Roy Furniture Company, 1-212-679-2565

➤ Boyles Furniture, 1-336-889-4147

➤ House Dressing International, 1-800-322-5850

➤ Broyhill, 1-800-327-6944

➤ Furnitureland South, 1-336-841-4328

Get Out to the Outlet

Another good route is to head for the clearance outlets. Most larger retail companies, such as Sears and JC Penney, operate such outlets where older, out-of-stock, or returned merchandise is sold for about 50 to 60 percent off retail. The selection is usually fairly small, and includes a lot of floor models with plenty of scratches, but most of the items are a real steal. You may have to deal with a few imperfections, but you'll get those anyway after a kick or two from the kids.

Furniture Kits: Dandy If You're Handy

If you can handle a paintbrush and work with a screwdriver, you can save up to 30 percent by assembling your own furniture from a kit. Simply put it together, do a little staining, and you have a new table or chair. While some of these do-it-yourself kits may contain poor quality veneer furniture that doesn't hold up well, it is an exception. The lower prices generally come from the manufacturers' savings on assembly, shipping, and storage costs, so you will find plenty of better quality oak and maple wood kits. They're sold at discount home warehouses, department stores, general discount stores, and also by mail from house and decorating magazines.

Computer Cheapskating

More and more Americans are jumping on the cyberwagon and buying personal computers. PCs can be powerful tools to help organize your life, but you need to be aware of some pitfalls.

It's very important that you seriously evaluate your specific needs before you plunk down two grand or more for a good computer system. Unless you're purchasing it for professional use, I recommend that you have at least three or four great uses in mind before you make the plunge.

You may need the computer for word processing, budgeting, library research, investing online, e-mail communications, spreadsheet capabilities, or perhaps a data base. If you own a business, you may find a personal computer invaluable. If you just want to play games, then I strongly advise you to buy a Nintendo or other TV-based machine. The graphics are better and you'll save hundreds of dollars.

IBM versus Mac

There are two main types of computers: IBM (or IBM compatibles) and Macintosh. I've had both types, and think the decision is a real toss-up. If you don't know a thing about Windows and you really want to work with graphics, then I suggest you go with a Macintosh. Macs are much more user-friendly, and famous for their superior graphics capability. One thing about IBM and IBM clones, though, is that it's the standard for most businesses, which means you'll have many more software choices. If you run a business, it's probably the better choice.

Buy for Tomorrow

Be very careful not to purchase a model that is old or out of date unless you only intend to use it for one or two simple applications. Computer technology is changing so fast that you may be left in the dust. Statistics show that the life of new computer technology lasts only about a year before it's out-of-date. When the technology changes, so does all the software, and you don't want to find yourself unable to run your favorite software packages. If you want to make an investment that will serve you well for several years, your best bet is to buy the latest computer.

Cheap Trick

To find out how a computer can help you, spend some time looking over software. Find a store that deals exclusively in software and ask a clerk to guide you to the best programs. If you choose the software first, you'll get an idea of how much power and speed you'll need in a computer. Many computers are sold with software bundles that may have just the software you want.

Cheap Shot

If you're making your first computer purchase, stay away from notebook computers. They have very small keyboards, are much more expensive, and frequently lack upgrade options (although that is changing rapidly). It's best to get a desktop computer and add a laptop later if you find you really need one.

143

What's the Damage?

For around $1,600, you can buy a computer system with decent speed and all the latest multimedia capabilities at an electronics discount store or through direct-order companies like Dell or Gateway. These last two companies also provide excellent online and telephone service and advice. Speed is all-important in a computer because it determines how well your software programs run.

➤ If you purchase an IBM or compatible, I suggest that you buy a Pentium microprocessor (the chip that runs the whole system) running at 50MHz (megahertz). Again, your decision rests on the tasks for which you're planning to use the computer. Make sure it has at least 16MB (megabytes) of RAM (random access memory) and a large hard drive to store all your applications. Your hard drive should be about twice the size you need to begin with.

➤ If you're looking for something inexpensive, check the local classifieds to find a good used computer. You may find one that's only a year or two old and has all the features you want. You can save about 50 percent or more by going this route. Make sure you check out the computer thoroughly before you buy. Have the owner hook it up, then spend an hour or so checking all the applications and printing out documents.

➤ Buying a computer is a big investment, and you should definitely comparison shop before making your purchase. Computers have come down in price considerably in the last few years, and all the retailers are out to beat the competition. I recently saw two different store ads in the same paper offering similar computer packages at a $200 price difference. I'm sure the more expensive retailer did not have a great day.

➤ Pick up a computer magazine and call a few discount computer vendors. Many of these warehouses can offer savings of 20 percent off what other retailers charge.

Deck the Walls

In the elite art world they say that you can't put a price on a work of art. They say this, but then do just that, and it's usually outrageous. I consider priceless to mean that it doesn't cost anything! No such luck. Even if you're not looking in the Rembrandt category, buying art can be costly and confusing. Remember that one of the cheapskate's guiding principles is: Keep it simple.

Paintings can be expensive, so try buying low-priced prints, posters, photos, maps, quilts, antique plates or platters. I've even seen framed drawings by children that are quite charming. Definitely avoid frame stores. If you frame all your artwork yourself, you can save a bundle. To find how-to books and framing supplies, check the local hobby shop.

If art is an area you must indulge in, instead of going to trendy galleries, check out local fairs where artists hang out and answer questions. If a particular artist's work catches your fancy, develop a relationship. Often, if you get to know them and send some business their way, they'll create something especially for you at a great price. Don't forget about nearby art schools. Just find out when their showings are and drop by to take a look. You may just find the next Picasso for pennies.

Rings on Your Fingers

When you shop for any kind of jewelry, especially engagement or wedding rings, if you aren't hip about how to bargain, you can really get taken. The best thing to do is first educate yourself by visiting as many dealers as you can. Keep in mind that jewelry is one of the highest mark-up items in the retail industry, with retailers often quadrupling their wholesale costs. Stay away from jewelry stores in malls, no matter how good their radio ads sound; they have the highest prices of all.

One way to save quite a bit is to buy your ring or unset stones from a wholesaler or at a designer show. You can then have them mounted in the setting of your choice. Don't ever spend more than you can afford; you can always upgrade later when you have a little more money.

Moving for Misers

Talk about big ticket items! The price of moving your household has begun to get out of hand. To add insult to the cost injuries you're bound to suffer, you can get stuck with one of the many incompetent and reckless movers that have sprung up in search of the fast buck.

Here are some common problems people have with movers, and ways you can avoid them:

Cheap Trick

Whether you negotiate with artists or art dealers, always ask if there's a discount for a cash sale. They'll often lower their prices by 15% for an up-front cash deal rather than wait on payments or checks to clear.

Cheap Shot

Many cheapskates buy their jewelry secondhand. Although pawn shops are highly regulated by state governments and often carry fine jewelry for 30% less than new, be careful. You can usually find great deals, but you should be sure the store is reputable by checking with the local Better Business Bureau. You can also find bargains in used jewelry sections of retail jewelry stores. Ask for an independent appraisal for extra protection.

Problem: You get socked with an add-on bill after the move because it took the movers longer than expected to get Aunt Mae's antique bed up to the third floor.

Solution:

➤ Make sure that all costs are detailed in writing in the estimate you receive, and ask whether there are any hidden charges. Have the mover write on the estimate, "There are no extra costs associated with this proposal," and initial it.

➤ Tell the mover in advance about any places in your new home that you think may be difficult to handle, such as tiny elevators and winding staircases.

➤ Above all, use a mover that has an excellent reputation in your town, preferably one that has been referred to you by a friend or relative. If you have to pay a few extra bucks, do it.

Problem: You have a prized oak table that now has a hole in it.

Solution:

➤ To avoid any handling problems, watch the loading and unloading. All movers will be much more careful if they know you're watching. Insist that they wrap or box all precious pieces. Be courteous about it and don't get in their way.

➤ Examine all your belongings and furniture before you sign the final check so you don't have to extract money from the company if you find a problem later.

Problem: The movers don't show up, or are late.

Solution:

➤ Call the company if they are any more than thirty minutes late.

➤ If they don't show up and it costs you money because of the delay, demand to be compensated.

➤ If you have major problems receiving any refunds from them, contact your local Better Business Bureau or consumer protection agency.

For Better and Cheaper

Whoever the dingbat was that said, "Two can live more cheaply than one," must have been single. While married couples often have two incomes, they also embark on an endless spending journey that will last a long time. Between buying and establishing a home and bringing up kids, mounting costs can start to look like Mount Everest.

Unfortunately, it's almost inevitable for committed cheapskates to have spats now and then with their spouses. The fact is that it's almost unheard of to find two cheapskates in a marriage. Opposites do attract when it comes to money issues, so there are bound to be money tensions in any household, especially when there's a committed cheap-skate involved.

It doesn't take a rocket scientist to figure out that most people want financial freedom, whether they're cheapskates or not. It's how to get there that puts dedicated cheap-skates at odds with their spendthrift partners. But all is not lost. With some foresight, you can sidestep a lot of potential disasters on the home front.

1. First, get off to the right start with a smaller wedding by deciding that you don't have to have ALL the bells and whistles. It doesn't matter whether you, your spouse-to-be, or either set of parents are paying for it: Keep it reasonable. For instance, you can have a very nice wedding with just over 100 guests, and a great honeymoon for less than $6,000. That's about half of what most people spend. All you have to do is make a mutual decision to try to cut costs. The money you save can go toward the down payment on a house or an Individual Retirement Account (IRA).

2. Above all, it's important that newlyweds talk about how they are going to handle their finances throughout the marriage. For instance, who's going to pay the bills? Are you going to get joint accounts or separate accounts? These are all important considerations in marriage and need to be worked out before you make the plunge.

3. The single worst thing you can do to your family's future is to get divorced. Divorce takes its toll emotionally, but keeping separate households is a also a huge financial drain. Try not to let your marriage spiral downward to divorce—all too common these days. If you work hard to keep it afloat, it will pay off in untold emotional as well as financial ways for both of you and, if you have them, your children. If your differences are clearly irreconcilable, consider mediating your property settlement instead of going to court. Mediation will cost half as much and produce half the emotional stress.

Cheap Thrills with the Big Stuff

➤ Once sneered upon as an option for jewelry, 10-karat gold is now considered a great buy. Not only is it sturdier than 14-karat gold with no noticeable differences, it retails for 20 percent less than its heavier cousin.

➤ Shop for audio equipment and TVs in January and February, just after the holidays. This is the time of the year when retailers need to clear out old models and make way for the new. After the first of the year, check the Sunday paper for clearance sales. You'll save as much as 30 percent just by putting off your purchases until then.

Cheap Trick

Home builders and other contractors get preferred pricing on appliances. If you build a house, make sure you buy all the appliances through the builder. Also, if you have friends or relatives in any kind of contracting business, look them up. Contractors generally get about 30% off the retail price of new appliances.

➤ To find fine china at great prices, call or visit a local restaurant supply house, or check the Yellow Pages under "Restaurant Equipment and Supplies" to find out what kind of china is available. You may have to visit several supply houses to find one that carries the kind of china you're looking for, but if you're lucky, you'll find quality merchandise at ridiculously low prices.

➤ When it comes to buying bedding, break the cheapskate rule for buying furniture and buy in sets. If you get the mattress and box spring at the same time, you'll automatically save about 20 percent. Your bedding will also last longer; the box spring is designed to support the weight of a matching mattress, so you'll get a better fit and avoid premature sagging.

Frugality Footnote

Tools can be very expensive, so shop wisely. Cheapskate do-it-yourselfers buy tools in bulk packages. For instance, a quality tool kit with 200 pieces can be bought for about $150, and will meet all your tool needs. If you purchased all the tools separately, it could cost you $500 or more. A cheapskate rule: Tools take a beating, so the better quality you buy, the longer they'll last. Also consider renting tools and equipment you'll only use once or twice a year.

➤ If you're the type who can't live without your own boat, shop the annual boat shows to get the best deals. You can generally save about 25 percent by taking advantage of promotional incentives dealers offer, including free optional equipment and engine upgrades. But take your time and be very cautious if you're buying; there are dealers who will lowball you at first and then talk you into buying a more expensive model. Boat shows are generally held in the winter in major metropolitan areas.

➤ If your furniture and appliance budget is limited, prioritize your purchases. Decide what is absolutely necessary right now and what can wait. By planning these major purchases, you can save by buying at the right time of the year and, if possible, paying cash. Some big ticket items, such as a quality stove or refrigerator, are essential. The fancy dining room furniture and decorative lamps you've had your eye on can wait.

➤ If you're in the market for sports equipment, check the classified section of your local newspaper. This is where you'll be able to get just about anything you need, from basketballs to the latest exercise equipment, at great prices. You may also want to check your white pages for a chain store called Play It Again Sports or other used equipment stores where you can save as much as 60 percent off retail.

The Least You Need to Know

➤ When you're shopping for expensive appliances and electronics, consider buying last year's models or floor models that may have some dings and scratches. If you can live with products that are not in mint condition, you can save hundreds of dollars on a single item.

➤ Consider calling mail order houses to get the best deals on furniture. Even after you pay for shipping, you'll come out way ahead. To be the best of cheapskates, purchase furniture kits, and assemble and stain it yourself.

➤ Computers are great if you have a clear idea of what you need them for. Think about what you'll use a computer for before you buy one. If you can handle everything a computer could do in about the same time, then don't buy one. Exception: if your children need to learn about computers and their school doesn't have one.

➤ Choose pleasing but less expensive forms of art to enhance your surroundings, such as prints, photographs, posters, and decorative textiles and objects. Buy unframed works, and learn to do your own framing. You'll save a bundle.

➤ Jewelry probably has the highest retail markup of anything on earth. If you're in the market, learn something about quality and cost, find the lowest priced wholesale outlet, and remember that, even there, given the markup, you can still haggle for a better price.

➤ Beware of rip-off moving companies that are becoming more and more prevalent. To protect yourself, make sure everything is in writing, ask for several references, and talk to as many as you can before you make a deal.

Part 4
Finally, Time to Lounge Around

Did you say gimme a break? You're probably wondering if this cheapskate thing is ever going to get to be fun—cut costs here, save a penny there, work, work ,work. Well, contrary to popular belief, cheapskates have a lot of fun. Why would they go to the trouble of saving money unless it's to enjoy the fruits of their strategies? When it comes to leisure time, cheapskates apply the same money-saving principles they operate on in their everyday cheapskate life. In Chapter 13, you'll find out how to keep up-to-date on all the best travel deals. Chapter 14 shows you how to have more fun for less around home base. Shop around for the best theater ticket deals, dine out for half-price, and scout out fun that costs practically nothing.

As with all cheapskate ventures, a plan is a must when it comes to the holidays. The best cheapskates know how to avoid getting sucked into the holiday shopping frenzy by budgeting and planning well in advance. They do the same for birthdays, anniversaries, and other celebrations. Learn how in Chapter 15.

So, no matter what your budget is, and whether you're going to a museum, taking a trip around the world, or celebrating Christmas or Hanukkah, you can find ways to enjoy yourself more for less cash. Go for it!

Chapter 13

Pack Those Bags for the Sunny Land of Discounts

In This Chapter

➤ Can a travel agent always help?

➤ When to train it, plane it, and bus it

➤ Extend your stay with low-budget bunks

➤ Cruising in savings paradise

➤ Up, up and away

➤ The cheapskate's scam tipsheet

Doesn't everyone need a good vacation? Sure, but the problem is that it takes "mucho dinero" to make it happen. If you're into good air travel and accommodations in fabulous vacation spots and you don't know what you're doing, you may just end up mortgaging the house to pay the bills.

One night's stay in a better hotel can cost as much as $200. Even so-called bargain motels can cost $50 or more a night. If you want to visit Disney World, you could pay as much as $500 for a single day of family entertainment. Could Walt Disney have imagined how difficult it would become for the average American family to visit the wonderland that bears his name?

If you're not a practicing cheapskate, you can really get burned by seductive, over-priced tour promotions. But there is a way you can have a great vacation without taking out a second mortgage. Some cheapskate know-how will get you the best rates on airfare, lodging, and entertainment, and cut hundreds of dollars off the bill for your vacation without cutting out any of its pleasures.

Can a Travel Agent Always Help?

Travel agents around the world have started charging fees to issue airline tickets, even though their main source of income is commissions on their sales. It's left a lot of cheapskates wondering if they really need a travel agent's services. As it stands now, the right travel agent can be a good bargain, but there are some things you should watch out for if you choose to use their services all the time.

Cheap Shot

Travel agents don't necessarily always have access to the lowest airfares. They can save you lots of time by instantly looking up the available fares on their computers, but they don't usually have instant access to charter flight fares or special promotional rates. Commissions on individual airline tickets are too low to make it worth their time to find the best deals unless you're a regular customer.

Cheap Talk

"Blocked space" is space set aside by a hotel or airline and made available when there are cancellations and last-minute emergencies. An agent can have access to this space when normal travelers can't.

Flyer Beware

Some large travel companies get special deals from certain airlines if they sell a great number of tickets. This can compel your agent to steer you toward an airline that may not necessarily be the best deal for you. To find out if you're getting the lowest rates from your agent, do some homework yourself. Metropolitan newspapers list the lowest rates for the week in their weekend editions. You can also call the airlines directly, and read the advertisements in the travel sections of Sunday newspapers to research the range of going rates.

How Discounted Are Those Digs?

Travel agents can sometimes get you good rates on hotels, but the best route for you is to become a member of one of the many discount travel clubs and coupon books in the country. The Entertainment book (Entertainment Publications: 1-800-285-5525) is a great choice. It offers a 50 percent discount on hotels throughout the world. Many cheapskates have used this service and saved a bundle.

Blocked Space: The Agent's Ace-in-the-Hole

The one area a travel agent can really help you in is booking a room, rental car, or airline ticket when the tickets are sold out. How do they do this? Many large agencies have the ability to access what is called "blocked space." They can also use their clout to book car rentals even when they have no special arrangements with the rental company.

Buyer Beware

If you're traveling on a package deal, call the company yourself and ask lots of questions to double check what your travel agency may have found out.

Don't think that you can hand over all the details of your special tour or vacation to your agent. Be prepared to follow up on many details yourself so you'll know what's going on before you leave. Even though I often use a travel agent, I like to do a lot of the planning myself. I save lots of money this way, and always feel confident that I know what's ahead of me when I walk out the door headed for some faraway place. You should use a travel agent to help you plan most excursions, but don't take their advice as gospel.

Cheap Trick

One way travel agents can help tremendously is if a flight is canceled or you're bumped. They have immediate access to computers that can instantly find you an alternative route. If you ever have an airline problem, it's better to call your agent or the airline than to wait in line at the airport with fifty other people.

Take the Rail or Road

Since the price of flying continues to go up, consider taking the train or bus next time you travel. Admittedly, Amtrak and Greyhound lack the thrill of a jet takeoff, but for shorter distances, they are just fine. When you add the time it takes to get to and from the airport, and additional time for layovers, train or bus travel can be quite appealing. Both Greyhound and Amtrak offer discounts which vary seasonally for kids, students, seniors, companions, and groups. All you have to do is ask.

On average, train and bus travel is about 30 percent cheaper than air travel and have the added advantage of being able to see the scenery. Also, seats tend to be a little roomier than on an airplane. On a personal note: It's a shame that America doesn't have the train service that Europe has, but what we do have is adequate and inexpensive for short hauls.

Frugality Footnote

Train and bus travel is, on average, about 30 percent cheaper than air travel. If you have the time, why not take advantage of the savings?

Low Budget Bunks

There are over 500,000 budget motel rooms in the United States. Many budget motel chains offer the tired traveler a good room at a fair price.

➤ *Best Western* is the world's largest company of independently owned motels, with about 2,000 in the United States and another 1,500 in 49 other countries. Each property has a coffee shop or provides a continental breakfast; most have swimming pools.

Rates average about $54 per night and there is usually no charge for children under 12. The motel chain has a program called Gold Crown Club International, which carries special services and awards for frequent guests. 1-800-528-1234.

➤ *Comfort Inns* offer free lodging for children under age 18 staying in their parents' room, a complimentary continental breakfast, and nonsmoking rooms. Many have swimming pools, fitness facilities, and restaurants or coffee shops on the premises. Rates average about $49. 1-800-228-5150.

➤ *Days Inns* offers rooms as low as $29 if reservations are made at least 29 days in advance, but generally average around $52. Children under 12 stay for free in their parents' room. Children also eat free when accompanied by an adult who is a registered guest. About 15 percent of the motels offer suites or below-budget rooms. Some offer free in-room movies, coin laundries, and on-the-premises cocktail lounges. These motels have the best senior citizen discounts in the market—20 to 40 percent off the regular rates. 1-800-325-2525.

➤ *Econo Lodge* has about 766 motels. Many have swimming pools, and rates average $36 per night. Rollaway beds cost $5 extra, and children under 18 stay free with parents. 1-800-553-2666.

Cheap Shot

When traveling on the highway, never stay at local motels unless it is absolutely necessary. Unless they have a AAA or Mobil stamp of approval, there is no way for you to know how clean or safe they are. Opt for national chain motels; most are highly scrutinized by their corporations.

➤ *Fairfield Inns* are Mariott's addition to the budget market. They have about 125 motels in 34 states. Most have spas with swimming pools, and offer complimentary breakfast. Rates range from $29 to $50, and are generally lower on weekends than on weeknights. Fairfield Inns are my runaway choice for the best budget hotel because they have the touch of Marriott at a great price. They've just gotten started, so we can look forward to more of them in the future. 1-800-228-2800.

➤ *HoJo Inns,* a spin-off of Howard Johnson's, has about 165 locations around the country. Rates average $40 per night and accommodations vary from place to place. Most have swimming pools. 1-800-446-4656.

➤ *La Quinta Inns* comprise 215 southwestern-style properties in 29 states. Guests receive free continental breakfast in the lobby, same-day laundry and dry-cleaning for a fee, outdoor swimming pool, fax machine, and free local phone calls. Most offer free shuttle service to nearby airports and have adjacent family restaurants. Rates average $50 a night. If you stay eleven nights at any time, you get one night free. 1-800-531-5900.

➤ *Motel 6* is probably the most popular of the motel chains and has about 650 properties. Who can forget the slogan "We'll leave the light on for you"? They offer bare-bones lodging. There are no breakfasts, coffee shops, or pictures on the walls. These motels feature an average per-night rate of only $31. Most do have pools and free local phone calls. 1-800-466-8356.

When you're traveling cross-country, first think of staying in a budget motel rather than a more expensive place. Make a few phone calls, and you'll probably be able to stay in a comfortable room for a lot less—and use what you save to extend your vacation.

Cruising for Big Discounts

If you're planning a vacation, you should consider a 4- or 7-day cruise. Cruising is one of the best vacation values available today. There's never been a better time to get a deal on a good cruise because many cruise lines are offering cut rates to compete in the market. Sure, cruise lines have had their share of troubles, but they are small compared to the thousands of successful voyages every year. Just make sure you travel on a cruise ship that has an excellent safety record.

Another great reason to take a cruise is the unique treatment you'll receive on board. On almost all cruise ships, food and service are top priorities; that means you get three gourmet meals a day, with luxurious snacks in between. A steward will clean your room twice a day, and if you need room service, someone's there in a flash. To get this level of service on a normal ground excursion, you'd have to pay a bundle. But since it's all included in a cruise package, it's very affordable. You'll be treated like a king on a cheapskate's budget.

Cheap Trick

Call *The Cruise Line* (1–800–327–3021) for discounted fares on cruises. The company will send you its cruise magazine with all the latest deals. The Cruise Line also has spur-of-the-moment cruises that are exceptional values. Or with some good planning, you can take a 7-day cruise to the Caribbean for around $800 per person, or a 4-day cruise to the Bahamas for around $500 each!

There's no better way to relax than on a cruise ship. You can take part in ship activities, go on shore excursions, or just sit around and do nothing. It's up to you!

Here are some tips on how to book the best cruise deals and most inexpensive cruises the easy way:

➤ Book your cruise a year in advance. If you book early, the ship is just beginning to fill its cabins, so they give great rates to get booking off to a good, fast start. If you book a year early, buy in at about three levels below the category cabin you want. Usually, people who book this far in advance get bumped up three or four categories since, eventually, many cheaper cabins will be sold.

➤ If you can't book early, wait until about two months before the cruise, when the cruise line is offering good deals to make sure it fills the ship before sailing. If you do book at this time, buy the cabin category you want, since it will be harder to get bumped up on such short notice.

➤ Ask your travel agent lots of questions about the particular styles of available cruises, and state your preferences. In other words, if you're looking for peace and quiet, a Spring Break cruise is the last place you'd want to be.

➤ If you have a choice of a late or early dinner seating on a cruise, pick the late seating. There's never any pressure to leave the dining room, and, when you do, the evening's entertainment will just be getting underway. You won't have to worry about any lag time between the dining and the fun.

Leaving on a Cheap Plane

Flying can be a hassle, but it doesn't have to be. You just have to learn what cheapskates know about how to make air travel much easier.

These are some great ways to take the turbulence out of air travel and save lots of money, too:

➤ Fly off-peak to get the best fares. Fares on domestic flights are usually cheapest on Tuesdays, Wednesdays, and Thursdays. Avoid flying between 6 a.m. and 9 a.m. on weekdays, when fares are high because of business traveler demand. For international travel, avoid flying on the weekends when fares are highest.

Frugality Footnote

Cheapskates often use an airport that's close to their destination, but less popular. For example, if they're flying into Washington, D.C., they save by going into Dulles instead of Washington National. A flight to Newark airport is generally cheaper than one into JFK (as long as you don't spend the difference getting to your ultimate destination). Ask your airline or travel agent about alternative airports that might get you a cheaper rate.

➤ Make a friend of the airline reservationist. If you're making your reservation through the airline rather than through a travel agent, the reservationist can be your greatest ally. Even though the reservationist's job is to get the plane filled, not get you the best deal, if you call at night or on the weekend when they aren't too busy, and make an effort to be nice, you just may get the cheapest ticket in town. Airline employees deal with angry business travelers all day long; a cordial voice is a refreshing change.

➤ Some questions you should ask: Would it be cheaper if I flew at a different time of day or a different day of the week? Do you know of any special fares that would save me money? Do you offer a family discount on this flight?

➤ If you're flying internationally, buy your tickets only from an accredited consolidator for international flights. You can save up to 40 percent on your ticket price. Consolidators buy seats at deep discounts, and then pass the savings on to you. Your travel agency can be a good source of reputable consolidators.

A common disadvantage with tickets bought through consolidators is that flights may have layovers, and tickets are generally nonrefundable. As with any agent you use, be especially careful about international consolidators; the airline industry has its share of scam artists.

➤ Avoid paying extra when you don't have a Saturday night stay. Under the airlines' ridiculous rules, buying two sets of tickets with a Saturday-night stay might actually be cheaper than buying just one set without a Saturday-night stay. Say you live in Chicago and want to visit Orlando. To get the better of this penalizing system, simply do the following:

Buy one round-trip ticket that flies you on the day you leave from your home city (Chicago) to your destination (Orlando) and back.

Then buy a second round-trip ticket that starts with your destination (Orlando) on the day you want to return, flies to your home (Chicago) and back.

When you fly, just use the first ticket from each set.

Cheap Shot

For added protection, always pay for travel arrangements with a credit card. Most credit cards have departments that will give you some recourse if you're taken by a travel promoter. If the outfit you're dealing with doesn't take credit cards, run away as fast as you can.

When the cheapest Saturday-night-stay tickets cost less than half the round trip with no Saturday-night stay, this is the strategy to use. If it costs you $1,000 for a ticket without a Saturday-night stay, and $400 for one with a Saturday night, then you'll save $200—and have two more tickets for another trip! You usually just have to pay a $50 reservation fee to reuse the other tickets. Confusing enough? The airlines have done it to themselves.

➤ Join frequent flyer programs and take full advantage of them. You don't necessarily have to be a jet-setter business traveler to benefit from frequent flyer programs. You can often get free upgrades and bonuses for just 5,000 miles of travel. When you make your travel arrangements, always ask for discounts or specials available through the airline's partners. These are companies that have set up special promotions on car rentals, hotels, florists, credit cards, etc. Not only do you get great deals in conjunction with air travel with these partners, you also accrue frequent flyer miles by using their services.

Traveler Beware!

Even though law enforcement agencies around the country have been beefing up prosecution of travel agency scams, deceptive promotional travel deals are still being heavily marketed. These promotions generally try to make you think you're a lottery winner when all you may be is a potential victim of a scam.

The people running these operations are pros at the con. A typical scam goes something like this: You receive a gold-leafed certificate in the mail that entitles you to a week's vacation at an exotic resort for only $199. The documents look very official. The sales material is so compelling that many people call to "check it out," even though it seems too good to be true. They explain the offer, and even give you references. Once you call the references (people or companies in on the scam), you're sold. You call back and purchase the "deluxe" package for only $399 because it's the best deal.

The reality is that you've just given your credit card number to a company you know nothing about, and now it has carte blanche to bill you for almost anything. You may get to go on the trip, but not without being subjected to a high-pressure sales pitch for a time-share property. You may not even get all the benefits of the vacation if you don't buy the time-share. This type of scam is very common.

Frugality Footnote

The latest certificate scam involves promoters using the logos of famous and respected travel companies, hotels, and tour operators. They simply pay for the rights to use the logos, and the big-name companies seldom have much control over how their names are used. Promoters use them to add credibility to their offers, which have nothing to do with these prestigious companies.

And Here's the Pitch

When you call, you may be told that you could have gotten the "special" price, but, unfortunately, you're too late. The offer was so spectacular that it's already sold out. If you would like to, though, you can upgrade to a "premium" package and still get a great deal.

The gimmick here is that the price of the upgrade more than covers the promoter's cost. But that's not the worst that can happen. There are promoters who will just take your money, close up shop, and move on to the next state to scam some more gullible customers.

Where's the Heat?

Promoters have adopted two tactics to get around the fraud regulations. First, the certificates they send out no longer say you've "won" a vacation. Instead they say that you "will receive" a trip. What you find out later is that, to get the trip, you have to pay for it.

Second, you'll probably see testimonials from former travelers. Some may be legitimate, which means it's harder for regulatory agencies to nail the promoter. Maybe there have been some satisfied customers, but don't be fooled by testimonials; many of them are setups.

Whatever the scam, and this is just a sample, if you get a letter that sounds like this, toss it straight into the trash can with the rest of the junk mail.

Cheap Thrills in Travel

➤ Use the Internet to find some of the best travel deals in America. Simply search with keywords "cheap travel" to find a slew of great sites. Three of my personal favorites: http//www.frommers.com, http//www.bestfares.com, and http//www.previewtravel.com. Check these three before you make any major travel plans. You can also find out about the best deals on hotels, car rentals, airfares, packages, and tours through Travel Smart Newsletter, 1-800-FARE-OFF.

Cheap Shot

If you use a pay phone at an airport, you can pay up to five times the normal cost of the call. Person-to-person calls can cost you even more. To avoid getting stung at an airport, always carry a calling card from your long-distance carrier. All you have to do is punch in your direct access code to be charged regular rates.

➤ Never pay an extra fee for plane travel insurance. It's nothing more than very high-priced life insurance. Walk by the airport machines that shoot out

"$100,000 worth of accidental death and dismemberment insurance for only $8.99." It sounds great, but the policy generally covers you for only one trip, so the odds are in the multimillions that your beneficiaries will collect. If your dependents need financial protection, you should already have plenty of life insurance that will benefit them however you meet your end, including a plane crash.

➤ At the airport, consider leaving your car in satellite parking rather than near the terminal. Though you'll usually have to take a shuttle to your terminal, you'll save a lot on parking. Also, many cities have bus services that will take you to the airport for far less than you would pay for parking. You can park your car in a safe area, or, if the bus stop is close enough, even leave your car at home. Of course, if someone can drop you off and pick you up, that's the way to go.

➤ Want to get free plane fares? Next time you schedule an airline flight, ask if the flight is almost full. If it is, book your seat. When it comes time to fly, arrive half an hour early and tell the ticketing agent that you're willing to be bumped onto a later flight. If the plane ends up being too crowded, you'll be the first one bumped, and get a free ticket for your next flight. Of course, you'd have to be traveling at a leisurely pace to give this a shot.

Cheap Trick

When you have more than one call to make from a hotel or pay phone and you're using a calling card, don't hang up after each call. Simply push the # button to stay connected to your current long-distance carrier. By doing this, you'll avoid being charged for another call. Most hotel computers cannot decipher the difference between single and multiple calls.

➤ If you buy travel insurance, get it through your travel agent rather than from a tour operator. The reason is simple: If the tour operator goes bankrupt, which happens with some frequency, your policy will be worthless and your money will be gone. When you buy a policy through a travel agency, it's often with a very stable and reliable outside insurance company. So, even if the travel agent goes under, the insurance company will pay off. When you buy a policy, check for any exclusionary clauses that would increase your liability or seem unfair. Ask lots of questions. Also, before you book tours through a company, make sure it is affiliated with a national consumer protection organization, which can help you in any kind of dispute.

➤ If you're planning a trip out of the country, you should get a small amount of the foreign country's currency before you leave. Call your local bank, which either has the currency or can help you get it. Once you enter another country, you may not be able to cash a traveler's check right away, and you'll usually need money fast to pay for a cab, food, and anything else you may need right away. You'll save by having local currency on hand, because exchange rates at foreign airports are horrendous. This way, you can manage until you're able to get to a bank or exchange where rates are much more reasonable. Rates are clearly posted, so become familiar with them before you change your currency.

➤ Most airlines do not allow refunds on tickets purchased as "super-savers." However, if you need to change your travel plans, don't assume that this policy is absolute. When you buy your ticket through an agent, the reservation is made immediately, but the agent may not pay the airline until several days or a week later. During that time, a good travel agent can cancel the reservation and give you your money back. Of course, they're not required to do this because, technically, "super-savers" are nonrefundable. Nevertheless, if they're pressed hard enough, some agents may give you a refund. It's not in their best interest to advertise these "exceptions," so let them know that you know that it's possible.

The Least You Need to Know

➤ If your travel agent doesn't seem to make an extra effort to try to find you the best deal on airfares and vacation packages, find a new agent. Better yet, spend more time doing your own travel planning, and see if you can learn how to find the best deals yourself.

➤ If you're planning a short trip to a city nearby, consider train or bus for something new and different in travel.

➤ For a great travel deal, look into taking a cruise. You can't beat the relaxation and the quality of service. When you take price and quality into consideration, cruises are perhaps the best bargains in the entire travel industry. But make sure you travel on a liner that is tops in safety.

➤ Next time you're driving across the country, try staying at budget motels instead of snazzy hotels. You can sock away some savings, or spend what you save on some vacation treats.

➤ If you fly, be aware of all the different discounts available to you. Also, don't be so sure that your travel agent is finding you the best airfares. Every once in while, do some fare checking yourself.

Chapter 14

Hit the Town for Half the Price

Everybody likes to have fun, even the biggest cheapskates, but the cost of entertaining ourselves is skyrocketing. The average American family spends about $3,500 a year going to the movies, eating out, seeing an occasional concert, and keeping up on our hobbies. That's about 20 times what we give to charities!

But it's easy to see why we spend so much. If you take the family out to the movies, you can rack up a bill of $30 to $40 for tickets and junk food. When you and your friend go to a restaurant, have a few glasses of wine, and then go out dancing, the tab will probably be at least $75. That doesn't include the baby-sitter, if you need one! And what about taking the whole gang to the ballpark? Between tickets, parking, and refreshments, you'll be doing well to get by with $100 for just a few hours of fun.

Fun can be expensive, but only if you don't know the cheapskate way to make it affordable. You can save money, and probably have a better time, if you know where to go.

Deals on Meals

If you like to eat out, use coupons, and take advantage of special deals whenever possible. Many restaurants participate in promotional campaigns that offer you some sort of discount. Two-for-ones are the best. Another great deal is a complimentary meal or sandwich after you've paid for a certain number of them. If you're planning a meal out for a birthday or anniversary, phone around and find out who's offering freebies and two-fers. Some restaurants even offer specially priced complete meals for special occasions.

Frugality Footnote

Cheapskates generally don't dine out except on special occasions. We've become a society of fast food junkies who automatically pull into McDonald's for a quick bite. The fact is that cheapskates save hundreds of dollars a year by eating at home.

That's Entertainment!

Each year, pick up an entertainment coupon book that's good for a year of discount dining and other entertainment in your area. You can usually get them at large department stores or through local charities, and some are even offered free in the mail. You can find out who's distributing them by calling Entertainment Publications at 1-800-285-5525. (They can also tell you where to buy them in other areas you may be traveling to.) The book is a great way to get two-for-one offers at local restaurants, and will be well worth what it cost when you use it on a vacation. And you get deals on more than just restaurant meals. At the back of the book, you'll also find coupons for cheap airfares and car rentals throughout the country

Stand Up for Savings

Take advantage of the current popularity of salad bars and buffets, where you can eat all you want at very low prices. Seek out all-you-can-eat cafeterias, and look for salad-only restaurants that have good, low-fat selections. Why should you pay six bucks for just one item on the menu when you can have anything you want for $4.99? It's not the cheapskate thing to do.

There's No Place Like Home

Sure, you can save a lot by staying home, but who ever said you can't have fun doing it? More people are opting for potluck dinner parties instead of taking on the enormous expense and hassle of throwing the lavish, formal kind. Invite three or four couples over and ask them to bring different entrees, paper plates, napkins, and utensils. Since everyone is contributing, you'll be left with less mess and more cash, and it's a lot cozier and more creative than a traditional dinner party or another humdrum restaurant.

More Movies for Less Moola

I wondered how the $1 movie theater could make money on such cheap tickets. Then I saw the line at the concession, and the prices! I'd love to own one. Don't ever buy soft drinks, candy, or food at the ballpark or movie theater. You can easily spend the price of a ticket and then some on this junk. Eat your fill before you go, and take along peanuts, popcorn, and drinks for yourselves and the kids; most movie theaters and sporting arenas allow it; just don't lug in a huge picnic basket.

If there's a dollar movie theater in your area (actually, some theaters now charge $1.50), consider going more often. I usually wait four or five months to see a movie because I just can't get myself to pay the $6 or $8 it costs when it first comes out. Think of the difference in expense for four or five people. The film may be a little scratchier, but there's not much difference in the theaters. Remember, if you buy junk food from the concession stand, you'll blow your whole "cheapskate" experience. You may want to split a soda, but that should be it.

Cheap Trick

Don't see first-run movies. If you wait a couple of months, you can usually rent it or see it on pay-per-view. Then the whole family can see a flick for far less than the cost of one first-run ticket. The bigger your family, the more you save! Also, check out your local library; many rent movies for free or as little as $1.

Theater the Thrifty Way

If you like to see plays and other live performances, there's a great way to get tickets for the whole family for practically nothing. Many local theaters have last-minute tickets available a day or two before performances. Granted, you may not get them for high-profile performances, but it works fine most of the time. Another strategy is to stand outside the theater a half hour before the performance begins and ask people if they have any extra tickets to sell. Odds are there'll be someone that has extra season tickets or one a friend couldn't use.

Frugality Footnote

Universities, colleges, and community colleges in many areas offer lots of events for the whole family. Chief among them are plays, dances, and recitals. Many of them are free or very reasonable. Call local schools and see if they'll send you their performing arts schedules.

Some theaters offer special discount days or specially priced performances. Often, tickets for matinees and specified weekday evenings can be bought at half-price. Don't forget to take advantage of any student or senior citizen discounts. Because every theater has a different policy, call several in your area to ask, get on their mailing lists at the same time.

Tipping Made Easy

When you go out to eat, do you always know how to tip the waiter or waitress? Always look for ways to keep the tips down, but be fair, too; they work hard for a living. That is, most of them do. I've been in restaurants where I've gotten bad service and been very upset about it. How did that affect my tip?

Here are some cheapskate tipping guidelines:

➤ Waiter/Waitress: 15 percent of the bill, before tax. Add another 3 to 5 percent if service is outstanding. If the service is less than adequate, leaving a smaller tip won't make the waitperson do a better job the next time; you'll just give cheapskates a bad name.

➤ Captain: If you get special attention from the captain, 5 percent of the check. Specify the amount that you want to go to the captain, or the restaurant will give the whole tip to the waitress or waiter.

➤ Hostess or headwaiter at a quality restaurant: If you want the best seats, tip them $5 to $10 in cash when you walk in the door.

➤ Bartender: 50¢ per drink or 15 percent of the total check.

➤ Restroom attendant, coat check, or doorman: 50¢.

➤ Valet parking, wherever it may be, $1 to $2.

➤ Hotels: Valet, room service, or bartender should all receive a minimum of $1 per transaction. Bellman: 50 cents to $1 per bag; this goes for skycaps at airports and train station porters as well.

➤ Sports arenas and concerts: A $5 to $10 tip should get you some unused reserved seats that may be better than the original ones you had.

If You Have to Take a Gamble

Gambling is just that—gambling, and everyone knows it's a high-risk game. Still, a large number of Americans play the lottery, bet on horses, and also go to a casino every once in a while. That's okay, as long as you see it as a way to have fun, and not as a way to make money. Unfortunately, many do view gambling as a money-making proposition, in stark contrast to us cheapskates. We all gamble enough just by living our lives day to day. Why add to our stress levels by blowing hundreds of dollars a year on the lottery or at the casino?

Solution: Spend a very small amount of money, an amount you're willing and able to lose. The best way to come out a winner is to ask yourself, "How much is this entertainment worth to me?" Then give yourself an honest answer.

Face it: You're a loser if you buy a lottery ticket; not a loser in general, but definitely a lottery loser. Don't even begin to think you'll win. In a normal lottery (six out of fifty-four numbers), you have a 1 in 12.5 million chance of winning. To put it another way, your chances of winning that lottery are less than getting hit by lightning seven times in your lifetime. No kidding! Do you think that could really happen? "Somebody's always winning!" cry the promotional ads, but it won't be you, no matter how many tickets you buy. Remember, if you want to play for fun, go right ahead, but if you're spending more than you should because you think you can win, you'll only be in for a letdown.

> **Cheap Trick**
>
> If you gamble and win 50% more than you started with, take your original bet and 50% of your winnings and stash them away. Do whatever you can to avoid dipping into your original bet. If you don't, you may want to head for the nearest ATM. By following the 50% rule, you'll have fun, and come out way ahead.

Cheap Plans for Sports Fans

Movie theaters aren't the only places that offer discounts at off-peak times. Bowling alleys, skating rinks, and swimming pools do it, too. Two-for-one deals are generally available when the kids can go, such as on weekday mornings and early in the evening.

If you or your family and friends like to swim, instead of paying high prices to join a club, opt for a summer-long membership at the city pool. You can usually get one for about $100—or less if it's an off-hours membership. Some community pools even offer free swim time at designated hours during the week. An added bonus if you go then is that there's less of a crowd.

Frugality Footnote

Cheapskates always buy the cheap seats at pro baseball and football games, and take their binoculars along. These days, most stadiums don't have that many bad seats in the house anyway, so opt for the nosebleed section and save some dough.

We all know it's getting very difficult financially take the whole family or go as a couple to a professional sporting event. Instead of forking out hundreds of dollars a year to see pro football or baseball, opt for minor league or amateur games. Most towns and cities have some type of minor league baseball team, and, of course, high school and college football teams. Do these games have the same thrill as pro sports? Maybe not, but if you go to a pro event a couple of times a year and amateur events the rest of the time, you'll save hundreds of dollars.

If you like to work out, consider joining your local "Y." Most of them are very clean and offer all the equipment you need for a good workout, including a pool if you like to exercise by swimming.

Let the Government Fund Your Fun

Cheap Trick

Local clubs and houses of worship can pack your calendar with fun and rewarding activities for the whole family, and it won't cost much. Consider joining one or more clubs or a religious community in your area, and take part in some of their many regular activities.

Flip through the government section of your local white pages and you'll be surprised at what you find. It's full of resources and facilities for your amusement and fun. Under "city listings," you'll find zoos, golf courses, swimming pools, recreation centers, parks, aquariums, dance halls, theaters, boating centers, and art museums. Under "county and state listings," you'll see parks and educational services. Under "public schools" you'll see a wide range of departments at local colleges and universities. Call the numbers that interest you and ask to be placed on their mailing lists of upcoming events. Most activities and events are free or low-cost.

Speaking of public places, libraries have become the hip place for cheapskates to be. They're not just there for books anymore; libraries provide videotapes, audiocassette learning courses, compact discs, how-to manuals, and much more. You can learn a new language, travel to the ends of the earth, listen to the latest CD, cook with the great chefs, or learn how to fix that leaky faucet—all under one roof. The best part is that most of it's free or at a nominal charge. The next time you think about buying a book or tape, or renting a video, first think of the library. You'll save a bundle. It's not a bad place to meet fellow cheapskates, either.

Credit to the College

Enrolling in an accredited course at a local university or community college is a great way to get the use of student privileges. A student ID card can get you into the gym free, which is much cheaper than joining the local health club. You can also use the library, obtain free entry to some school events, receive cheap rates on university movies, performances, and sporting events, and maybe even obtain free health services. And don't forget all the things you can use a student ID for around town: movies, plays, concerts. Enroll in a class you'll truly enjoy and consider your student ID a fringe benefit.

If you can't think of any courses you'd like to take, call the university or college and ask them to send you a catalog. Courses at most schools range from chemistry to tennis; something is bound to pique your interest. Here are some good suggestions:

➤ Aerobics

➤ Basketball, volleyball, tennis, golf

➤ Childhood development

➤ Cooking

➤ English literature

➤ Family planning

➤ Film and theater

➤ Foreign languages

➤ Golf

➤ Investing

➤ Massage

➤ Painting

➤ Personal finance

➤ Photography

➤ Pottery

➤ Public speaking

➤ Sewing and needlework

➤ Woodworking

Thirty-Five Cheap Ways to Entertain Yourself

Don't base how much fun you have on the amount of money you spend. Look for activities that are inexpensive but also enjoyable for you and for your family and friends. Here are 35 ways to have a great time without digging too deeply into your pocket:

➤ Visit the local zoo and feed the monkeys.

➤ Go to a free concert in the park.

➤ Pack a picnic lunch and drive to an out-of-the-way spot.

➤ Window-shop at your favorite stores (don't buy anything!).

➤ Eat early-bird specials at local restaurants. Then go home and watch a movie on TV, or read.

➤ Dress up and enjoy a special dinner at home, complete with wine, music, dancing, and candles.

Cheap Shot

Beware of events that advertise themselves as free. Call the organizers and ask if there are any hidden costs. For example, some summer concerts may be free once you get into the concert, but you may have to pay $10 for parking, or donate $20 to a charity. It might still be worth it, but you need to know the cost in advance.

➤ Go hiking or camping.

➤ Go gallery hopping. See the latest art exhibits.

➤ Go to your public library and hang out in your favorite section. Catch up on reading you've been putting off, or listen to some CDs or tapes.

➤ Take a drive in the country and enjoy the scenery. Visit stores and restaurants to soak up some local color.

➤ Visit friends in a nearby city (for those of you who are obsessive cheapies, plan to arrive around lunch time!).

➤ Eat dinner at home, then go out for dessert and coffee, and maybe a walk.

➤ Seek out restaurants that offer great lunch specials. Avoid eating out for dinner if possible.

➤ Use two-for-one coupons when dining out.

➤ Go to free lectures, seminars, and concerts offered by local museums, libraries, and other community centers.

➤ Invite friends over for a video or game of cards. Have everyone bring a favorite dish.

➤ Take an afternoon stroll with a good friend.

➤ Instead of a high falootin' dinner party, have friends in for pizza and beer.

➤ Whip out the old Monopoly and Trivial Pursuit games, or try your hand at chess or backgammon.

➤ Learn to paint, sculpt, or do some sort of craft.

➤ Find a field near the airport to lie under the paths of incoming planes; listen to your heart race.

➤ Do do-it-yourself projects around the house.

➤ Teach yourself aerobics with a workout tape.

➤ Get involved in a local political club.

➤ Play poker with friends for penny stakes.

➤ Learn to be a great cook. Share your results with friends.

➤ Go to area tourist sights you've never visited.

➤ Get involved with your local church or other house of worship. Join the choir, and keep your eyes peeled for free concerts and lectures offered by other area religious communities.

➤ Learn a foreign language with audiotapes.

➤ Join a choral group, or try out for a play.

➤ Go to a high school football or basketball game.

➤ Spend time reading books bought at discount warehouses or used book stores.

➤ Play nine holes of golf at a public course. Use public courts to play a set or two of tennis.

➤ Spend special time with your family and friends just talking about the events of the day.

Cheap Trick

If you love music, but don't love the price of CDs and tapes, try swapping with one or two relatives or friends. They must have tastes similar to your own and be willing to buy a CD now and then. You can simply swap CDs back and forth, and even tape the ones you really like.

Cheap Thrills in Entertainment

➤ There is no such thing anymore as a cheap night out on the town. By the time you add up dinner, a few drinks, and a movie, a couple is looking at a cost of around $60. If you really want to go cheap, invite a few friends over, have dinner, and watch a video. Next time, they'll invite you to their humble abode, and the night will be on them. You can even make it a game to see who can throw the cheapest VCR party. I think you'll find this type of evening much more relaxing and a better way to spend time with friends.

➤ Rent, never buy videotapes. Collecting a library of videotapes is really a waste of money when you can easily rent a tape any time you want to see your favorite movie. Most new movies average about $20. You could rent a movie and watch it about six times for that amount. How many movies do you want to see six times? Maybe *The Wizard of Oz* or *Gone With the Wind,* but that's about it. If you absolutely can't do without a movie, buy it used at the video store.

173

➤ When you dine out, consider splitting an entree or appetizer with a family member or friend. Most restaurants these days give you way more than you should be eating, so why not share, and save a few dollars. If you have to have your own meal, at least split that huge mega-chocolate dessert. Also, avoid buying soda, and opt for water. Remember to use coupons and go to restaurants that offer great lunch deals. Take home any leftovers.

➤ There may be no such thing as a free lunch, but there is such a thing as a free dinner. Many restaurants have bars that offer free hearty appetizers on certain days and hours. For instance, better Mexican restaurants that serve alcohol usually have "happy hours" where they offer free tacos and burritos. A smart cheapskate will buy a Coke or stick to one beer, and have a complete meal for free.

Cheap Shot

Don't fall for record clubs that offer you ten CDs for 10¢. Some may be a good deal, but most make you buy five or ten more CDs at higher than retail prices. The devil's in the details, so read the fine print thoroughly. Cheapskates generally try to buy their CDs on sale at local discount electronics or used record stores.

➤ Do you really need the 200 channels that your cable or satellite TV company provides? It's a good idea to cancel your subscription, buy a good local antenna, and make do with less channels. You'll be surprised to find out that it's just about the same as having tons of them. It's true what they say about there being nothing on even when you have hundreds of channels. Besides, watching less TV will give you more time to expand your mind by reading or enjoy talking with your family.

➤ Take advantage of all the free entertainment there is during the summer months, such as concerts and plays. Some of it's great and some really bad, but it can be fun anyway, and what do you expect for free? Check your event schedules and watch the papers for what's going on nearby.

➤ If you're a senior citizen, don't forget to ask for discounts wherever you go for fun. Many restaurants, movie theaters, bowling alleys, and sporting events offer discounts.

➤ If your employer has a gym or shower facilities, consider bicycling or jogging to work, or working out two or three times a week in the gym. An obvious added bonus to bicycling or running to work is saving transportation costs.

The Least You Need to Know

➤ Next time you think about meeting friends out at a local night spot or restaurant, invite them over for a potluck dinner instead.

➤ To save money when you dine out, purchase an entertainment coupon book and save 50 percent on many restaurants in your area. Also, search the Sunday paper for valuable coupons.

➤ For an inexpensive night out, go to a restaurant that has a happy hour with free food, then take in a dollar movie instead of one that just opened.

➤ If you must gamble, do it with entertainment, not making money, in mind. Play with a small amount of money you are prepared to lose, because that's what you're most likely to do.

➤ Visit your local library and take an informal tour. You may be shocked at the services they provide and how much fun you can have there.

➤ If you're a sports fanatic, search out places around town where you can see amateur sporting events and even semi-pro games for much less than pro events. Often, they're even more fun.

➤ Consider taking a course at a local college or university to have fun learning something new and at the same time receive student discounts at events at school and around town.

BETTER WATCH OUT!!

DECEMBER

Chapter 15

Caution: Holidays Ahead

In This Chapter

➤ Christmas à la cheapskate

➤ The savvy giver's gift list

➤ Ways to save on every celebration

➤ Happy (low-budget) birthday, kid

If you're like most Americans, you approach the holiday season with a mixture of anticipation and dread. It starts earlier every fall and sets off a spending frenzy that lasts for the rest of the year. Holiday spending accounts for a good chunk of all retailers' annual profits, so of course they pull out all the stops to get you to buy. But do you have to buy, buy, buy, to have a festive holiday? On this subject, cheapskates are of the unanimous opinion that the answer is no.

With a little savvy planning, you can have just as good a Christmas or Hanukkah— throw parties, give gifts, have big holiday dinners—without running up bills you'll be paying off until the next holiday season hits. If you've had it with the financial hangovers that come from overspending, turn a blind eye and ear to the hundreds of sales pitches you'll be battered by every day, and make up your mind to follow the cheapskate holiday spending strategy of doing it all for far less.

Think Fun Instead of Funding

An important part of celebrating big holidays like Christmas, Passover, Thanksgiving, and Easter is the preparation that goes into them. If you start getting ready for the big day far enough in advance, it will cost you a lot less to celebrate it the way you want to.

Set aside time to prepare holiday decorations and treats, and get family (especially kids) and friends to help. You'll save time and money by avoiding last-minute buying and, who knows, it may even help get you into the spirit.

Cheapskates go shopping on the days following major holidays because they know how much they'll save on next year's expenses.

Day-After Savings

Item	Pre-Holiday Price	One-Day-After Price
Box of assorted Christmas cards	$12.95	$4.95
Roll of quality wrapping paper	$6.00	$1.95
Christmas tree garland	$12.00	$6.00
Quality ornament	$10.00	$3.95
Bag of Halloween candy (freeze for next year)	$4.00	$1.95
Easter basket (good candy, cheap)	$6.50	$2.95
Bottle of quality wine	$12.00	$7.00

Dashing—and cashing—through the snow is par for the holiday season, of course, but it doesn't have to be that way.

Here are some great ways to make Christmas and Hanukkah cost less but be no less festive. Doing things cheapskate style could even add to their significance:

1. Try setting up ground rules with friends and family about what should be spent on Christmas gifts. If you have a big family or wide circle of friends, you may want to draw names from a hat so that each person gives and gets just one gift. You'll make it much less stressful for everyone, and create the opportunity for people to give some thought to what the person whose name they've drawn would really like.

2. Never let children choose their gifts from catalogs. It can be disappointing and frustrating for them (and us) if they don't get exactly what they circled. Instead, ask them for a list of four or five things they really want, and give them two of them at most. That way, they'll still be surprised.

3. If you live anywhere near a wooded area, pick up large and small pinecones, spray paint them with silver and gold, and use them as ornaments on your tree, garland, or wreath.

4. Make ornaments from inexpensive felt. First, get some holiday cookie cutters and trace around them on the felt. Cut out your basic design, and duplicate it in different colors. You can then create a colorful ornament by gluing two felt designs together. Try stuffing some cotton inside before you glue if you want a three-dimensional look.

5. Save the boxes from gifts you receive, and always ask for boxes when you buy gifts. The reason: The right-sized boxes can be very hard to find and very expensive to buy. It's worth using some storage space to have boxes on hand when you need them.

6. If you're handy in the kitchen, consider giving jams, desserts, or other food items as gifts. The fun part about this is getting creative with the packaging. You can give your gift a homemade look, with checkered ribbon and a white box, or use a gold box and silver ribbon for a touch of elegance. It doesn't cost much to make jam, cookies, or cake, so you can spend a little more on packaging.

7. Popcorn and cranberries are traditional standbys for holiday garlands, but why not try using something different, such as pasta? It comes in so many different sizes and shapes it can be a fun decoration, especially if you dip it in food coloring.

Cheap Trick

You can usually buy Christmas lights and ornaments for 50%–75% off after December 25. Candy drops dramatically after Halloween and Easter. Wine and liquor prices are excellent right after New Year's.

Cheap Shot

Thieves like the Christmas and Hanukkah season because they know there's extra loot around. Be cautious during this time of year and, if you have to, buy an inexpensive motion detector for added protection. Just the fact that you have a system and advertise it with stickers and signs will be enough to make burglars move on to the next house.

It may sound tacky, but you should think about trying to make your holiday meal a "pot luck" event. It can really work well—far better than anyone could do it alone—if your parents bring a traditional dish, your friends bring their specialties, and the kids mash the potatoes. It not only spreads out the cost, it takes the pressure off you, and is a lot of fun.

Give More, Spend Less

It's a good idea to have gifts in mind all year 'round, whenever you're out shopping. If you see things on sale that would make great gifts later in the year, buy them and keep them in a special gift closet so you don't have to rush to the store a day or two before the birthday or anniversary and pay top price. You can save a tremendous amount of money (not to mention anxiety) by avoiding last-minute shopping. If secrecy is a problem (those nosy kids), store gifts in a lockable chest or at a friend's house.

Get an early start on thinking of gifts that will mean something without necessarily costing you a lot. There are endless ways to give that will cost you nothing but time, and mean a great deal to the receiver.

1. Instead of rushing out to buy something, consider giving a family member a gift of your time and energy—a backrub or foot massage—or a gift certificate for the same experience performed by a professional.

2. If you hate to cook, make a special effort to prepare a celebratory dinner for the birthday person.

3. How about making an anniversary gift of offering to baby-sit a time or two for your neighbors' kids?

4. Buy an inexpensive scrapbook and have everyone in the family write special notes in it about how important Grandma and Grandpa are to them. Your grandparents would appreciate a gift like that much more than some wine glasses or dish towels.

5. Put old family pictures in a photo album—a great gift for anyone in the family. If you have videotaped footage from several holidays, having it copied onto a cassette makes a great gift.

Frugality Footnote

If there's someone in your life who is really passionate about a hobby or sport, put together a theme basket for them. For example, if they like to fish or cook, buy several little gifts to put in the basket, such as magazines about cooking or fishing. Theme baskets may be a little more expensive, but the thought that goes into them makes them very meaningful gifts.

There is cheap and there is cheapest. Here are some of the best, cheapest gift ideas a cheapskate could ever want:

➤ Make copies of audiotapes or CDs to give to people you know will like them.

➤ If you have a half-price coupon book, remove some of the better coupons and give them as gifts enclosed in a card or letter. People especially love "buy one, get one free" offers. It costs you practically nothing and gives the recipient a good time out.

➤ Make a package of all the ingredients and the recipe for something you make that the recipient loves, and give it as a gift. If you have a good hand, try writing the recipe in calligraphy on fine parchment.

➤ For a sentimental and thrifty graduation, wedding, anniversary, or Valentine's gift, buy a blank scrapbook and fill it up with pictures and souvenirs that the recipient can enjoy year after year.

If you have a garden:

➤ Dry roses and other flowers to make pot-pourri. To add some extra fragrance, spray them with a floral scent. Put the potpourri in a basket or attractive glass container decorated with a bow.

➤ Save attractive bottles to make your own herbal oil and vinegar gifts. For herb vinegar, fill the bottle with a quality vinegar and add fresh sprigs of any herb. Do the same with olive oil. Add a bow and a label detailing the ingredients.

➤ Give gifts of fresh flowers arranged in baskets or inexpensive vases.

Cheap Trick

If you have a backyard, prepare for Halloween by growing your own pumpkins. Instead of carving a jack-o'-lantern or buying one, tie a strong mask to the pumpkin when it starts to grow, and let the mask do the creative work for you.

Say Congrats All Over Again

Uh-oh, what do I do with all the wonderful Christmas cards I received this year? Consider recycling. Cut off the backs of the cards and turn them into postcards for next Christmas. Make clean cuts so there are no ragged edges. You can save on cards next year, and on postage, too. Mailing postcards is 30 percent cheaper. You can even save time because you won't have the space for those long stories about how the year has gone. A word of caution: Write the card before you cut off the back, so you don't send it to the person you got it from last year. How embarrassing!

Gather old magazines, scraps of fabric, glitter, glue, construction paper, and markers, and make your own creative holiday cards to give to others. These are great gifts to give to relatives on any special occasion and they say a lot more than a store-bought card.

Good Value Valentines

How about some ideas to cut your costs on Valentine's Day? The best route may be to stay away from the traditional gifts, and do something special instead. Why not prepare breakfast in bed for your valentine, fulfill a special wish, or agree to do all of the day's household chores? Your gift could be making a promise to stop doing something that has been driving your valentine batty, such as always arriving a half-hour late.

If you feel you must buy roses, don't plunk down $50 or $60 when you can buy them for $15 at a discount shop. A lot of the more expensive ones drop their heads just as soon. Also, consider buying less expensive flowers, such as red carnations; spending less doesn't have to mean that you care less.

Happy (Cheapskate) Birthday, Kid

Most people spend way too much on birthdays for their kids. Does little Johnny really have to have Bozo the Clown entertain at his party? And do you have to rent out a restaurant to have some great fun? Learn how to throw a great party that's also affordable. As long as there are lots of relatives and friends, a simple cake, some candles, and a few games, it can add up to the best birthday any kid could have.

To make the day extra special, develop traditions the kids know they can expect year after year. For example, let them pick the kind of cake they want, open presents in bed, or let them be the boss of the house for a day (within reason). It doesn't really matter what it is, just as long as it's one of the special things they know they get to do on their birthday.

Cheap Thrills for the Holidays

➤ Homemade toys and games can add a special, personal touch to any holiday. Go to a local hobby shop or arts and crafts store to get kits with all the materials you'll need. Wooden toys can be especially smart gifts because they're so durable.

➤ Kids love to get involved in any aspect of holiday preparations. Put them to work carving pumpkins, making Easter baskets, and writing valentines' cards.

Frugality Footnote

If you tend to send lots of cards to people, buy boxed assortments to save money. You can get them at about half of what it costs to buy cards individually. Get an assortment to cover all the bases, and buy an assortment of wrapping paper and ribbons to have on hand for any occasion.

➤ At Eastertime, instead of dyeing hundreds of eggs and making a big mess, try reusable plastic ones. They usually twist apart into two sections so you can stick all sorts of candy and gifts inside. Kids will like them a whole lot better than those hard-boiled eggs anyway.

➤ Cakes can be an expensive element in any special event. For a wedding, consider buying a sheet cake instead of the multi-tiered variety. You'll usually save about 70 percent, and it'll be easier to cut. Use sheet cakes for children's parties, too. You can decorate them yourself very easily or have it done where you buy it.

➤ If you're planning to travel over the holidays, make plans well in advance. Holidays are the busiest travel times of the year, and if you don't plan, you could find yourself paying loan shark travel bills.

➤ If someone is particularly hard to buy for, get them a gift certificate at their favorite store.

➤ Buy a quality artificial Christmas tree that will last for years. You'll be amazed at how lifelike many of the new ones are; some even come with a bottle of pine scent! Since they look so good, why not make a one-time buy and never have to worry about the mess and cost of a tree again?

Cheap Shot

Gifts are a luxury. Use a credit card to buy them only if you foresee a hassle if they have to be returned. Don't buy on credit because you're strapped for money. Budget for gifts and pay cash.

➤ A year-long gift that anyone will enjoy is a subscription to their favorite magazine, or a membership to a local club or organization. Many museums, for example, allow unlimited access for the small amount a membership costs.

The Least You Need to Know

➤ To save the most money on gifts, cards, and decorations, plan and prepare well in advance. It's worth taking the time to find new and creative ways to celebrate that won't break the bank.

➤ During the holiday season, make a special effort to spend less on gifts, especially if you have a big family or a lot of friends. Let them call you Scrooge; spending more money doesn't necessarily make for a better holiday.

➤ To save a bundle, consider making as many holiday decorations as you can yourself. Not only will you save, it's a great way to get everyone into the holiday spirit.

➤ Make buying gifts part of your shopping routine throughout the year. That way, you can take advantage of sale prices, and give better gifts for far less. For instance, when you're at the outlet store shopping for yourself and you see something at an incredible price, consider buying the same item as a gift for someone (as long as it's not a dress for your sister).

➤ The best way to make the holidays and birthdays special is to establish traditions that will be carried on every year. Once in a while, add a new touch to keep your celebrations lively.

Part 5
More Down-and-Dirty Tactics

So, you need more cheapskate tricks and techniques? You got 'em; with cheapskates, there's no end to great ideas for saving bucks. In this section, you'll learn easy ways to save money on all kinds of things. In Chapter 16, we'll take a look at great techniques for squeezing some cash out of your kids; maybe they can't go out and earn a living, but there sure are ways you can spend less on all the things they need. You'll learn how important it is to stay in good health in Chapter 17, and avoid medical expenses by having regular checkups. How can you get the best health plan for the fewest bucks? It may be at your workplace, where you can also pick up some extra cash by learning more about deductions and company benefits in Chapter 18.

Education is one of the biggest expenses families face, and cheapskates have no shortage of ideas for how to help the kids get that piece of parchment. Chapter 19 will show you when and how to start a college savings plan, how to get financial aid, and how to get the kids to pitch in on funding their higher education.

Chapter 16

Care for the Kids at Half the Cost

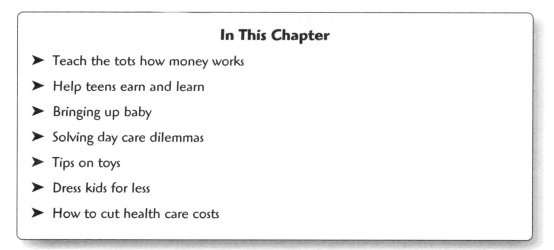

In This Chapter

➤ Teach the tots how money works

➤ Help teens earn and learn

➤ Bringing up baby

➤ Solving day care dilemmas

➤ Tips on toys

➤ Dress kids for less

➤ How to cut health care costs

Kids can be as costly as they are priceless. If you're a parent, you're probably so busy that you've never sat down and figured out just how much the kids really cost you.

Between fast food and overpriced tennis shoes, according to government statistics, the average American family spends about $8,000 per child annually. That covers feeding them, but doesn't factor in the major expenses that go with the territory, having to get a bigger house and a minivan, for example. A few calculations would show you that you'll spend about $200,000 from the time Junior or your little princess comes out of the womb until they're shipped off to college. Of course that's when you REALLY get to spend money! (See Chapter 19.)

Well, it's a little late to send them back and get a dog, but you can breathe a sigh of relief. Good cheapskates have lots of tricks up their sleeves for saving thousands of dollars a year on the cost of shepherding your little darlings to responsible adulthood.

Mommy, Where Does Money Come From?

Managing our financial lives is getting more and more complex every day. Cheapskates know the best ways to prepare young people to handle their finances in the future, so start teaching your kids smart money moves early on. As they grow up, you can do more than set a good example; be alert to questions and situations that present opportunities for you to teach them more about the ins and outs of being a cheapskate.

Frugality Footnote

According to government statistics, households with kids under 18 on average cost about 27% more to maintain than those without them. Families with children spend 45% more on housing, 40% more on clothing, 35% more on entertainment, and 32% more on food. It's no wonder the average American family never seems to get ahead—it costs a lot to raise kids.

Teaching Kids About Cash

Cheap Trick

Make sure your children get a regular allowance for work around the house. It's best to start this routine at about age 6 or 7 with $2.50 every week. Of course, you need to raise the amount as they get older. An allowance is a great way to teach a child the value of work and money.

When your children reach the age of 10 or so, open a savings account for them, and agree to match whatever they sock away in their account. This is a great way to give them an understanding of money and the incentive to save. Suggest that they put an occasional cash birthday or holiday gift in the bank; the fact that you'll match it should give them a good grasp of the art of the deal.

You can find creative ways to teach children about the rewards that come from having the discipline to save. Examples are best. When I was a kid I wanted a tricycle, and my father encouraged me to save up for it. I put away my pennies, dimes, and quarters religiously for a long time, and my father kept tabs on my savings and matched every penny. He was so impressed with the discipline I'd shown that he bought me the tricycle for my birthday AND let me spend what I'd saved at the local amusement park. Obviously, his lesson in the rewards of disciplined saving stuck.

Help Teens Learn as They Earn

When your daughter or son gets to be about 14, if they haven't thought of it themselves, suggest that they get a part-time job to help pay for their social expenses and special treats.

An after-school or summer job can help teens develop a sense of responsibility and accomplishment; they'll also learn what it's like to sweat for a buck. It also will teach them about taxes, since they will have to file a return if they make over $2,150.

Share the Burden of College Costs

Cheap Shot

Resist giving your children everything they ask for. Saying no can be harder for you than for them, but it will have a positive effect on your children in the long run. They'll learn when they're young that getting everything they want when they want it is just not how life works.

When it's time for college, have a talk with your son or daughter about the costs involved. Decide together on a manageable college expense for your freshman student to take on, such as books or social expenditures. It doesn't matter if you can afford to pay the whole tab; sharing in the financial responsibility is a good way for your child to learn about the cost, and value, of higher education.

Work Well Done

Most kids are expected to do certain chores, if you ask them to do things that are beyond the call of duty, such as painting the house or helping with the family business, it's reasonable to pay them. Giving them the opportunity to make some money this way means that they can buy some of the things they want for themselves. When you pay your children for their work, it's important not to be too critical, especially when they're younger. If you give them time to learn the ropes of the particular job, they'll stay interested, and get better and better at it.

Cheap Trick

Give kids your best cheapskate advice about how to spend what they've earned, but if they overspend, don't bail them out. Along with their troubles they'll get another valuable lesson in financial management.

You may be among many who believe that it's unwise to attach cash rewards or penalties to routine chores or schoolwork, but there may be exceptions. Things such as cleaning their room or brushing their teeth don't provide kids with very tangible, immediate rewards. Why not give a child a small amount of money or a special treat as a pat on the back for a sustained effort? The key is to do this when they're younger, and form lasting habits more easily. As personal responsibilities become part of their routine, you can continue to create new ones, and make small gestures to show them that you're pleased. The fact that you keep track of how they're doing may be a reward in itself.

Bringing Up Baby, Cheapskate Style

If you're thinking of having a baby, check out the maternity coverage attached to your health plan. Even if you don't anticipate adding to your family for a year or more, it's wise to pay the extra premiums for maternity coverage just in case. To keep birthing costs down, use a hospital that encourages early discharge if things progress smoothly in the first twenty-four hours. You'll also save if you choose a hospital that allows you to keep the baby in the room with you. An added advantage is a lesser likelihood that your child will catch a virus from the other babies, or be switched (it DOES happen).

Although 85 percent of households use disposable diapers, using cloth diapers is a much better idea. Most diaper services charge about $10 to $15 per week for washing and delivering eighty or so diapers, and less as the child gets older and doesn't need as many. If you use disposable diapers it will cost you about $25 to $30 per week to start, but as your child gets older and needs larger ones, the price will get higher. A diaper service also generally provides you with storage cans which they will pick up. And last but not least, cloth diapers help save the environment. So what's a smart cheapskate to do? This is a no-brainer.

Cheap Trick

If you're dead set on disposable diapers because they're so convenient, always go with a store brand or generic diaper to save big. They're about 40% cheaper than name brand competitors. Buy them at large discount stores to save even more. Do some comparison shopping to see which brand fits your baby best and saves you the most.

To get a low-cost child car seat, contact the highway patrol office nearest you. Since most states have mandatory car seat safety laws on the books, they go out of their way to make sure that every motorist with a child has one. If your highway patrol has a program like this, don't be surprised if you can get a new car seat for under $20.

One way to cut spending on baby accessories is to hope you'll get just about everything you'll need at the baby shower. Another is to look for used cribs, high chairs, and strollers. Since most have been used for only a year or two, they won't show a lot of wear and tear, and you can get them for half the price of new ones. The best places to find used baby accessories are close to home: through family and friends, and, of course, at garage sales and used baby furniture stores. Check your local Yellow Pages for a store near you.

Day Care Without Care

One of the most important decisions you'll make as a parent will probably not be based on financial factors: finding quality child care. Spending some money is inevitable—a reputable day care center may charge as much as $30 a day for full-time care, and even a baby-sitter you call in when you want a night out will run about $5 an hour—the challenge is to find the right care for your child or children.

A good option is to find someone in your neighborhood that does private day care. They may not be licensed with the state, but you can still deduct 30 percent of the cost on your taxes. Arrangements with these individuals are generally informal, and can save you as much as 15 percent of what you would pay at a day care facility. What's great is that they'll usually come to you, so you won't have to haul the kids around. But be very careful and check your state laws to see if there are licensing requirements for all daycare workers.

If you put your children in a day care facility, ask if you can provide breakfasts and lunches for them to take with them. Even though they make a healthy profit on meals, most centers won't object. By sending a touch of home along with your child, you can save about $20 a week. Most centers give discounts for two or more children from the same family. You mean, the more kids, the more you save? You got it! Just ask; you could get as much as 20 percent off. Especially if you're new in the area, you should try to get a combined discount by signing up your kids with a friend's.

Cheap Trick

It's not a good idea to put your child in a day care center that asks for a large up-front deposit to "hold your spot." Don't pay any more than $100. The reality is that most reputable centers require only a small deposit and a signed contract. Get at least ten references, and call several before you entrust your child to any day care facility.

The government has several programs to help those who can't afford quality day care. Depending on your income, generally below $20,000 per year, you may qualify for one or more of them. Even if you don't, check out local churches and other organizations to see what low-cost programs they provide. You can save as much as 15 percent if you can find such a program and are eligible.

If you go out frequently, baby-sitting can set you back a few bucks. The best way to cut costs is to share sitters, either with other people who are joining you or with friends or relatives who may be going out on the same night. Another trick is to swap out baby-sitting with neighbors or relatives. You baby-sit their kids one night, and they do the same for you.

Tips on Toys

Any parent who's watched their child tear apart a new, expensive toy knows how frustrating it can be. You might just as well have given the kid the box to rip to shreds and taken the toy back for a refund. Studies show that the average child has gone through about a hundred different toys by the age of 6. The best way to cut down on this number is to buy toys that will last much longer.

Do-It-Yourself Toys

Save big bucks by making whatever toys you can. Here are some ideas to make long-lasting and fun playthings for your kids:

➤ Show your girls how to make inexpensive necklaces and bracelets by stringing together different types of pasta. They can paint them to add some color.

➤ Make blocks out of wood scraps you can find at any lumber store. Just have the store cut them into the sizes you want, then sand off the rough edges. Break out the paint or food coloring again, and have the kids help decorate them.

➤ You can have a homemade basketball court just by hammering an old trash can to an unused area of the house. Use a small, lightweight plastic ball in place of a basketball, and make sure the can is low enough for the kids to reach in and get the ball out by themselves.

➤ Buy do-it-yourself toy kits at hobby stores to make toys that can last just about forever.

Toy Scouting

To buy toys as cheap as they come, look no farther than your own neighborhood. Just keep your eyes peeled for garage sales, where they're the most popular items; they are by far the best places to buy. With just one outing, you can probably outfit the kids with all the toys they'll need for many months.

One of the greatest cheapskate toy strategies is to call local libraries and ask if they have toys you can check out. You're bound to find at least one in your area that does, and it can be a great way to find out which toys your child does and doesn't like without paying for them first. Kids often stop playing with a new toy after a week or two anyway. Some children's hospitals have systems set up to loan out older toys. See if there's one in your area that does.

Cheap Shot

Head injuries from bicycle accidents are increasing every year but can easily be avoided simply by wearing a helmet. Make your kids aware of how seriously they can be injured if they don't. Cheapskates are always looking to avoid medical expenses, but it's even more important to keep your child from suffering a needless head injury.

Best Bike Buys

Bikes are probably about the highest priced toys you can buy; their cost can leave your head spinning as fast as their tires. It doesn't make sense to get a fancy new bike for a kid under the age of 7; opt for something as cheap as possible. Why? They outgrow their bikes as fast as they do their shoes, and they really don't need special features. Buy a decent bike that they can learn on at a garage sale or Goodwill. When they get a little older, invest in a quality bike. Older kids tend to be rougher on their bikes, so get a good bike if you want it to last for a few years. Older kids also ride faster, so they'll be safer with a better quality bike.

Deals on Kids' Clothes

One of the simplest ways to save money on kids' clothes is to make sure they really like something before you buy it for them. The fact that you may like it is not going to get them to wear it often enough to make it a good buy. Before you buy something, be sure you hear more than just a "yeah, it's okay"; something like "that's so cool" means there's little chance that you'll have to return it, or that your child will get sick of wearing it anytime soon.

Here are some good ways to keep their clothes budget to a minimum:

➤ Inventory your child's clothes just as you do your own. For instance, when school time comes around, go through all their current clothes, make a list of what they absolutely must have, and stick to it. Try to limit shopping for them to a couple of times a year.

➤ When you buy for infants, buy only clothes that can be worn by both sexes. They'll make more flexible hand-me-downs.

➤ When your children get older and start to want trendy clothes, convince them to buy basics in neutral colors and go for colorful accessories. You'll save a bundle by not having to buy them a whole new wardrobe when there's a color trend change.

➤ Cheapskates buy a lot of white clothes. Why? Because white clothing can be bleached clean when the kids do their number on them.

➤ Buy cheap T-shirts with imprinted team names and hip logos. The kids love them and they cost practically nothing. Don't fall for designer T-shirts, though.

➤ Always, always buy clothes and shoes that are a little larger than kids need so they have some growing room. It's also a good idea to buy clothes with elastic waist bands and adjustable straps.

Health Plans for Kids

Obviously, the health insurance your kids have is only as good as yours, so make sure the coverage you have protects them adequately (see Chapter 17).

Many county health facilities offer free immunization shots for kids. They may include vaccines for diphtheria, pertussis, tetanus, measles, mumps, rubella, polio, and certain strains of influenza. Most of them are required before children can be entered in school. Check the blue pages in your phone book for a clinic near you that provides free shots.

Frugality Footnote

Cheapskates try to keep their kids out of hospitals and clinics by making sure they have a healthy diet and good quality all–natural multivitamin supplements. You can find quality supplements specifically designed for kids at many health food stores. Stay away from One–a-Day and other name brand vitamins. They are synthetically made and provide very little nutritional value.

Your children may also be eligible for free or low cost physicals, hearing tests, and eye exams at the county health department if your family meets certain financial require-ments set by the federal government. If yours is a middle- or lower-income family, it's worth checking your eligibility. Don't be scared off by the fact that these clinics are run by local governments. They are among the cleanest and best-equipped facilities you'll find.

Whatever you do, don't buy an insurance policy on your child's life. Insurance agents give you all sorts of reasons to insure children, such as the possibility of having to pay for their funerals, providing guaranteed insurance when they become adults or using the paid up policy to build a college fund. Hogwash. If you want life insurance to provide for your kid's college costs, make sure you have plenty of it—on yourself and your spouse. That way, if one of you dies, your child can still afford to finish college.

Cheap Thrills for Kids

➤ Are you fed up with the high cost of kids' haircuts? Go to a local cosmetology school, and you can save as much as 60 percent, but you will lose some time. It takes longer than it does at a retail shop because students check and recheck their work, and usually have it checked by a manager. If you don't mind the wait, you can get your kid's hair cut for about $5. Take a friend and their kids along and make a party of it! Check your Yellow Pages for schools nearby.

➤ Want to cut your day care bill even more? Ask the center if they need any extra help. If you work there even on a part-time basis, your costs will almost disap-pear, especially if you can negotiate a special staff rate.

Frugality Footnote

Don't overlook discount warehouse clubs for buying all sorts of children's clothes, food, and toys. You'll save about 15% off retail on many of the things kids need most. You won't find generic products, but you'll save if you buy in bulk.

➤ If there's a professional service you can offer, try bartering with a day care center manager or even your teenage baby-sitter. If you're an accountant, offer to do some light bookkeeping, or if you're a good tennis player, see if your baby-sitter wants to swap services for tennis lessons.

➤ Day care woes and scandals are front-page news these days. If you or your spouse work in a corporate or institutional setting, it's a good time to lobby for an in-house day care program where employees can place their kids with greater confidence. Stress the fact that they can get much more productivity from their workforce by providing good child care options. If an onsite facility isn't feasible, ask your employer to arrange for discounts at a local center, or help you find the right one for your needs.

➤ Restrain yourself from buying expensive designer clothes for kids. Sure, you want little Jane or Johnny to look good, but you're being a better parent by buying less expensive clothes and putting the money you save into a college account. Cheapskates never buy designer clothes for their kids.

➤ Instead of buying your kids Halloween costumes that cost as much as a whole new outfit, make them yourself, and get the kids to help. It's crazy to spend $20 or $30 on a costume that you'll toss out the day after Halloween. Work with your kids to come up with some good costume ideas.

➤ If your child wants to move back home after college, unless it's for a short time, insist that they pay rent. That may sound harsh, but it's the only way they'll learn how to survive on

Cheap Trick

If you have children who use your car, give them a dose of reality and an incentive to drive safely at the same time. Insist that, if they cause an automobile accident, they pay the deductible. Also have them agree in writing to pay any deductibles or premium increases that result from their use of your car.

their own. Once you start charging, they'll probably get the point fast and find a place to live before you know it.

➤ Take advantage of a kid's early years, from ages 1 to 6, to give them inexpensive, used merchandise instead of buying new. At that age, they don't really know the difference between new and used, nor are they as fixated on brand names as their older siblings. Once slick advertising gets to them, it won't be so easy.

The Least You Need to Know

➤ Teach your kids the value of a dollar at an early age by encouraging them to save up for special things that they want or need.

➤ Introduce your children to bargain-hunting for clothes at thrift stores and garage sales. Make it fun! Never buy them designer clothes; if they get hooked on labels, there won't be any cash left for college.

➤ Buy, or consider making, sturdy toys that will last a lifetime instead of cheap plastic gizmos that won't last a week.

➤ Quality day care is a mounting problem. Protect yourself by searching out the best possible day care center or individual in your area, then finding ways to cut costs.

➤ Take advantage of free shots and other health services available to your kids at your county health center. Use their services as often as possible to save considerably on children's health costs.

➤ As soon as they're old enough, encourage your kids to go out and find a job, or pay them for special jobs around the house. As soon as you can, start getting them used to the idea that money comes from working for it.

Chapter 17

Good Health and More Wealth

In This Chapter

➤ Preventing illness means preventing bills

➤ Holding down hospital tabs

➤ How to trim your pill bills

➤ Health insurance for half the cost

➤ Cheap eye care and dental do's

Rising health care costs are enough to make any cheapskate sick. The $500 billion-a-year medical industry, politicians, insurance companies, and lawyers are all getting a piece of the action while we struggle to stay healthy without going broke.

There seems to be no end in sight to the skyrocketing cost of health care, which, if we stay on our present course, will probably rise about 10 percent a year for the next ten years. It won't be long before we're spending a trillion dollars annually on health care—about 15 percent of the country's gross domestic product!

Health care is not exactly prime territory for bargain-hunters—let's face it, open-heart surgery is just plain expensive no matter where you have it done. But don't despair; if you're a cheapskate you can save hundreds of dollars a year and still get good quality care. Get started with the strategies in this chapter.

An Ounce of Prevention

Some cheapskates can be 60 and look 45 and others look 60 when they're only 45. Sure, biological traits are a factor, but you can have some control over how well or badly you age. With a positive attitude and a healthy and active lifestyle you can live longer and, with a little luck, not do it in an expensive hospital.

Frugality Footnote

Average Americans don't get the nutrition they really need in their regular diet. That's why an increasing number of doctors and other professions recommend supplementing your diet with a good quality, all-natural multivitamin. These vitamins can give you all the essential nutrients you need for your body to run at peak performance. Just remember that vitamins are not a substitute for a proper diet and regular exercise.

Cheap Shot

Beware of diets that promise such spectacular weight losses as "30 pounds in 30 days." Sure, they may work, but the process will shock your system and starve your body of needed nutrients. Then you'll bounce right back to your original weight and probably put on a few extra pounds for good measure.

You know what to do: Eat right, exercise regularly, and keep stress down by getting plenty of relaxation. If you get an early start at living a healthy life, you have a better chance of avoiding illness and the high costs that go with it. Staying in good shape also makes you feel better about life, which decreases your chances of having to cope with a stress-related illness.

The latest studies on exercise suggest that more is not necessarily better, and that three 45-minute walks a week can be an adequate exercise program for most people. So don't feel like you have to go out and run a marathon or do massive amount of aerobics to keep your body in shape. If you're overweight, don't try to burn fat by working out; there aren't enough hours in the day for it to have much of an effect. Changing your diet and the way that you think about food is what works, along with a light workout schedule. No sweat, right?

Holding Down Hospital Bills

The average cost of a hospital stay is about $1,000 per day, and it's rising fast. Bottom line: Stay away from them if you can.

Do you really have to go to the hospital? Given the scandalous practices uncovered every day in the health care industry, it's a fair question. Before you go into any hospital, discuss other options with your doctor, such as going to an outpatient facility that may be able to deal with your problem for far less money. If it's feasible, you'll save over half the cost of surgical procedures and all of what you would have paid for an overnight stay.

If you don't need a special diet, find out if the hospital will allow you to provide your own meals. High-priced hospital meals are rarely appealing, and their cost is right up there with popcorn and candy at the movies—without the movie! The best thing about having your own food brought in is that you won't have to face that awful green Jello.

Never pay a hospital bill right when you check out. Do it the cheapskate way: Take time to scrutinize it for erroneous charges—not an uncommon occur-

Cheap Trick

If you must go into a hospital, find a non-profit center. You can save about 15% on your bill. Nonprofits may not have the most space-age equipment available, but if your ailment is something less compli-cated than brain surgery, you can usually get the same quality care as you would in a for-profit hospital.

rence. If you have health insurance you may think the charges don't matter; that's a prescription for disaster. You could get a call or letter months later from your insurance company telling you that you owe them for the erroneous charges. If you don't review the bill before the insurance company pays it, you are responsible for the extra costs.

Trimming Your Pill Bills

Most prescription drugs have doubled in cost over the past decade, outpacing inflation more than sixfold since 1980. Under one of the many proposed health care reform bills, prescription drug costs would be capped at levels determined by drug manufac-turers, but it probably won't happen anytime soon. In the meanwhile, there are several ways you can fight mounting drug costs:

➤ If your doctor says that your prescription can be filled with a generic, do it by all means. You'll pay around half of what a brand name would cost.

➤ Check out the costs at different pharmacies. Chain pharmacies are generally cheaper than the corner drugstore, and they have a wider variety of drugs. Comparison shopping can save you as much as 20 percent.

➤ If you use certain medications frequently or on a regular basis, look into mail-order pharmaceutical houses. You can save as much as 15 percent. Ask your doctor, or search on the Internet with the keyword "discount prescriptions" or "discount drugs."

➤ If you have health insurance, be sure that you're taking full advantage of the benefits. Many policies cover prescription drugs, but don't necessarily shout it from the rooftops. Millions of dollars are spent on drugs by people whose insurance could have paid for them.

➤ Many insurance companies now offer separate prescription drug benefit plans. Some let you buy at participating area drugstores and others are set up with mail-order houses. Check with your employee benefits department to see if they offer a good plan and, if not, suggest it.

Frugality Footnote

Doctors are addicted to prescribing brand-name drugs. This may be because doctors get "perks" from pharmaceutical companies if they sell enough of their products. Vacations to conferences and golf clubs for birthday and Christmas gifts are just a few of them. That's why it's always important to ask if a generic can be substituted.

Cheapskate Formula for Longevity

Looking to increase your longevity? Here's how champion cheapskates extend their lives:

➤ Sleep seven to eight hours nightly.

➤ Keep your weight to no more than ten pounds over what is recommended for your height, build, and age.

➤ Get a half hour of moderate aerobic exercise every other day by walking, swimming, or participating in some other active sport.

➤ Don't smoke.

➤ Eat as much fat-free food as possible.

➤ Don't drink alcohol, or limit yourself to one drink a day.

Health Insurance for Half the Cost

The average cost of health insurance for a family of four is a staggering $300 per month. If you are one of the 50 percent of Americans who does not have an employee-paid plan, or if you believe you're getting a good deal from your employer, read on.

How Good Is the Company Plan?

If you're in a company health insurance plan, study your policy, and keep up with changes in benefits. Chances are that whoever handles the employee health plan was fully trained by the insurance company, so don't expect the advice you get to be entirely user friendly. It's up to you to be sure you're getting maximum protection for the lowest cost.

Coverage at Half the Cost

Cheap Talk

In an insurance policy, a *deductible* is the amount of medical expenses you are responsible for before the insurance company starts to pick up the costs. A *stop-loss* is the percentage of medical expenses you are responsible for after your deductible is met.

Have you had an insurance agent tell you that a low deductible is great because it reduces your out-of-pocket expenses? It's true; it does—on the back end—but what about now? You may be paying as much as $1,500 more a year for your plan so you'll have the advantage of paying $750 to $1,000 less if disaster strikes! That just doesn't make sense. Cheapskates know better than to go for a low deductible; they look at what their total out-of-pocket cost could be in a major medical emergency.

If you raise your deductible from $250 to $1,000, you can save as much as 50 percent on your premiums. If you're a real cheapskate, you'll set aside what you save on premiums every month for just six months, and have enough money to cover the higher deductible if you have to!

Next, pick a stop-loss amount that's reasonable. I suggest an 80/20 plan up to $5,000. That means that you'd be responsible for 20 percent of costs (after you meet your deductible) and the insurance company would pay for 80 percent. If you chose a $1,000 deductible and an 80/20 stop-loss, your maximum out-of-pocket expenses would be $2,000, even if you had a major medical catastrophe in the family.

Where and What to Buy

Ask the insurance company you're dealing with if it is rated A or better by A.M. Best Company, an independent rating service. You want to feel confident that they're dependable and pay their claims on time. A good rule of thumb is to find a company that operates in at least forty states; that means they've been around for a while. If you buy insurance from a company licensed only in a few states, you'll be taking a big risk.

Ask the potential insurer for references, and talk to several randomly selected policyholders. It's a bit unconventional, but you'll learn a lot about what you may be getting into.

There's a long list of "don't buys" that goes with most types of insurance.

In the case of health insurance, don't buy:

➤ Maternity benefits, unless you are paying for it as part of your policy. It's generally way overpriced and provides very little coverage.

➤ Dental care and prescription drug benefits. They are usually less expensive when you buy them separately from your policy.

➤ Accident coverage, unless you're very active and prone to injuries such as a broken ankle or torn ligament; otherwise, forget it.

Frugality Footnote

Medigap insurance is health insurance that takes up where Medicare leaves off. To make the best use of it, decide which benefits you're most likely to need. Many policies cover a variety of services such as nursing home co-payments, out-of-country emergencies, prescription drugs, etc. Understanding the premium structure for different policies is important, since so many companies offer similar benefits. Also, check out the cap on premium adjustments; companies can get you locked into a rate, and then bump up the premiums 20% or more the second year. Ask for a guarantee of the lowest percentage increase possible. Finally, check to see that the insurer will bill services they don't cover to Medicare directly so you won't have to file forms and pay bills yourself.

If you're under 65 and you and your family are in good health, buy a high-deductible, low-premium policy as described above. Pay for minor medical services, such as yearly checkups and routine doctor's visits, but be completely covered for the kind of major illness or injury that would otherwise wipe you out financially. Chances are you'll come out ahead at the end of the year.

Economical Eye Care and Dental Do's

If you wear glasses, look into good old-fashioned glass lenses. Some plastic lenses that are scratch-resistant and lightweight don't hold up as long as glass, which is hard to scratch and very durable. The only exception would be if you are very athletic and are worried about them breaking. Get wire metal frames, not plastic. Plastic is much more brittle and gets damaged more easily. When you need new frames, it doesn't mean that you have to buy new lenses; find frames that fit or are smaller than the originals, and ask your optician to cut your glass lenses down to size.

Contact Lens Contacts

If you wear contact lenses, get the prescription from your eye doctor, and have it filled at a discount store, price club, or mail-order house. You'll save around 30 percent. Some doctors won't give prescriptions to their patients because they make such a large profit on lenses. Go to one who will, and just pay for the exam. Regular eye exams are important; just buy your contacts elsewhere!

Spend Less on Dentists

Many or most major dental problems could have been prevented with proper care. Just as your dentist says, brush and floss your teeth regularly; you'll avoid a lot of pain, much of it financial! One of the things you can do for your youngsters is take advantage of modern science and get their teeth coated. Once their teeth are sealed, they won't get cavities; it's not cheap, but it's a good investment when you consider how much dental work costs. Also, consider dental insurance if it provides free checkups on a regular basis. If not, you may be paying $20–$30 per month for something you will not use.

Cheap Trick

Whether you pay a lot or a little for sunglasses, they won't protect your eyes unless they have proper UV sun protection. Most cheap plastic lenses do; just look for the UV seal on the label before you buy. Perfectly good and safe sunglasses shouldn't cost more than $15.

Cheap Thrills in Health

➤ Potatoes are extremely healthy, being virtually fat-free, low in sodium, and a great source of carbohydrates. They're cheap, too. They can usually be bought in 5-pound bags for less than the cost of most vegetables. Potatoes, especially the skins, are full of vitamins, minerals, and fiber, but watch out for the toppings, such as sour cream, gobs of butter, and salt. Instead, try topping them with fat-free cheese, sour cream, or some herbal seasoning. There are hundreds of creative ways to prepare potatoes, so fight the urge to fry them, and hit the recipe books.

Cheap Shot

Note the number of grams of fat listed on food labels; calories are not as important. Eating fresh foods with as much fiber and protein and as little fat, salt, and other additives as possible is the best eating there is.

➤ If you smoke, now is the time to stop. You already know about the health risks to yourself and possibly to those around you; think about what you could do with all the bucks that are going up in smoke. Cigarette prices are bound to go up every time the state needs some new revenue, so bite the bullet now. (You'll pay less for health insurance, too.)

➤ For relief from the pain and itching caused by insect bites, poison ivy, sunburn, and other skin irritants, use 100 percent aloe vera plant gel. If you have the plant available, just cut a leaf in half and squeeze the balm onto the affected area. You can grow aloe vera in the house very easily, or just buy aloe vera lotions which work quite well. Look for products that have the highest pure aloe vera content. Linseed oil is also another surprising all-purpose skin soother that reduces inflammation and relieves itching.

➤ Popcorn is fairly nutritious, low in calories, and reasonably high in fiber. It is also about the cheapest snack you can buy. Without added oil or butter, a 3-cup serving can cost as little as three cents. If you want the healthiest popcorn possible, use an air popper and avoid all those fatty oils. Name-brand microwave popcorns are expensive unless you can find a special deal, and there's really not much difference between the so-called gourmet popcorn (give me a break!) and the generic stuff. Try cheap, healthy popcorn, and lay off the potato chips, cheese doodles, and other more expensive snacks.

Cheap Trick

Avoid the misery and major life disruption of the flu by getting a shot from your doctor before the flu season sets in. Most flu shots won't ward off all strains, but they come darn close. Doctors know which strains are prevalent in their geographic area, and will give you a shot that protects you best.

➤ You know it's cold-and-flu season when just about everyone you talk to either has or has just gotten over a bug. When you're shopping for over-the-counter remedies:

Get single-ingredient products, such as suppressant, expectorant, or decongestant, depending on the symptoms you have.

Generics are as effective as name brands and can save you as much as 40 percent.

Make sure you look at warning labels to see if the remedy causes drowsiness.

Try using home remedies such as drinking plenty of fluids, gargling with salt water, or rubbing your chest with pure peppermint oil.

If your symptoms persist for more than a week, see a doctor; you may need a prescription for an antibiotic.

➤ Get a complete physical once a year; it's expensive, but it can save you money in the long run. Many of today's diseases and illnesses can be successfully treated if detected early enough. One of the surest ways to cut medical costs is through preventive care.

➤ If you shop like a cheapskate, it doesn't cost any more to eat healthy, and it will increase your vitality and improve the quality of your life. Think fresh fruit, vegetables, and breads, not prepackaged frozen meals.

➤ In the spring, watch for a community health fair, where you can get your cholesterol checked, a blood pressure screening, be tested for colon cancer, etc., absolutely free. You'll save yourself a trip to the doctor's office, and a hefty bill if you don't have health insurance that covers preventive testing. Going to a health fair is also a great way for kids to learn about science and medicine. Call your local hospital or community health center if you want further information.

The Least You Need to Know

➤ If you haven't already done so, start on a regular exercise program and healthy diet.

➤ Next time you need to buy prescription drugs, if your doctor gives you the option, choose a generic instead of a name-brand drug.

➤ Review your health insurance policy to make sure you're not paying too much. If you have a low deductible, raise it to $1,000 to save a significant amount on your premiums without sacrificing coverage.

➤ Opt for glass lenses in your next pair of glasses. Glass doesn't damage as readily as plastic, and will last years longer. Metal frames will also hold up longer than plastic.

➤ If you can't stop smoking, you'll never be a good cheapskate. The reason: Not only is your money going up in smoke, you're also setting yourself up for tremendous health bills down the road. Do whatever it takes to stop.

Chapter 18

Finders, Keepers: Keep More of Your Pay

In This Chapter

➤ Find more pay in your paycheck

➤ Is your workplace working for you?

➤ FICA (Social Security) tax twists

➤ Discover more allowable deductions

➤ Could your fun hobby increase your funds?

➤ Maximize your business tax deductions

If you want to take this business of being a cheapskate seriously, look at every area of your financial life for ways to make and save more money. If you have a regular job with a steady paycheck (and the same old salary), chances are you haven't thought about the many ways you can get more pay out of that paycheck.

Even if the kind of work you do includes extra salary and fringe benefits, you may have overlooked a workplace savings plan that would make great financial sense without cramping your lifestyle. The right financial approach can work just as well if you're self-employed; either way, getting more financial breaks will make you more productive. It follows that your earnings will increase; all you have to do is follow the cheapskate strategies in this chapter.

Find More Pay in Your Paycheck

Are you getting all the pay you can out of your paycheck? Check out this list of ways you may be able to take more home without earning more.

Review your paycheck stubs, starting with your gross salary before deductions, and see if you can find any ways to increase your take-home pay:

➤ Are you withholding too much in taxes? Most Americans withhold much more than they have to. You should adjust your deductions according to how much you'll deduct at the end of the year. To come up with a rough idea of this figure, ask yourself a few questions:

Are you going to take an IRA (Individual Retirement Account), medical, or mortgage deduction? If you plan to take all or any of these deductions, calculate them into your allowable withholding allowances. Why loan Uncle Sam the money when you could be earning interest on it for a year? (See section in this chapter on W-4 withholding for more details.)

➤ Do you really need all the insurance you're paying for through payroll deductions? Most paycheck stubs are littered with mostly unnecessary insurance deductions. You may be able to get it cheaper someplace else, or at least have a trustworthy insurance agent check out your employee coverage.

Does your spouse have coverage, and are you paying to duplicate it unnecessarily? If any of this applies to you, after you adjust your coverage, you may be able to go home with an extra $50 to $100 per month. (See Chapter 21 for insurance advice.)

➤ If you changed jobs within the year, you may be over-withholding on FICA (Federal Insurance Contribution Act). FICA is simply the part of your paycheck you pay to the government for Social Security benefits. Employers are required to begin withholding afresh when you start a new job, but the most they can base their withholding on is $37,000. If you've been earning $40,000 for most of the year and you switch to a job paying $45,000, make sure you're not paying too much FICA tax. You'll get it back when you file your return, but why wait? If you get that money immediately, you can put it to work in a good cheapskate investment plan! No matter what you do, you can't stop FICA withholding, but you can claim additional allowances and reduce it by visiting your company's personnel department (see section on FICA taxes in this chapter for more details).

Cheap Trick

Are you due for a raise? If it's been a couple of years since the last one, now is a good time to ask. Ask yourself if you're being paid what you could get elsewhere, and, if not, consider looking for another job in your spare time. As long as you don't quit your present job, what can you lose?

➤ Are you taking maximum advantage of any company-sponsored retirement plans? These plans are a great way to reduce your tax burden and help you start a savings program for the future. Many employers will match your contributions, which makes saving doubly rewarding (see section on employer-sponsored retirement plans in this chapter for more details).

➤ If you need money in an emergency, try borrowing from your company's 401(k) plan or your employee credit union. The rates are usually more favorable than a bank's, and you have the advantage of dealing with your employer rather than with some unknown banker.

Cheap Talk

Tax-deferred savings means that your accumulated investment return is not taxed until you withdraw funds from your retirement account. It doesn't always mean that your contributions to the account will not be taxed. Check with your employer to find out about the tax consequences associated with your account.

Review your paycheck with your company's personnel department or your office manager as soon as possible. You may find out about some company benefits you've overlooked or forgotten about, or discover that you're withholding too much. Take a good look at your paycheck at least twice a year to make sure you're getting the most out of it.

Is Your Workplace Working for You?

When was the last time your boss, or anyone, said to you, "Let's sit down and make sure you're saving enough for retirement"? Making your retirement nest egg grow is your responsibility, and your employee retirement plan could make that egg golden.

If your employer offers a 401(k) plan or a simple pension plan, contribute the maximum amount. If you're a teacher, government employee, or work for a nonprofit and have access to a 403(b) plan, contribute the most you possibly can. By contributing the maximum allowed per year, you can accumulate enough money for a very comfortable retirement through the power of tax-deferred savings.

As an example, if you take one penny and double it every day, after thirty-one days, you'll have $10,747,000. If Uncle Sam comes along on the fifth day in and demands taxes on 28 percent of your savings, that will eat into the earnings considerably. If he asks for more taxes on days 10, 15, 20, 25, and 30, your money will be worth only $1,500,000. You would lose about $9 million! Who wants an uncle who does that to you? Could there be a better reason to take tax-deferred savings in your employee retirement accounts?

The following table shows you the results of investing $4,000 a year in your company retirement plan. The first column indicates the age at which you begin contributing.

$4,000 Investment Per Year Before Taxes*

Present Age	Account at Age 65
20	$6,088,871
25	3,440,570
30	1,937,852
35	1,085,170
40	601,336
45	362,795
50	171,013
55	82,618
60	32,461

12% compounded annually in tax-free retirement plans

Here are some more details about the plans your employer may offer, and guidelines to see if you qualify for them:

➤ 401(k) and 403(b)—You can contribute up to $10,000 annually to these plans and your employer also has the option of contributing. Contributions are made before taxes are taken out, and your money grows tax-deferred until it's withdrawn. You can't beat the advantages of these plans, especially if your employer matches funds. Sometimes they're limited by your employer's investment choices, but it's worth the price for such great benefits.

Cheap Shot

Don't ever invest retirement fund money in accounts that pay low interest, such as 4% or 5%, unless you're close to retirement age. For the long haul, park your money in equity investments and let compound interest do its work. Low rates of return won't even keep up with inflation over the years.

➤ While most employers offer some sort of 401(k) plan, general pension plans still exist. If your employer provides a pension plan and you can contribute, it's not a bad idea, but you may find that a straight pension plan only allows for employer contributions.

➤ If you have ten or more years until retirement and have control over your plan, invest in equity securities; they'll outperform other investments in the long run. A no-load mutual fund is an excellent option, and a good company plan should give you mutual fund options. Choose one that provides a good return on your money over the long haul over an option with outstanding short-term gains.

Once you've done your homework, if you see that you need to contribute more to attain your retirement goals, try to work it out. The retirement years are when you'll need the money most and will have the time to enjoy it. Use all your available employee resources and you may find that even an early retirement is not an impossibility for a smart cheapskate.

Follow Your FICA

You or your accountant should check your FICA account on a regular basis. FICA stands for the Federal Insurance Contribution Act. Your FICA account was established to set money aside for you for your retirement years.

Frugality Footnote

The Federal Insurance Contribution Act established Social Security during the Great Depression when Franklin D. Roosevelt was President. During the FDR administration, Social Security was seen as the foundation of a good retirement plan, not the only source of income for retirees. Though it was never intended to provide more than 25% of what people would need to live on, many Americans still mistakenly expect their Social Security benefits to see them through their later years.

These days, the $13,000 maximum Social Security benefit will not even come close to paying the bills of most retirees. Assuming that the system continues to make payments at the present rate, as the inflation rate rises, it's likely that benefits will buy less and less.

FICA is the most elusive of all taxes, because you never even see the money that is being credited toward your Social Security benefits. And as if paying the tax weren't bad enough, there's a chance that it's not being credited properly. Many people find errors in their Social Security reports, so don't just assume that all that money will be there for you when you retire. Over the years, Congress has raided the Social Security fund regularly for loans to pay the government's bills.

Murphy's Law—that anything that can go wrong will—might have been invented to describe FICA. There is an almost infinite number of errors that can affect your account. Companies move, merge, are sold, change their names, and go out of business every day. Any or all of these occurrences can result in lost and fouled-up records. Women who interrupt their careers to have children, and part-time workers whose hours may not have been properly credited, are particularly subject to accounting mistakes.

Don't Donate to the IRS

Tax refunds sound great, but the reality is that all you're getting back is what you loaned the IRS—without interest! Many Americans use their tax refunds as a forced saving to help pay bills, but does it make sense to give the IRS a $1,000 or $2,000 interest-free loan every year?

Cheap Trick

To determine whether your FICA account is accurate, obtain form SSA-7004 from your local Social Security Administration (SSA) office (if you want one sent to you, call 1–800–772–1213). A few weeks after you mail it in, you will receive a report detailing all credits in your file. If you find an error, report it to the SSA with all the necessary documentation to back it up.

There is a better way. If you're getting a refund this year, please, please, put it in the bank for a rainy day. Then go directly to your human resources office at work and ask them to help you rework your W-4 statement. After you adjust the form to include only allowable deductions, you'll start getting more money in your paycheck—it's kind of like an instant raise! You can use it to pay your bills on time and avoid interest penalties, or put the extra cash into your monthly savings or investment account. Whatever you decide to do with it, IT will be more than you would have gotten back as a tax refund.

Could Your Hobby Be a Tax Haven?

There are definite advantages to running your own business from home. If you have a hobby or trade that you're good at, think about starting part-time on building a business. You can generate a substantial second income, get great tax breaks, and—who knows?—you could even end up a full-time entrepreneur.

There really is no formula for creating a successful business, but there's a lot you can do to give yourself a fighting chance. If you're considering going into business for yourself, these are the keys to mobilizing your energy, vision, and skills.

Keys to Starting a Successful Business

➤ Do a tremendous amount of research in advance. Talk to people who are in the industry you're looking to get into, and ask lots of questions. Spend time at the library and on the Internet reading and researching. If you decide to launch your business, do a lot of the legwork beforehand such as opening up bank accounts, preparing a business plan, filing for a business license, and setting up your books. This will free up your time to focus on generating income when you do get started.

➤ The worst time to start a new business is when your life is in turmoil; ironically, that's when most people think about it. If you experience a family breakup or other major emotional letdown, the timing can appear to be right for a radical change like starting a business. It's not; wait until you've got your balance before you take on such a great risk.

Frugality Footnote

Be prepared for the ups and downs in your business; they go with the territory. A slow quarter or even a slow year is not uncommon. You need to stick with it for as long as possible to give it a chance. If after two years your business shows little sign of growth, it's a good time to reevaluate your options.

➤ Try to start your business on a part-time basis at home. It may not be possible, but if circumstances allow it, you'll get a chance to test the waters while you still have a regular job.

➤ Start out as an extreme cheapskate. Don't spend money on management consultants and market researchers when you can do the research yourself. While it's true that it takes money to make money, the new business owner tends to make better money decisions when there's not a lot of cash to play around with. Solving problems creatively with the least amount of capital can get your business through the difficult early years when most new enterprises run out of cash before they've had a real chance to succeed. It is vital that you spend money on a good lawyer and accountant, though. They'll save you a lot in the long run.

Cheap Trick

Make sure the product or service you're going to sell has compelling advantages over the competition. Just because someone is making a killing in the same business doesn't mean you will, too. Don't wait for business to come to you; it never does. Get out there and hustle!

Any expense related to the running of your business can be deductible. There are actually eighteen categories of deductible expenses, including advertising, bank charges, bad debts, office and utility expenses, as well as "other expenses." You can also deduct the cost of resold inventory, and interest expenses if you borrow money to finance equipment purchases and operations.

Depending on the business you go into, some other potentially tax-deductible items are:

➤ Autos

➤ Auto expenses

➤ Cost of workspace in your home

➤ Utilities

➤ Computers

➤ Travel

➤ Professional books and subscriptions

➤ Calculators, typewriters, and recorders

➤ Education expenses

➤ Uniforms

➤ Stationery and business cards

One of the best things to do is run your business from a spare room in your home, and deduct the mortgage or rent and utilities for the space on your taxes—if you use it exclusively for business.

Cheap Thrills at Work

➤ Think twice about working for a company as an independent contractor. A positive is that you can take deductions that an employee can't, but there are negatives.

As an independent contractor, you'll automatically pay both the employee portion and what an employer would otherwise pay for Social Security tax, which will double your FICA tax liability.

Depending on the company, you may be missing out on thousands of dollars worth of benefits, such as health and disability insurance. If you have a choice, compare the financial aspects of being an employee with being an independent contractor to determine which is more advantageous.

➤ If you have an office in your home with a fax machine or e-mail account, when you can, use them instead of mailing correspondence and making long-distance calls. They cut down on wasted money and time spent on postage and chit-chatting. To save even more, send your long-distance faxes automatically late at night when the rates are cheaper.

Frugality Footnote

Work for employers that provide generous benefit packages, typically the larger ones. Fringe benefits can add considerably to your bottom-line salary, and aren't taxed. For instance, if you receive a salary of $30,000 per year, with the benefits, it may look more like $35,000. Always factor in the additional value of the benefits when you consider the salary for a job you're offered.

➤ You can take a tax deduction for traveling to a job interview, and nothing says you can't spend a few extra days in the area. As long as the interview is for a position in your field, the cost of the trip is fully tax-deductible. The deduction includes airfare, rental car, and passport fees.

➤ If you need life insurance, see what your employer has to offer. Companies often have special rates on term life insurance (see Chapter 21) through their employee benefit packages. Group insurance frequently comes with attached life insurance benefits.

➤ Eat your breakfast at home or take something with you to work. Lunches are expensive enough; why shell out another $5 a day for breakfast?

➤ If you move to another city for a new job, don't forget to take advantage of moving deductions on your next tax return. If you're an employee of a company and they don't pay for the move, it's about the only deduction you can take.

➤ Get a job as close to home as possible. Commuting costs a lot and can also be emotionally taxing. If you're in the process of looking for another job, try to find a company that's within a few miles of where you live. An added advantage if you're married is that you can often get away with just one car.

Cheap Trick

If you work for a larger company and like to travel for fun, always ask for corporate discounts. Often airlines, hotels, and rental agencies have special discounts of 10% or more for employees of large companies. Even if there aren't special rates for your specific company, you can usually get a corporate rate anyway just for asking. Cheapskates take what they can get.

➤ Why not extend the cheapskate spirit to your work? Look for ways you can help your company reduce expenses, and you may find your efforts returned tenfold when they're noticed.

The Least You Need to Know

➤ Immediately review your last pay stub to analyze any possible deductions you may be taking needlessly. Look at insurance, retirement plans, and day care costs and make adjustments where needed.

➤ If your employer offers quality retirement plans, by all means contribute the maximum amount to them. Often employers will match your contributions, and help you get to retirement that much faster.

➤ Check your W-4 at work to make sure you're taking the proper amount of deduction allowances. They'll be correct when you don't get any money back from the IRS at end of the year. No use in giving Uncle Sam an interest-free loan.

➤ Check to make sure that the right amount of money has been going toward your future Social Security benefits by requesting form SSA-7004 from the Social Security Administration office. Mistakes are common and should be corrected immediately.

➤ If you are in need of extra money and have a hobby or craft you are good at, consider making it a part-time business. A home-based business can generate lots of income and also plenty of tax deductions.

How Much for That Piece of Parchment?

The average cost of sending a child to college for four years is about $70,000—twice that if it happens to be in the Ivy League. And that's right now; the costs are expected to double every decade, so if you have a tot or two, double those numbers. But there's hope if you're a cheapskate and know how to take advantage of the cost-cutting opportunities that abound on college campuses.

How Can I Afford College for the Kids?

Parents may say that sending their kids to college is their number one priority; even more important than saving for their retirement, but the fact is that only about 10 percent of parents have a savings program for their children's college education. Some parents just never made enough money to save, but more often, they aren't aware of how costly college is, or don't know how to go about saving for it. And then there are the spendthrifts who figure that their kid's education will take care of itself.

Plan It or Can It

If your child or grandchild is planning to pay some college expenses, don't think you have to earmark every penny you save for their education. Just be in a position to pay a large proportion of the tab if you want to give them a good start in life. Plan to cover tuition, room, board, and books if they'll cover extracurricular activities, or find some other combination that works for you and the student.

Baby Steps in Saving

The general guidelines for a college savings fund are to sock away $2 a day for a newborn child. Triple the amount when the child is 5 ($6 a day), and triple it again every five years ($18 at age 10, etc.). This is just one way to approach a savings plan; how much and how often you save should be something that suits your circumstances.

If your daughter or son goes to a private college, plan to pay about double of what a public institution would cost. A good compromise is for your child to go to an inexpensive local college or a community college for a year or two and then transfer to an expensive private college to earn a diploma. After all, resumes list the school someone graduates from, right? So why not save some money on the first two years of college and be able to afford the last two at a school with a great reputation?

Cheap Trick

More than $100 million in education financial aid offered by the government goes unclaimed every year simply because people don't know about it. To find out about every loan and grant available, contact: College Financial Planning Service, 1010 Vermont Avenue NW, 4th Floor, Washington, DC 20005. They have a listing of about 200,000 different sources of funding, including many obscure ones.

Frugality Footnote

How much do you need to save for college? In about fifteen years from now, the average cost for four years at a public college will be about $125,000. The cost for a private school will be about $250,000. The reality is that you'll probably be able to come up with only about 50%–60% of the money your child will need to cover the cost of college. Most likely, you'll also have to take out loans to cover all the expenses. The important thing is to start saving now if you want to contribute even partially to your children's education. Even the partial contribution you're able to make will be extremely important as education costs continue to rise.

If you haven't started to save for your children's college education by the time they've hit high school, be prepared for a struggle. To pay a good proportion of the cost of a public college or university, you'll have to start saving about $600 a month immediately; that's why you're so much better off if you start much earlier.

Bottom line: If you don't save, your kids' options, and ultimately the quality of their education, will be greatly diminished. When they see you taking steps to prepare for their education, the kids may take college, and the idea of saving, more seriously, too.

Financial First Aid

If you don't have enough savings for your children's college costs, student lends are a blessing. The government lends, and also gives away, billions of dollars every year to help students pay for college. If your assets are positioned properly, you may be able to qualify. For example, paying down your mortgage or contributing more to your retirement plan would leave you with less available cash for college bills—and give your teen a better shot at a loan.

There are several forms of financial aid:

➤ Gifts or grants

➤ Low-interest loans

➤ Work-study loans

Cheap Shot

Be careful to fill out all applications for student loans completely and truthfully. Often, students forget important facts, or intentionally omit information, which can lead to the immediate calling of the loan, or even fines or imprisonment.

They are offered through state or local governments, colleges, and private institutions. The best way to find out about available programs is through the financial aid office of the school your son or daughter will be attending; do it early to make sure you meet deadlines for applications.

College Aid Sources

➤ Gifts and Grants: These top the list because the money doesn't have to be paid back. Gifts and grants can include scholarships (generally for gifted athletes or students), or Pell Grants given to students in families with an annual income of $32,000 or less.

➤ Student Loans: Government loans, such as Perkins Loans and Stafford Loans, offer below-market interest rates and excellent payback terms. Often, a student won't have to make payments until they've finished school, and can stretch the

219

Cheap Trick

When you apply for a Pell Grant, you may also automatically qualify for another government grant called the Supplemental Education Opportunity Grant (SEOG). They are awarded in $100 increments up to $4,000, but you won't get one if you don't apply.

payment period to ten years or more. Most banks back loans of this type, and may also offer their own versions. To find out about all the student loans available, simply call the Student Loan Aid Information Center at 1-800-433-3243.

➤ Work-Study Programs: These programs are generally sponsored by the federal government or individual schools. They combine schoolwork with work the student does in their field of study or other area to help defray college costs. Other programs allow the student to work half the year in their chosen career field, and attend classes during the other half. These programs are great because they give students hands-on experience in their field, which gives them a big advantage when they start job hunting. To find out more, contact the National Commission for Cooperative Education, 360 Huntington Avenue, Boston, MA 02115, for a listing of schools that offer these programs.

The amount of financial aid a student receives is based on a set formula which determines the maximum amount the family is able contribute. When you apply for any type of aid or grant, it's within your rights to adjust your financial profile to minimize your cash assets at the time of application. And remember, you must apply for a new loan every year.

How do you structure your assets and savings to your advantage?

➤ Don't save money in your child's name, because a dependent child is expected to pay about 35 percent of their assets toward school. Parents only have to pay 6 percent.

➤ If you haven't fully funded all your available retirement funds, do so before you apply. Funds in retirement accounts are not counted as assets.

➤ If you want to cash in any investments you've made money on, do it in your child's junior year of high school, and take your gains before the child's college years.

These moves may seem shady, but they are perfectly legal, and any smart cheapskate would take advantage of them.

Pay Now AND Pay Later?

Yes, believe it or not, there are many colleges that offer prepaid college tuition plans, that allow you to lock in payment at the going rate at the time that you pay. You can do it when they're still toddlers; they just have to meet minimum admission requirements at the time of admittance. If they don't meet those requirements, most plans will refund your money plus interest.

Sound great? Sure, except that, once you've signed on the dotted line, your son or daughter is committed to attending that school, and there are a lot of things that can get in the way of that happening.

Frugality Footnote

A type of prepayment plan that makes sense allows students to prepay all four years of college the first year they enroll. It locks in current costs for tuition, room and board, and other expenses. Many colleges make loans available to pay for these plans and, with this arrangement, you don't have the pressure of choosing a school for your kids years before they're college-age. If you take advantage of such a plan, ask about your right to a refund if the student changes schools or drops out during the four years.

If something does go wrong, you may be able to get some kind of refund, or you may not, especially when you can't be sure that you'll actually end up saving money on the tuition rate. Some of the pitfalls are:

Making a college choice for a young child. What happens if the kid wants to major in something that particular college doesn't offer, or decides not to go to college at all?

The college you choose may no longer exist in fifteen years! Many of those that pioneered prepayment plans didn't do such a great job at investing the funds they raised.

Bottom line: Don't opt for a prepaid college plan. Your best bet is to begin a college savings fund for each of your children when they're young, and put money into that plan on a regular basis. Or make a lump-sum investment in a growth-oriented mutual fund. A year or two before you have to commit the capital, preserve it in a less volatile investment.

Cyber-Ed

Computers are here to stay, and any cheapskate who refuses to learn about them will be left in the dust.

One of the fastest growing segments of the computer revolution is online service and the Internet. Installing a modem in your computer allows you to access huge data

banks offering services to help you at home and work, along with e-mail communications and live interactive chats on the keyboard.

If you aren't plugged in but are thinking about it, or are considering changing services, check out these options.

The Online Revolution

The following is a listing of the most popular online services and a brief evaluation of each:

➤ America Online (1-800-827-6364): The cost is $21.95 per month for unlimited access. America Online is by far the fastest growing service today, the costs are reasonable and they offer many diverse services. You'll find the travel, sports, and leisure services extremely helpful and "chat rooms" are fun. These live, online conversations between subscribers on the system are interesting, entertaining, and informative. The investing and finance sections are very basic, but do provide some good cheapskate tools. America Online also has easy access to the Internet and it's included in your monthly cost.

➤ CompuServe (1-800-848-8199): The cost is $9.95 per month for five hours and $2.95 for each additional hour. CompuServe offers more services than any of its competitors. It's easy to use, but beware of add-on pricing for some types of information. The investing and finance sections are great for us cheapskates, and the basic services are better than the competitions'. Travel, news, and sports and leisure are also very good. CompuServe offers the most comprehensive service, but it's not as user friendly as the others.

Cheap Trick

If your child needs a computer at school, an older, used one will probably do the job. About the only thing college kids need computers for is word processing, so you don't have to get them the latest, fastest model. A few software packages and a printer, and they'll be up and running.

Cheap Shot

A word of caution about the Internet: Even with today's software advances, it can still be difficult to navigate. If you don't like computers or have some knowledge of them, the Net may not be for you. But it won't be long, perhaps just a few years, before several hundred million people will be on the Internet and you'll *HAVE* to be one of them!

➤ Prodigy (1-800-776-3449): The cost is $19.95 per month for unlimited access. The graphics are not the best, and advertising is everywhere, but they do provide some top-notch services. Access to the Internet is included in the monthly fee.

If you prefer, and have some computer savvy, you save some cash by bypassing the online services and getting directly onto the Internet. Just call an Internet Service Provider (ISP) and hook up; most major cities have providers available, and you can find them in the Yellow Pages. An Internet Service Provider will provide the software you need for direct access, and you'll have no online service to mess with. Make sure the service has a local access number so you won't be paying long distance rates to be connected.

Beat the Cost of College Books

Books can take a big bite out of the college fund. Students should check out the campus bookstore for used textbooks sold on consignment, and resell their books when they've finished a course. And there are always used bookstores near colleges where the savings can be great.

Cheapskate Books in General

College isn't the only place we need to save on books. Next time you think about enhancing your own education buying a book, you may want to keep the following cheapskate pointers in mind:

➤ Look in the Yellow Pages for chain discount book stores in your area. They discount most books and also have deep discount racks. You can save as much as 30 percent if you shop selectively. Some of these stores offer discount cards that provide even greater discounts if you purchase a certain amount of merchandise from the store over a specified period of time.

➤ Check local wholesale clubs that sell in high volume. Their prices are excellent on recently published and best-selling books.

➤ Consider joining a book club if you read a lot, *but* only if you read a lot. You generally get a certain number of books for $1 or $2 plus shipping when you join the club. Then you receive new releases every month or so. You can save $50 or more a year if you tend to read one book or more a month. Make sure

Cheap Trick

The single greatest way to save on books is to use your local library. And you don't pay a dime, unless you take the books back late. We're so used to buying things that we think there's nothing worth a darn for free. Don't sell your local library short; it's a cheapskate's paradise. They even sell books cheap from time to time.

you're dealing with a reputable company, and by all means read the fine print at the bottom of the contract before signing on. You also must be prepared to send a notification to the company if you don't want the latest month's selection. Some clubs just send you the book, and if you don't like it, you have to send the whole package back. What a hassle. Again, read the tiny print at the bottom of the application. Also, keep track of what you really spend with these clubs to see if you're getting the savings you expect.

➤ Great places to get bargains on books are garage sales, community bazaars, and used book stores. You'll be amazed at the number of quality books available at garage sales. People just want to get rid of the clutter on their bookshelves. A cheapskate should be able to negotiate most books for less than a buck, even a hardly read recent bestseller.

➤ Talk with friends and relatives who are avid readers about working out some kind of exchange. It's a great way to read lots of books for half the price, and you can have fun discussing them afterward.

Cheap Thrills in Education

➤ When it's time to send the kids back to school with new clothes, donate their old ones to charity. It means a tax deduction for you. If you give away items valued at $500, you can generally take a tax deduction of over $150. This isn't chump change. Don't trash old clothes when someone else's kids can get some wear out of them and you can make some money to boot.

Cheap Shot

Taking a car to college is a major expense for any student. As difficult as it may be, determine whether your child really needs this added expense. Sometimes having a car is a great convenience, but often a student can get along just fine using campus and public transportation, and hitching rides from friends.

➤ Many civic clubs such as the Scouts, Rotary Club, and Kiwanis offer some type of college assistance program. Also local churches, synagogues, and foundations offer grants.

➤ Unless your child pays to live in a cramped house with a bunch of other college kids, a dormitory is probably their best bet. One of the things they may want to do is live off-campus, but it can be a big mistake, especially at the beginning of their college careers. It's better for them to live closer to campus where all their education resources are within walking distance and they're in an environment that will encourage them to study harder.

➤ If your child has a penchant for the military, encourage them to investigate further. If money is tight, they can enlist in the Army for four years and get about $25,000 toward their college education paid for by Uncle Sam. Another option is to become a part of ROTC (Army Reserve Officers Training Corps). Your education is almost entirely paid for and you're only required to spend eight years in the Reserves after college. Being in the Reserves is not a full-time commitment, but you will need to be ready in time of a national emergency.

➤ Don't pay dues to join campus organizations. There are plenty of free activities. For instance, you can get involved with campus politics, volunteer to help manage a sports team, join a singing group, etc. There are great ways to enjoy your free time at college.

Cheap Trick

Be a big fish in a small pond rather than a minnow at some Ivy League college. Less prestigious colleges offer many more honors programs and more financial aid options. If your child is a good student, don't automatically send them to an upscale college when they may just get a better deal and a better education at a school with a lower profile.

The Least You Need to Know

➤ Evaluate your family's need for college funds. If you have more then one child, you could be in for a major shock come college time if you have't been saving. If you don't have a savings plan, start one today.

➤ If your savings fall short of paying for college, evaluate your other payment options. Use the resources provided by your school's financial aid office to help you find the right loans and grants for your child.

➤ It may be worth your time to investigate prepaid college plans, but most are very risky. Ask your school if they have a program that gives you a discount if you pay all four years in advance, and be sure to find out what their cancellation provisions are.

➤ To learn about computers and take advantage of the vast research material available in databases around the world, consider subscribing to one of the many online services, or hook up directly to the Internet.

➤ Bargains on books abound. Check garage sales, used book stores, community fairs, and thrift shops. Your kids can save money on school books by scouting out used bookstores that carry college books.

Part 6
Cheap Money Management

My dad always told me that it's a jungle out there. He must have been talking about saving and investing. It is, without a doubt, the most confusing part of most people's financial lives. But for the savvy cheapskate, sound money management isn't that different from managing the grocery shopping; you gotta have a plan. If you follow the advice in this section, you can easily eliminate paying outlandish fees to bankers, stockbrokers, and so-called financial consultants, and make wiser investment choices. Follow the cheapskate example and keep money management simple; it's the best way to take charge of your financial future.

Are you sick of finding new fees on your bank statement every month? Learn to fight back and win at the banking game in Chapter 20. Let cheapskates show you how to find your way through the maze of insurance options and cut your costs by as much as half. Chapter 21 describes the best and worst insurance deals, and tells you how to talk back to your agent. Paying taxes is something everyone hates to do, but you won't hate it as much after you learn the great cheapskate tax tricks in Chapter 22.

You don't have to have a bundle to become an investor; first learn to save, and then use the advice in Chapter 23 to increase your savings magically through compound interest. You'll find out how easy it is to start with a small investment and learn how to build it up over the long haul. No matter how little you start with, your money will be working for you all the time, and you can have a nest egg that will give you a lot of choices in your retirement years.

Chapter 20

Get the Best of Your Banker

> ## In This Chapter
>
> ➤ The skinny on banking schemes
>
> ➤ The plague of the killer fees
>
> ➤ Play to win the banking game
>
> ➤ Make friends with your bank's ATM
>
> ➤ Uncle Sam's got you covered
>
> ➤ Getting real about your estate

Banks are in the greatest business of all—selling money at good prices. No one's happy with their service or their rates, but the banks stay in business anyway. We accept the fact that, yes, gone are the days when your banker was a confidante and ally in the life of your family and business. Banking, like every other industry, has undergone tremendous changes over the decades. Cheapskates take a dimmer view: They see a business that preys on customers who don't know the ropes, and they fight back.

Squeeze More Bucks Out of Your Bank

You have a lot of banks, bank services, and products to choose from. If you want to get more control over your money and squeeze a few more bucks out of your banker:

> ➤ Don't pay unnecessary service charges. Fees vary since deregulation has occurred. Call your bank and find out what the fees are on your accounts. Then call around to other banks in the area and see if your bank is competitive. If you find a better

Cheap Talk

A *money market mutual fund* is completely different from a *money market account* offered by banks. *Money market mutual funds* are administered by hundreds of mutual fund families across the country and usually offer a higher rate of return than a bank *money market account*. Always put your idle cash in *a money market mutual fund* for similar liquidity (ability to get the funds) and returns that are higher.

Cheap Trick

Deposit your paycheck by direct deposit if your employer allows it. Not only do you save the time and inconvenience of going to the ATM machine every week or two, the money becomes "good funds" faster. Most companies that have direct deposit also allow you to send a portion of each paycheck to an investment vehicle of your choice. It's a great way to budget.

deal somewhere else, tell your banker that you're going to take your business elsewhere; they may just lower or eliminate the excessive fees they've been charging you. Be firm, and don't be intimidated by the banker's nice suit and big office.

➤ Never let money pile up in non-interest-bearing accounts, as many checking accounts are. Have your money working for you at all times. Most interest-bearing accounts have minimum balance requirements.

➤ Set up a money market mutual fund with a good mutual fund family rather than a bank savings account. You'll get a higher rate of return on your savings. Most money market mutual funds offer a small book of checks if you need to withdraw money quickly.

➤ Make regular deposits in your money market mutual fund and use this money as your emergency fund, that is, as readily available cash if an emergency crops up in the family. It should contain the equivalent of at least three months' income. If you have excess money building up in your checking account, transfer it over to your money market mutual fund. When you have more money in your money market mutual fund than necessary, look into a 6-month or 1-year CD (certificate of deposit) at your bank, or a short-term government security.

➤ Take advantage of no-fee or interest-bearing checking accounts and other service packages. The packages quite often include safe deposit boxes, free traveler's checks, and more. Senior citizens should look for banks that cater to their specific needs. Check out your qualifications for fees associated with different balances in your accounts.

➤ If you belong to an organization that has a credit union, take advantage of its lower borrowing rates and fees.

➤ Save time by banking on-line.

The Plague of the Killer Fees

As banking has become more and more competitive, most banks have been scrambling to find ways to make money. To the chagrin of all cheapskates, one of the ways has been to increase fees gradually, year after year. Instead of charging higher interest rates or huge fees on loans, they're nickeling-and-diming us to death. Many major banks have upped the cost of their basic services tremendously. It's not uncommon to have to pay $10 to $15 for a cashier's check or a simple bank check these days. How about $30 for a bounced check that costs the average bank only 79¢ to negotiate! Many banks even charge YOU $30 if someone else writes you a bad check. A banker I know recently told me that over 30 percent of his bank's profits were from these nickel-and-dime fees.

Basic services is just the beginning. How about the bogus fee for account research? You notice an error on your account statement from a few months ago, you call the bank, and you're told that, because your question is not about a current bill, they're going to charge you a $20 "account research fee" to look up the archived information. This is not a joke! Hundreds of banks around the country are bilking naïve customers this way every day. If a customer objects, they're usually blamed for not catching the error sooner.

Many banks have developed elaborate ways to conceal their extra profits on loans. Instead of charging a single, blatantly excessive fee for handling the loan, they add three or four small fees for things like "document handling" and "computer expense." These administrative expenses are part of the bank's overhead, and are already calculated in the profit they make on the loan. They're only $20 to $30 apiece, but they add up for the customer, and are just pure profit for the bank.

The only way to combat excessive fees is to get up to speed on what your bank charges fees for and how much they are. Ask for a fee disclosure statement and figure out how much your banking habits could cost you. If the bank is charging excessive fees for the services you use regularly, start shopping for another place to stash your cash. Ironically, the banks that charge the highest fees generally have the worst service. If you're banking at one of them, you'll never run into a cheapskate.

Playing to Win the Banking Game

The cheapskate's dream checking account would have no monthly service charges, no minimum and average balance requirements, no per-check charges, and no ATM fees. It would earn a good rate of interest and offer higher rates for higher balances. This may sound impossible but here's the complex strategy to making it happen: Just ask!

Only true cheapskates know that many bank services are negotiable. Banking is like any other business (a bit stuffier, perhaps), so if you can show them how it's in their best interest to change a few things, they may just do it. The next question is, how do you make it in their best interest?

Frugality Footnote

Avoid making any kind of regular purchase via a monthly automatic debit on your credit card or through your bank account. An example would be cable TV service. By letting a company debit your account, you lose financial control. You're also setting yourself up for problems if you ever want to cancel or change your product or service options. Quite often, the company debiting the amount takes too much money, fails to comply with a cancel request, or gets your account confused with someone else's. If you do experience problems, automatic debits are very difficult to void. There have also been many recent cases of fraud perpetrated by company employees who use numbers on customer cards and accounts to take themselves out for a night on the town—and worse!

➤ First, offer to have your paycheck deposited directly into your account on a regular basis. Arrange it with your employer, and the funds from the check will be automatically deposited and available on payday! No fuss for you means no fuss for the bank either. Make them aware that you know they'll save money on you this way, and ask them to waive their monthly minimum charge if you agree to direct deposit your check.

➤ Second, open up a savings account and put $300 or $400 in it. Explain to the bank you intend to deposit thousands more in the account in the coming months. If you're considering buying a car, tell them you intend to get your auto loan from them, and maybe even your next mortgage. You can tell them you'll do all these things if they're willing to give you free checking with interest. They may balk, which is their right, but point out to them that you intend to do business with them only if they can meet your small requests. If you're talking to the branch manager or someone else in charge, you'll generally get what you want.

Six Steps to the Best Bank Accounts

1. Compare several different banks for the best fees and features.
2. Pick a bank that has a short holding period on deposited checks.
3. Look for an institution that will contact you before they bounce a check.
4. Check on the bank's customer service. For instance, how many tellers do they have working at peak times, and what are their hours of operation?

5. If you want a one-stop bank to handle all your finances, check into their interest rates on certificates of deposit (CDs), and their loan rates.

6. Take only the services you need and don't pay for anything else. Often banks add perks with an account, such as a credit card or insurance; they add to the cost of the account but may be of no benefit to you. Get only what you need.

Banking for Two?

If you and your spouse have good credit, it's best to put all your funds into one account and use it for all your income and expenses. If one of you has a credit problem, consider splitting up your accounts until you have it under control. Otherwise, with a joint account, you're both held liable for any debts the other has. Discuss your options before you decide on the type of account you should get; money is the number one problem in most marriages.

One thing to be aware of with joint accounts is that they can trigger some inheritance problems. Too often a surviving spouse may need help with financial matters, and open a joint account with a child. Though it may not be intended, upon the death of the parent, the joint-owner child becomes sole owner of the parent's account. If the joint-owner child fulfills the parent's known intention to share the money equally with the other siblings, their shares will be subject to gift tax. To avoid this problem, sign a durable power of attorney and make one or more children agents to sign. Leave the bank account in your own name, and specify in your will that the account will be divided equally.

Check Mate

Most people think they have to buy their checks from their bank or they won't work. Cheapskates know it's not true. A check is just a piece of paper with some printing on it.

Instead of buying the bank's overpriced variety, contact Current Check Products, P.O. Box 19000, Colorado Springs, CO 80935. Phone 800-533-3973,

Cheap Trick

Keeping separate financial files if you're married can be advantageous if either spouse has poor credit and you want to get a loan or credit card. Just get it in the name of the spouse with the best credit history.

Cheap Talk

A *durable power of attorney* is a legal document giving someone the right to act in accordance with someone else's wishes. For instance, an elderly cheapskate may be unable to take care of their finances for health reasons. They can appoint someone else through a *durable power of attorney* to write checks, sign documents, and do anything they need to in the cheapskate's best interest.

and ask for a color brochure of check choices. Not only are the checks half the price that most banks charge, they have some great designs, like the Elvis edition, animals, and landscape scenes. My favorite is the check that looks like a dollar bill.

Another good company is Checks in the Mail, Inc. at 800-733-4443. If you're looking for business checks, you can save even more because banks really gouge businesses on them. Why are these check companies cheaper? There's no bank as the middleman.

Make Friends with Your Bank's ATM

Cheap Shot

If you deposit cash into an ATM machine, be careful. The receipt you get from the machine is not valid proof that you made the deposit in cash. If the teller makes an oversight opening the envelope and counting for final deposit, you're at the mercy of human error. Deposit cash at the teller's station inside the bank where a valid receipt is proof of deposit.

ATM's are really an incredible invention. It's amazing to drive up to a little machine and withdraw, transfer, and deposit money, all within a few minutes. It's just like having the bank vault right at your fingertips. As great as they are, though, a cheapskate won't pay $1 to $2.50 just for the "privilege" of using the machine. If you use an ATM twice a week, that's a minimum of $100 a year just in fees! If your bank charges fees every time you use your ATM, you're getting ripped off.

If your bank charges fees for your ATM, you owe it to cheapskates everywhere to raise a stink about it. The only time you should ever pay a fee associated with ATMs is when you use a bank other than your own. If that's how most banks in your area work, use only your bank's ATM, unless they charge you for transactions. If they do, switch banks. The bottom line is that you should never have to pay an ATM fee.

Safe Deposit Box No-No's

Be careful about putting cash, savings bonds, and stock certificates in your safe deposit box. Safe deposit theft is on the rise in metropolitan area banks, and if you're unlucky enough to have your box hit, you'll have a hard time proving that you had any negotiable currencies in it. Invest in a sturdy fireproof safe, and tuck it away in an unlikely place at home. If you're concerned about having valuables at home, make copies of all negotiable documents and put them in your safe deposit box. Having a backup never hurts.

Has Uncle Sam Got You Covered?

Your retirement nest egg may not be fully covered by the FDIC (Federal Deposit Insurance Corporation), which is the federal agency that insures your bank deposits. The maximum covered limit for bank deposits in checking, savings, IRAs, Keoghs, and 401(k)s is $100,000 for all accounts ($100,000 per bank).

Frugality Footnote

Some may wonder about the Federal Deposit Insurance Corporation and their ability to pay back depositors $100,000 per account. The fact is, if something catastrophic happened in the economy, it's doubtful that everyone would be covered and get the money they had in the bank back. The FDIC is primarily there to protect against small bank failures. If we have some sort of economic collapse, you'll probably be out of luck (like a lot of other people), but it's nice to know that if your bank makes some major mistake, the FDIC will be there to bail you out.

If you have $85,000 in an IRA and $90,000 in a Keogh account at the same bank, the FDIC insures only $100,000 of your entire savings in that bank. That leaves a whopping $75,000 uninsured. It's important to keep track of how much money you have in the bank, and if you have more than $100,000, spread it around to several banks to guarantee its safety. Keep tabs on your accounts to make sure they don't go over the limit.

Getting Real About Your Estate

Why discuss how to handle your estate in the banking section? Because banks often handle a large portions of people's estates through their trust departments. This is an overview of the basics of protecting your assets before you die. In no way is this small section a substitute for seeking out a competent estate lawyer to make sure everything is in order.

➤ First, every cheapskate should have an updated will to protect them from the possibility that their estate may go to probate. Probate means that the state decides how your property will be divided up. It is clearly an option you'd want to avoid.

➤ Another alternative to a will is setting up a family trust through a local bank. A trust is a great way to pass on your estate to your heirs and give specifics on how the money is to be properly divided. Trusts are much better than wills because they are more detailed and harder to contest. You also can change beneficiaries at any time.

➤ For most people, a revocable living trust is the best route to go. It's a painless way to pass on your estate, and you can revoke the trust if you feel it's not up to your expectations. You have complete authority while you're alive, and you choose the trustee who will distribute your estate when you die.

➤ If you want your spouse to have a steady income after you die, and then have the trust distributed when he or she dies, consider a QTIP (qualified terminable interest property trust). Sounds scary, but it's not that complex. The trust is managed by the surviving spouse and the trustee. The surviving spouse gets income from the trust and can sometimes even get a portion of the principal. However, the surviving spouse cannot change the beneficiaries who will receive all the assets from the trust after he or she dies. You should review your trust every couple of years to make sure it includes all your assets.

Cheap Shot

Try to spare your heirs property disputes after you've checked out of this world: Mark as many valuables as you can with color-coded stickers that designate who they'll go to. Include items that don't have a lot of value; the little things can sometimes be the most confusing for heirs to divide. You don't need to tell anyone your plan; just make sure your wishes are clearly spelled out in your will.

➤ Also consider a pre-nuptial agreement before you get married, so you can get around strict state laws that dictate how your estate will be distributed. If you're already married, draw up a post-nuptial agreement to do the same thing. The key to the success of either type of agreement is that both parties are honest and understanding about the need for it.

➤ At the very minimum, make sure you have an updated will to give your heirs at least some protection. If you get a trust, you'll still need a will that makes provisions for any assets the trust may have excluded. Ask friends and relatives if they know a good estate lawyer to help you get started.

Cheap Thrills in Banking

➤ This advice may sound negative and cold, but never, ever lend money to a friend. (Of course, some emergencies will override this rule.) If you decide to lend money to a buddy, be prepared for the worst. Nine times out of ten you don't get paid back, and the friendship could also be jeopardized. Look at the situation this way: If your friend can't get the money by traditional means, you can bet that you're making a high-risk loan. Just say no.

➤ Take advantage of overdraft protection if your bank offers it at no cost. It usually consists of giving a credit card number to your bank or tying your checking to a savings account. If you happen to get overdrawn, they'll charge the extra amount against your card or take it out of your savings. Of course, cheapskates would never need such a thing, but it never hurts to be prepared in case some mysterious person happens to miscalculate in the checkbook. You've never done that, have you?

➤ If you're thinking of moving your money to another bank but are concerned about its safety, check out this company for a complete solvency report: Veribanc, Inc., P.O. Box 461, Wakefield, MA 01880, 1-800-44BANKS. They charge just $10 for an instant rating of any bank, and $2 for additional ratings. For $45, you can get a complete report detailing more than anyone would ever need.

➤ Consider depositing money in a certificate of deposit if you want the safety of your principal but a better return than a savings account or money market would give you. It's best to buy a CD when you have funds you don't need to have for a year or two and you want to maximize your return. If you can do without the money for more than two years, consider investing in conservative stock and bond mutual funds (see Chapter 23).

Cheap Trick

Slow mail delivery can cost you money in unexpected interest charges and late payment fees from your bank and creditors. In your checkbook, note dates that you sent checks. Also, be aware of the dates that bills reach you in the mail; you can then call the company immediately and tell them when it arrived. They may allow a grace period on your account.

➤ A bank offering you pay-by-phone bill paying service can save you hours of time and many dollars every year. Simply by dialing the phone, you can automatically pay any bill and transfer money from one account to the other. Also check to see if they have an Internet site where you can look up balances, transfer funds, and pay bills.

Frugality Footnote

You may not even need a bank. If you're a member of an organization that has a credit union, you should put your money there. Credit unions generally have more liberal lending policies, fewer fees, higher interest on accounts, and cheap financial services. If you can put your money in one, you'll be a lot better off than those of us who are stuck with regular banks.

The Least You Need to Know

➤ To find the bank that's right for you, look into several in your area. One of the first things to check is the bank's fees. Generally, the bank with the lowest fees will also have the best customer service and cheapskate-friendly products.

➤ To check a bank's fees, simply ask for a disclosure statement. Most states require that banks disclose all fees up front to consumers.

➤ The cheapskate's checking account will have no monthly service charges, no minimum and average balance requirements, no per-check charges, and no ATM fees. You can find all the same advantages if you look hard enough.

➤ Buy your checks through mail rather than through the bank. Buying direct will always save you money.

➤ To avoid estate troubles for your heirs, set up a trust with a qualified lawyer, to be administered by your bank. Also, make a will to take care of any small matters your trust may leave out.

Chapter 21

Cut Insurance Costs Without Cutting Coverage

In This Chapter

➤ Choosing the right life insurance

➤ Is your home coverage enough?

➤ Put the brakes on car insurance costs

➤ Providing for income if you can't work

➤ Smart moves for policy shoppers

➤ Types of insurance you shouldn't buy

➤ The complete insurance makeover

Cheapskates hate insurance because they're paying for something they hope they'll never use. But they never consider being without it. Having insurance is one of the things we're stuck with, so the only thing to do is get over it, and learn how to buy the right insurance for the right price.

Whether you're insuring your car, home, or health, if you shop smart, you can have all the coverage you need (and sometimes more) and still keep your costs low. If you take a hard look at your coverage, you should be able to trim the costs to about half of what you're paying now—and get better quality coverage!

A Matter of Life and Death

Oh no, the life insurance agent is coming! Yes, we all need life insurance, but do we have to go through the ordeal of high-pressure sales presentations? Speaking from a lot of cheapskate experience, I can give you some pointers that can prepare you for your next encounter with an agent or—better yet—simply eliminate an encounter altogether. We do need life insurance; we accept that. But to make the right choices, it helps to understand why—and what life insurance really is.

Frugality Footnote

Ben Franklin was the first person to come up with the idea of mass-producing "death insurance" (as he called it). It does seem like the appropriate name for insurance that pays off when you die. But the guys who started to market the grimly named item couldn't make any sales, so they came up with the brilliant idea of calling it "life insurance." Overnight, life insurance became the hottest ticket in town, and soon the coffers of many insurance companies were overflowing—as they are to this day.

When insurers saw the cash they were raking in from life insurance, naturally they started to dream up other products to sell. That's when they invented "whole life insurance"—a mixture of insurance and low-interest investment that reaped interest for insurers at many times the rate they paid out to the policyholders who'd given them the capital. Insurance companies did so well that, when the Great Depression hit, they were the only ones left standing. Today, insurance companies are quietly the most influential in the world, and have billions more in assets than any other industry.

Cheap Talk

Whole Life insurance is a fancy term for a life insurance policy that has a savings element attached to it. It's a broad term that covers Universal Life, Variable Life, etc. If it is life insurance with a savings component, it's *Whole Life.*

Hold the Whole Life

Why do you need to know this? For starters, so you'll NEVER, and I mean NEVER, buy insurance as an investment unless you want to make a voluntary contribution to your insurer's portfolio. Any whole life or universal life policy will cost you far too much in fees and lost interest and is, in a world full of far better investments, a senseless place to put your capital. You should buy life insurance for one reason only: to protect your loved ones after your death.

What To Do with Your Whole Life Policy

If you already have a whole life policy, it's not any wonder. Some insurance companies pay their salespeople as much as the entire first year's premium in up-front commission! You have to become insurance-savvy to know when someone's just selling whatever they can or steering you in the right direction. If you have whole life, use the following information to decide whether or not to keep it:

1. If you're having difficulty coming up with the money to pay the premiums every month, you're probably paying too much. Whole life can cost a fortune, especially if you're older. Term life policies are generally much cheaper. Remember that life insurance is not an investment; it's death protection for your family.

2. If you've had your whole life policy for many years and the premiums have dropped considerably, consider keeping it. By now, you've paid many of the fees associated with the policy and can receive adequate benefits.

3. Make sure the return you're receiving on your savings portion of the policy is consistent with competitive bank CD rates. Read the fine print to make sure fees and other stipulations won't negate your return completely.

Cheap Trick

If you're considering canceling your existing whole life policy or just want inexpensive term life insurance, contact these two companies for some of the cheapest rates in the country:

Matrix Direct, 1–800–690–3884

SelectQuote, 1–800–343–1985

4. Check several insurance companies in your area to compare rates. Many companies rely on the talents of their sales force to sell overpriced policies. If you know the competitive prices, you can approach your current insurance agent about having your premium reduced.

5. If you know you don't have enough coverage and can't afford more with your current whole life policy, consider canceling it and shopping for a cheaper alternative. Or keep it, and get term coverage as a supplement. At a minimum, have coverage that is at least five times the breadwinner's salary, and about half of that for a non-working spouse.

6. Keep tabs on the financial well-being of your insurance company. Call once a year and ask for its annual report. Take a look at the balance sheet to determine if the company is profitable. If you smell something fishy, you can call your state's insurance commissioner and ask about your insurer's solvency.

Put Your Trust in Term Life

The only life (or should I say *death* in honor of Ben) insurance you should buy is straight death coverage, called term life insurance. You pay for a certain amount of coverage, when you die, your beneficiary receives that amount—plain and simple. Get annually renewable term and make sure it's guaranteed, which means that if your medical condition changes, the insurer still must renew your policy. If you're under age 50 and have a family, the best amount of insurance to own is about five to six times your gross annual salary. If you're a two-income family, both partners should be insured. If you're over age 50, you may not even need life insurance if you have substantial assets; technically that means you're self-insured.

Whatever you do, don't insure your child with his or her own life insurance policy. Think about it: You are buying life insurance on your child in case they die, and who gets the money if that happens? Do you think you would feel comfortable profiting on your child's death? If you are concerned about paying for their funeral expenses, start socking away $25 a month in a mutual fund. The most likely scenario is you will have thousands of dollars in the fund by the time they go to college to help with expenses.

And don't fall for accidental death coverage insurance for the kids. The chances that they'll die in an accident are very slim, and if they do, would you feel good about getting a chunk of cash afterward?

Insurance Mistakes You Shouldn't Make

In general, you should never purchase any of the following types of insurance. If you have a concern about not having some of this coverage, look for alternative ways to protect yourself, such as more life insurance, or an umbrella insurance policy.

Seven Secret Insurance Rip-Offs

Insurance	Coverage	Annual Cost
Extended warranties	Electronics and appliances	$200
Auto service contract	Auto purchase	500
Credit life	All personal/business loans	300
Credit disability	All personal/business loans	300
Mortgage life (MIP)	Any mortgaged property	1,200
Credit card insurance	All credit cards	200
Accidental death	Similar to life insurance	600
Dental and pharmacy	Health insurance should cover	200
	Total Loss:	**$3,500**

If you've been holding off on buying term life insurance for a while, then now is the time to buy. New laws are going into effect across the country that will make life insurance more expensive, and require insurers to set aside large cash reserves to make sure extra money is available for claims. The new reserve requirements will directly impact the bottom-line profits of the insurance companies, so rates are probably as low now as they'll ever be. Look for guaranteed annually renewable term policies or level term policies. Level term may be better because you can lock in a rate for ten or fifteen years as protection against major rate increases.

Cheap Shot

While it's the cheapskate's style to look for ways to save on insurance, never sacrifice cost for coverage. Many cheapskates are adequately insured in some areas but lack coverage elsewhere. Review every insurance policy you have to make sure you're well-covered.

Frugality Footnote

If you decide to cancel any insurance policy for any reason, wait until your new policy is in force before you cancel the old one. Don't let your coverage lapse until your new coverage begins. If you do, and something happens during that period, your family will be out of luck.

Is Your Home Coverage Enough?

If you don't have the right kind of coverage, homeowner's insurance can leave you high and dry. Even if your insurance covers the whole house and all your belongings, don't assume that you're completely covered for all losses. Chances are you're not, because it's so expensive. Assume that your policy doesn't cover much, then determine the value of your home and possessions, and get coverage that insures 50 percent more than the value you've set. Make sure you know the provisions of the policy—particularly what's NOT covered. If you have valuables, buy supplemental coverage, such as a personal items floater; and don't forget special coverage if you have your business in your home.

If Your Home Is a Rental

If you're a renter, be sure to have a renter's insurance policy that covers your belongings. They're usually inexpensive, and offer quite a bit of protection. Apartments and townhouses are easy targets, so insurance may pay off in the long run. If you have expensive possessions, such as computers, jewelry, or fancy electronics, make sure the insurer knows about them and includes a special rider in the policy to cover them.

Cutting the Cost of Insuring Your House

Cut insurance costs on your house by purchasing a property that is readily accessible to fire and emergency services. If you buy a home in a remote spot, chances are that your rates will be dramatically higher. To lower them further, do the following:

➤ Install fire and theft alarms hooked into a central monitoring location.

➤ Install a temperature alarm that sounds when temperatures get low enough to burst pipes.

➤ Install deadbolt locks, smoke detectors, and a fire extinguisher.

➤ Ask your insurer for any discounts that may apply if you make your house completely safe.

Put the Brakes on Car Insurance Costs

If you have a car more than five years old or worth less than $1,500, drop your collision and comprehensive auto insurance coverage. Being covered for what you'd pay for repairs from an accident probably doesn't justify the extra you're paying for collision. Even if it's a major accident, after your insurer subtracts the deductible, you could be left with a pittance anyway. If you eliminate collision, you can save 50 percent or more on your annual premium.

Cheap Shot

If you decide to eliminate collision and comprehensive car insurance, don't drop your liability coverage. Without it, if you cause an accident and seriously hurt someone, your financial future could be ruined.

If the Kids Drive Your Car

If you are keeping your collision and comprehensive insurance, pick up the phone and call your insurance company to discuss an overhaul of your coverage. If your deductible is under $500, it's costing you a lot extra in payments and making the insurance company richer; ask the agent to raise it to $500 or $1,000. If you get into an accident, what you're saving on premiums will cover your costs. Look at car insurance as protection against major damage or loss, and don't file small claims; they'll drive your premiums up.

Stopping the Coverage Gap

If you lease a car, look into gap insurance, which protects you if the car is significantly damaged or totaled in an accident. It covers the difference between what the insurance company rewards you in claims and the cost of repairs, which is often significantly more. Many leasing companies offer gap insurance, but you have to inquire about it. You can also find gap insurance at banks and credit unions if you ask.

Safety First

When you buy a car, make sure it has plenty of safety features. They'll not only protect you and your passenger, features such as air bags, seat belts, and theft devices will significantly reduce your auto insurance premiums. Another way to trim costs is to suspend your coverage if you're not going to be using the car for a while. See if your insurer provides this option; it's a favorite with senior citizens, who are often away for long periods.

Because most states don't require insurers to disclose their underwriting guidelines, most applicants who are rejected can't find out why, and policyholders aren't told what's required of them to maintain their insurance. It's easy to lose your coverage unwittingly if you don't know what the drill is. If your coverage is suspended and you feel you've been treated unfairly, petition your state insurance commissioner to have your policy reinstated until the dispute is settled.

Cheap Trick

Eliminate overlapping car insurance coverage. For instance, don't pay extra for medical coverage if you have health insurance that covers your medical expenses in the event of an accident. Or, do you really need towing and road service coverage if your car is newer? You can save about 30% annually by dropping what you don't need.

Providing for an Income If You Can't Work

Most insurance agents try to sell life insurance, where the big commissions are, so even cheapskates can overlook disability coverage. The reality is that, if you're young or middle-aged, you're much more likely to become disabled than to die. At age 40, disability is four times more likely than death. Particularly if you're a breadwinner, disability insurance can be invaluable. If you become unable to work for any reason, you and your family will be provided for by a regular income.

Cheap Talk

Disability insurance provides monthly benefits if you are injured or contract an illness that keeps you from earning an income. Based on premiums you've paid, a policy will generally replace all or a portion of your income for a set period of time.

Disability Coverage: Wise, but Not Cheap

Unfortunately for us cheapskates, disability coverage is extremely expensive. It can cost as much as $1,900 a year for a middle-aged man to get about $2,000 in monthly benefits if he becomes disabled.

Don't Count on Your Company

Most employers' disability coverage is not very good. You probably won't be covered until you've worked for a company for several years, and many policies have limits of $500 maximum per month in income replacement. Employer policies are primarily meant to supplement your own disability coverage.

Deciding What to Buy

If you're thinking of buying disability coverage, carefully evaluate how much you need. Most experts say that it should equal about 60 to 70 percent of your gross pay. Benefits won't start until ninety days after your disability occurs, so you should have emergency savings on hand to cover your expenses during the uncovered time (called the elimination period). The coverage should continue until you're 65, when you can get Social Security. Buy your disability insurance with money you've already paid taxes on and any benefits you receive will be tax-free. If you're hesitant because of the cost of a policy, you can lower your premiums by extending the elimination period for another three months; you'll save as much as 25 percent. Just make sure you have enough in savings to take care of expenses for six months.

Find a policy that defines disability precisely, and offers benefits if you are incapacitated and cannot work in your current occupation. Otherwise, the insurer will try to deny your benefits if you can work in another occupation but choose not to. Also insist on a guaranteed renewable policy, which means that the premiums on your policy can't be canceled or increased for any reason. And make sure that the company you select to insure you has an excellent reputation. Check with the insurance commissioner in your state about their past claims' performances and complaint record.

Frugality Footnote

An option to consider in a disability policy is a cost-of-living adjustment. With this rider, the amount of your benefits increases yearly to keep pace with cost-of-living increases. The adjustment can make a big difference during times of inflation.

Smart Moves for Policy Shoppers

Always be truthful when you fill out an application for insurance. Reveal any conditions that may affect your ability to get coverage. Insurance companies are sticklers for things like smoking, drinking, and any medical problems. Insurers may not bother you while you're paying the premiums, but if a time comes when they have to start shelling out the bucks, they'll do a thorough investigation. Any inconsistencies, and you can say good-bye to the pay-out. Another no-no is getting similar policies from two different companies. The insurers have a way of finding out about it, and generally won't pay duplicate pay-outs.

The average American family spends a bundle on different types of insurance every year. The following is an example of what you can do as a cheapskate to lower your costs considerably and overhaul your coverage using some of the strategies outlined earlier. We'll assume a family of three in which the father works full-time and the mother part-time:

A Complete Insurance Overhaul

Type of Insurance	Annual Cost Before	Cost After	Savings
$20,000 whole life insurance on 3 children	$480	$0	$280
$150,000 whole life insurance on husband	$2,800	$0	$2,800
New term life insurance on husband of $500,000 and $200,000 on wife	$0	$700	$700
Auto insurance (2 cars)	$1,800	$980	$820
Private mortgage insurance (see Chapter 9)	$1,200	$0	$1,200
Homeowner's insurance	$425	$230	$195
Disability insurance	$0	$1,400	-$1,400
Health insurance (see Chapter 17)	$4,200	$3,000	$1,200
Costs Before Overhaul:	$10,905		
Costs After Overhaul:		$6,310	
Total Yearly Savings:			$4,595
Extra Policy Refunds in First Year:			$1,260

Cheap Thrills with Insurance

➤ If you rent, unfortunately landlords are required to have insurance only on the property, and general liability coverage in case someone is injured on the grounds. You're best off to purchase your own renter's coverage for personal possessions, and liability if someone has an accident inside your apartment. Rates vary from company to company, so check around.

➤ In most areas of the country, the best approach to insuring your home is to insure the house for its replacement value rather than its market value. Replacement policies are generally less expensive. Part of the market cost in your home is the land, so if your house burns to the ground or a tornado blows it away, the land will still be around so you can dig a new hole. A guaranteed replacement policy is your best bet.

247

Cheap Trick

Always pay an extra premium if your son or daughter drives your car, even occasionally. If one of your children is in an accident and you haven't notified the insurance company, you can be denied payment for costs of the accident and lose your coverage. For full protection, let your insurance company know if anyone under age 21 will be driving your car.

➤ If you're in an area sanctioned by the Flood Disaster Protection Act, you can buy flood insurance through the government. About 20,000 communities in the United States qualify under this Act. Contact the Federal Insurance Commission at 500 C St. SW, Washington, DC 20472, to find out if your area qualifies. Most houses can be insured for replacement cost plus any household property.

➤ Generally it's a bad idea to buy any kind of insurance that advertises cheap deals on TV and in mail solicitations. Exceptions are some of the quality companies, such as those noted in this chapter, that sell cheap term life insurance. Most insurance companies that do mass advertising offer a teaser policy and rip you off on other policies later. It always pays to check out a company thoroughly, and comparison shop before you buy.

The Least You Need to Know

➤ Call your car insurance agent today and raise your deductible to $500 or even $1,000. You'll save on premiums and still be fully protected. Your savings will add up fast.

➤ If you don't currently have life insurance and know you need it, determine how much you should carry, and purchase cheap term life insurance only.

➤ If you have any form of whole life insurance, pull the policy out and review the fine print. Use the guidelines discussed in this chapter to determine whether you're paying too much and should drop the coverage. Don't forget: Never cancel your old policy until the new one is in force.

➤ If there are any discounts you may have overlooked in your homeowner's policy, contact your agent immediately and request a rate reduction.

➤ Check into the possibility of purchasing disability insurance coverage, particularly if you do work in which there's a greater risk of injury.

➤ If you rent, purchase an inexpensive renter's policy from your insurance agent to cover you in case you're burglarized, or anyone has an accident on your premises.

Chapter 22

Take an Ax to Your Taxes!

In This Chapter

➤ Do-it-yourself taxes

➤ Being prepared pays off

➤ The top ten cheapskate tax deductions

➤ The most overlooked ways to save on taxes

➤ Staying one step ahead of the IRS

➤ Your odds on getting audited

Tax season is stress season for most people. There's worrying about them, assembling documents, maybe having to find money to pay the bill, filing returns, and then worrying again. Taxes are very—well—taxing. (They sure got the word for them right.) Since we know that they, along with death, are the only certainties of human existence, all we can do is try to make dealing with them easier on ourselves. And it can be a lot easier if we know what we're doing, all year 'round.

Nothing is going to make you ENJOY dealing with your taxes, but this chapter will help you eliminate a lot of the stress of filing, and show you how to keep a lot more of what you earn. The average American (not the millionaires) now pays about 40 percent of their gross income in taxes if you add up federal, state and local, sales, and property. Sure, we're willing to pay our fair share, but most of us are paying more than that, and it's time to fight back.

Smart cheapskates know how to take care of Uncle Sam and all the other uncles who get a piece of the action, AND keep as much money as they can in their own pockets. They pay their share, but they know better than to pay MORE than their share. Most Americans wind up paying more than they have to because they just haven't done their homework. Homework is what cheapskates do best, so, if you want to save a bundle next April—no cheating—check out what's in this chapter.

Cheap Trick

If you have a personal computer and want to make your tax filing fly, purchase an inexpensive tax program specifically for doing your taxes. Two of the best are Turbo Tax and Tax Cut, and you can buy them for about $25 around the first of the year in any store that carries software.

Do-It-Yourself Taxes

No one can save money on your taxes as well as you can yourself, and I'm not just talking about the cost of paying an accountant—the annual *Money* magazine contest for tax preparers has proven that most of them are way off anyway. The reality is that no one knows the ins and outs of your financial situation as well as you do. So, once you learn the ins and outs of the tax regulations, no one, absolutely no one, can save you more on your taxes than you can yourself.

Frugality Footnote

If you're not in the habit of doing your own taxes, try it for a year or two to get a grasp of your tax picture. If you want to learn a lot but still play it safe, keep paying your tax preparer to do them, then compare the returns. Even if, after that, you decide you don't want to do your taxes yourself, chances are that you'll be able to alert the preparer to a lot of deductions that you caught. No matter who does your taxes the following year, you'll save hundreds, or even thousands, on your tax bill.

Try preparing your own taxes; you'll be frustrated at first, but the process gets easier as you go along. You'll be learning all the way, and if you get stumped or just want to abandon it, you can always call your preparer.

The IRS has free publications that can help you do your own taxes, and a toll-free information line to answer your questions: 1-800-829-4477. Don't call during March and April, because they are absolutely swamped. Along with this book, I also recommend J.K. Lasser's *Your Income Tax* manual that you can buy at any bookstore.

How Cheapskates Cut Their Tax Bills

There are many things you can do to cut your tax bill and have more money in your pocket. Good cheapskates are on top of their finances and files all year 'round, and they keep up with all the latest tax changes.

Here are some ideas sure to make tax time less taxing:

➤ The key to saving money on taxes is to be organized. If you have a personal computer, buy an inexpensive money management program to keep track of your finances throughout the year. One of the best programs is called Quicken and can be purchased at all stores that carry software. At the end of the year, just print out a summary report and you'll have all the information you need to do the paperwork. If you don't have a computer, put together a good filing system for organizing your receipts, canceled checks, and bank statements. At the end of each month, write a short tax report for your files so you can refer to it at the end of the year.

➤ Invest in every tax-deductible retirement plan you have available to you. You can double the power of your year-end bonus by putting it into an IRA, 401(k) plan, or a similar tax-deductible and tax-deferred savings program. Start with whatever tax-deductible plan you have, and invest as much as possible in it. If your employer offers any matching funds, don't say no to a free lunch. If you invest now, you'll be investing in your future financial security, and you won't need to pay taxes on your employer's contributions.

Frugality Footnote

Don't waste your time filing electronically; it speeds up your refund by only a week or two. And make sure you're using the correct filing status; either joint or single could save you as much as 20%.

251

➤ You can legally double the tax deduction on your kids by putting them to work in your part-time or full-time business and paying them a salary. You can keep the dependency exemption and also take an employee salary deduction for your business. The kids can do a lot of things like filing, stuffing envelopes, stapling, cleaning the office, etc.

➤ Make sure you're investing at the right time of the year. For example, it's a good idea to purchase stocks and mutual funds on the day after dividends are declared and distributed. If you buy before distribution, the value of your investment will drop when it's distributed, but you'll be responsible for taxes on the higher, pre-distribution value (Uncle Sam is a devil). Always SELL just BEFORE dividends are distributed to get a better share price.

➤ The IRS is nice enough to give you a deduction of 12 cents for every mile that you drive to and from charity work. If you do a lot of work for your church or synagogue or the local shelter, don't overlook this great deduction.

➤ If you want to give away an asset to a charity, donate something that has gained in value. You avoid the capital gains tax, and can deduct the entire current value of the gift. If you have an asset that has lost value, sell it, use the loss to offset any other capital gains, then give a cash contribution and take a charitable deduction.

Property Tax Nightmare

If you are fed up with rising property taxes, contact your local tax assessor's office to get information about these deductible areas you may fall into:

➤ The "Homestead exemption" could cut about 20% off your bill.

➤ A personal property tax exemption could enable you to deduct "necessary household items," such as a washer and dryer or refrigerator.

➤ There is a veteran's exemption of up to $50 a year.

➤ You can take a home-business exemption if you operate a business from home.

➤ A senior citizen's exemption is available to people 65 or older.

You can appeal your property tax assessment if you feel it is unfair or in error. You may be paying too much.

Top Ten Tax Deductions

When it comes to tax deductions, there's a lot of homework to do, but what are the most important ones to remember? These are the top ten:

1. If you donate your old clothes to charity, you can save at least $50 on your taxes. You may not think those old suits and dresses are worth much, but the IRS will if you value them properly and get receipts for your donations. Generally, if they're in decent shape, you can value old clothes at about 10 to 25 percent less than you bought them for. The staff at your local Goodwill or other donation center can usually help you get a handle on how much your donation is worth.

2. Child-care credits can be claimed on your tax return for expenses beyond what you spend on day care but only payments to nurseries and kindergartens are included in this credit. You cannot include payments beyond kindergarten unless they pertain to child care exclusively and not education.

Cheap Shot

If you're considering taking deductions that may be questionable, think again. The IRS has many different ways of identifying what is and is not a valid deduction. We are privy to some of their methods, but most of them are outside our realm. Your best course of action is to take only those deductions that you're 100% sure are legal and allowable.

3. If you and other family members are supporting a dependent in your household, decide early in the year which one of you should claim the individual on his or her taxes. Only the claimant can deduct the dependent's paid medical bills on her or his tax return. However, if, for example, you and your siblings jointly support an aged parent for whom none of you pays more than half the support, you can file a multiple support agreement and receive a dependency exemption.

4. If you bought a house within the last few years, you could save some big bucks on taxes. The IRS has ruled that seller-paid points (the amount you pay to buy down the mortgage interest rate of your buyer) can be deducted for house purchases beginning December 30, 1990. Previously, only points that a buyer paid could be deducted. If you paid on a house you sold and are entitled to a claim for deductions in any previous years back to 1990, just file an amended return on form 1040X, which you can get at your local IRS office. In the top right corner, write "seller-paid points." Attach a copy of your settlement statement with the amended return. Make sure you remember this deduction; you could get several hundred dollars back.

5. Self-employed individuals can get one of the greatest tax deductions of all; they can deduct as much as 15 percent of their net profits up to $22,500 per year through a Simplified Employee Pension Plan (SEP-IRA). What's great about a SEP-IRA is that it works just like any other IRA. It's simple to set up and simple to invest in.

Frugality Footnote

The IRS has new rules and tighter controls over tax shelter promoters, and may disallow tax shelter losses on investments that cannot be authenticated as valid ventures undertaken for economic profit, rather than tax savings. Tax shelter promoters are required to register the shelters they organize with the IRS, and to provide the registration numbers to investors. Investors are required to report the numbers on their personal returns. Failure to do so can result in a $250 penalty. Deductions for tax shelter partnerships are also limited under the new laws.

6. Take advantage of any tax-deferred investment plans available to you as an employee. Not only will you get a tax deduction, you can begin to prepare for retirement. Take a deduction for IRAs, 401(k)s, or 403(b)s.

Cheap Trick

If you have stock you've been holding onto for a long time that just keeps slipping down in value, consider selling it. Wait until the end of the year, sell it, and then claim the loss on your taxes. This is an especially good strategy if you could use a deduction against your income.

7. With all the confusing rules these days, you may not be sure if you're able to deduct your IRA contribution (information on how to determine deductibility is contained in Chapter 23). Don't be discouraged if you can't do it this year. When you put money into an IRA, it continues to compound, tax-deferred, until you withdraw funds. When you do, you'll owe taxes on only the investment returns or income received over the years. The principal you invested will not be taxed. Keep accurate records of all deductions you take, and report nondeductible IRA contributions on IRS Form 8606. When you withdraw funds in the future, you'll be able to determine your taxable portion easily if you have all the information on hand. Keep socking that money away.

8. Becoming self-employed enables you to take hundreds of tax deductions you had no idea existed. For example, you can deduct a portion of your mortgage and utilities if you run your

business out of your home. You can also deduct part of your auto expenses, and any business-related travel, books, and seminars. (See Chapter 18 for employee deductions.)

9. If you aren't self-employed, deduct every expense related to doing your job, and not reimbursed by your employer. Just a few ideas: auto expenses, dues and subscriptions, education expenses, entertaining clients, portion of equipment you purchase for yourself but use for job, and job searches.

10. You can take a charitable deduction if you donate professional services to a church or charitable organization.

Commonly Overlooked Deductions

When you prepare your taxes, determine whether you qualify for any of these commonly overlooked deductions:

➤ Tax preparation fees

➤ Safe deposit box fees

➤ 25% deduction for self-employed health insurance

➤ Subscriptions to investment and trade newsletters and investment-related books (yes, this book can be deducted if you use it to help you invest)

➤ IRA trustee fees

➤ Moving expenses associated with a new job

Do Cheapskates Get Audited?

You bet! For the first time in many years, the odds of being audited are up, and will probably increase as computer technology continues to make it faster and easier for the IRS to put the pieces together. Nevertheless, considering all taxpayers at different levels, the audit rate averaged out to an amazingly low .85 percent for 1996, the most recently compiled statistics.

Pretty soon, this rate will be old news. With its new computer equipment, the IRS will be doing almost double the amount of audits it now performs, and make an extra $10 billion a year for Uncle Sam. There will also be more "live" audits done in the field. If you have any shaky deductions or under-reported income in your returns for recent years, make sure you can square it with the IRS.

Cheap Shot

Be cautious about how you send correspondence, tax returns, and money owed to the IRS. To avoid problems, it's best to send everything by registered mail, with return receipt. It's the only way to be sure that what you sent was received, or prove that it was sent if they say it wasn't.

This table shows 1996 data for your chances of getting audited. It reflects all field and office audits for the year. For 1996, the IRS reviewed 1,058,966 individual tax returns, a slight increase over the number of returns audited in 1995. The big news is that audit percentages for Schedule C filers (self-employed) increased in all income categories.

1996 Percentage of Returns Audited	
*Individuals (Non-Business)***	**Percent Audited**
Under $25,000	.71%
$25,000 to $50,000	.58
$50,000 to $100,000	.88
$100,000 and over	4.03
Self-Employed (Schedule C)	
Under $25,000	2.24%
$25,000 to $100,000	2.41
$100,000 and over	3.91
Farmers (Schedule F)	
Under $100,000	1.06%
$100,000 and over	2.06%
Partnerships	
All income categories	.61%
Corporations (Assets)	
Under $250,000	1.33%
$250,000 to $1 million	3.94
$1 million to $5 million	9.35
$5 million to $10 million	19.04
$10 million to $50 million	23.31
$50 million to $100 million	25.56
$100 million to $250 million	31.15
$250 million and over	52.11

***The overall U.S. average audit rate for all individuals is .85%*

Uncle Sam Is Watching You

The IRS looks for red flags when they process tax returns. If one or more surface, their computers may bounce your 1040 form and return it to you for an audit.

The following are some of the items that draw the most attention to a return.

Home Office Deductions

This area is one of Uncle Sam's favorite targets. The IRS has gone to court repeatedly, winning support for its tough stand on rejecting taxpayers' home office deductions.

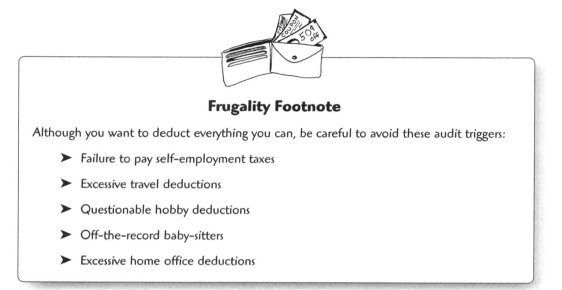

Frugality Footnote

Although you want to deduct everything you can, be careful to avoid these audit triggers:

➤ Failure to pay self-employment taxes

➤ Excessive travel deductions

➤ Questionable hobby deductions

➤ Off-the-record baby-sitters

➤ Excessive home office deductions

To take a deduction on part of your home, or a portion of your rent for the space you use as a home office, you must satisfy several requirements. First, you must be able to prove that you use the room regularly and exclusively for business. It must also be the principal place of your business, used to meet with customers. If you take work home from a primary place of employment, or if your office doubles as the family room, your deductions probably won't hold up.

Travel and Entertainment

Entertaining prospective customers in the hope of winning their business can be a valid expense. However, the IRS knows that many people tuck their personal tabs in with their business receipts. They estimate lost revenues of about $1.5 billion due to this practice—no small potatoes. You can write off only 50 percent of the cost of business meals and entertainment. Keep an organized file of documented receipts and corresponding diary entries that note the business purposes of the meals and entertainment claimed.

Taking a Personal Interest

There are several sets of rules for interest write-offs. The most favorable are those for home mortgage interest, which is generally 100 percent deductible.

Another group of regulations limits the allowable deduction for interest on funds borrowed for investment purposes (such as margin accounts used to buy securities). Investment interest is deductible only to the extent that it is matched by investment income, a category that includes interest, dividends, and capital gains (subject to restrictions).

The toughest rules obviously prohibit any deduction on Schedule A of form 1040 for interest paid on personal or "consumer" loans. This grouping includes credit card and charge account debts, college fees, auto loans, and overdue income taxes.

The IRS suspects that many taxpayers misclassify their interest deductions. For example:

If you incur interest on a loan from your brokerage account and then buy a car, you cannot claim your interest as a deduction.

If you have a sideline business and properly file a Schedule C for the self-employed, you cannot deduct interest on a personal debt as a business expense.

Cheap Trick

If you dispute any item on your tax return, have your documentation organized, and be prepared to summarize your arguments. Have all your calculations in written form so the IRS can understand them easily. Demonstrating that you're in control of your finances should work in your favor.

What to Do When the IRS Drops In

When issues with the IRS arise, many cheapskates choose to deal with them directly, rather than use an accountant or lawyer. If you make the cheapskate choice, here are some tips:

➤ Be very businesslike. Most IRS employees have seen it all and just want to hear the facts. You will not win their indulgence by telling jokes and being charming; you may even annoy them.

➤ Stick to the basic tax matters at hand. Don't get sucked into a discussion that's over your head. You're better off admitting that you need the advice of a professional before you can respond.

➤ Above all, be totally forthright and honest in your dealings with the IRS. Don't try to cover up the absence of documentation or facts that may work against you. They've seen it all, so don't try to con them, or they'll be on your back for a long time.

If you're called to an IRS office audit, don't panic. The Service is usually just checking to make sure that the deductions you claimed have proper supporting documentation. If you have the appropriate supporting papers, you have nothing to worry about.

Office audits are routine; field audits are a different story. The IRS usually asks for a field audit if you have discrepancies and major questions on your tax return. Most of them are performed on medium-sized businesses or individuals who have part-time income from small businesses. They often involve many technical and legal issues, and should not be approached lightly. If you get a field audit, seek the counsel of a good tax advisor, and if the situation is complicated, request that the advisor be present for the audit.

Cheap Shot

When you pay any type of taxes, always keep a copy of the check and the paperwork that you sent with your payment. If your paperwork goes astray, you'll avoid a tremendous amount of confusion by having copies of what you sent.

Cheap Thrills with Taxes

➤ The computer system the IRS is developing will give it better access to private databases to call up profiles on taxpayers. The new system will have access to commercial lending sources, state and local licensing authorities, construction contracts, currency and banking reports, financial transactions from state and local governments, and information on significant financial transactions reported in newspapers or other media. Bottom line: Do your best to stay off their hit list.

➤ Keep good records of house-hunting efforts you may make in advance of a move. If you or members that contribute income to your household have expenses related to finding a new job in a new city (meals, lodging, and transportation), they may later be deductible as moving expenses.

Cheap Trick

If you can, make IRA contributions regularly rather than waiting until the end of the year—or worse—April of the following year. Why? You'll pick up tax-deferred interest along the way instead of waiting months to begin to put your money to work.

➤ If you're married, you may be better off filing your returns separately rather than jointly. It's always best to figure it both ways to make sure you aren't giving the IRS any more than you have to.

➤ Most cheapskates are generous givers. Any money you give to charity can be a tax deduction, so give freely. Your church or synagogue, local children's hospitals, or charitable foundations are great choices, and true cheapskates give from their heart, not just for the tax deduction.

The Least You Need to Know

➤ If you don't prepare your taxes yourself, make an effort to do so for at least a year or two. You'll add knowledge about the tax system to what you already know about your own financial situation—an unbeatable formula for coming out ahead.

➤ Get organized! The surest way to save money on your taxes is to have the deduction value of your activities in mind throughout the year, and know where receipts and canceled checks are filed. At the end of the year you'll have a great advantage.

➤ Get out last year's tax return and see whether you took all the deductions you could have. Use this chapter as a guide to help you pinpoint what you may have missed. Make a note of any deductions you may want to take for next year's return.

➤ To reduce your chances of getting audited, pay special attention to the red flags discussed in this chapter. If you avoid these common mistakes on your return, you'll be much less likely to be audited by the IRS.

Chapter 23

Two, Four, Six, Eight, Make Your Dollars Propagate

In This Chapter

➤ How to make compound interest work for you

➤ Smart small investments

➤ The earnings are mutual

➤ Five investments to avoid

➤ How to find the right money manager

➤ Your retirement rainbow's pot of gold

If the extent of your investing has been to put a few extra bucks in your savings account now and then, it's time to look at better ways to make those hard-earned dollars grow. Sure, the bank's a good safe place for them, and the idea of investing may make you a little nervous. Join the club; a lot of people have been scared off by horror stories about slick-talking brokers and financial advisers who fleece naïve new investors. And then there's the dizzying number of options to choose from. The cheapskate's philosophy on investing is this: Keep it simple and try to do it yourself. Yes, you have to learn a lot about investment before you can make the right choices, but it's the only road to your future financial security. You don't have to spend all your free time sorting and tracking your investments; after you've done some research and made some selections, all you have to do is keep an eye on their progress. You can find ways to make a good return and still be able to sleep at night, and you don't need to pay an investment adviser if you're willing to do a little leg work yourself. It can be interesting, and even fun, and you'll save on fees and commissions.

The Magic of Compound Interest

Did you know that you're pretty much guaranteed to be a millionaire in your lifetime? It's true. Even if you have an average annual household income of only $30,000 for forty years, you'll make about $1.2 million. Pretty incredible, isn't it? So it's not how much you make, but how much you keep to invest.

Frugality Footnote

Einstein was once asked what he felt was the most incredible force of law in the universe. His reply was "compound interest," and he wasn't joking. He was astounded at the capability of a single dollar to grow exponentially and eventually produce another dollar.

If you're not saving at least 10 percent of your gross income, start as soon as possible. It may seem like a lot at first, but once you get into the saving habit you may find yourself looking for ways to free up more money to invest. Smart cheapskates save about 25 to 30 percent of their gross income, even on modest salaries. It takes a lot of time and patience to get to that point, though. If you can't manage 10 percent, save what you can. Even the smallest amount of money saved systematically over a period of years will grow astoundingly—through the power of compound interest.

Putting the Power to Work

You need only three things to use compound interest to your advantage: time, a little money, and some discipline. Every one of us has time on our side (some people more than others). If you use just a few of the money-saving strategies outlined in this book, you're guaranteed to find an extra dollar or two to get started with. And once you've set your sights on a goal, you'll develop the discipline you need to save.

I used to think interest was simple; put $1,000 in the bank at 5 percent annual interest, have $1,050 at the end of the year. Then, if you got 10 percent interest the next year, you'd get double the $50, or $100. Wrong! Actually, the second year, you'd receive $105 because the 10 percent rate is calculated on $1,050, your total balance after the first year. This process is called *"compound interest"* because new money keeps growing geometrically from the old money. The following table shows you the "magic."

One-Time $1,000 Lump-Sum Investment

Interest	20 Years	30 Years	40 Years
5%	$2,653	$4,321	$7,039
10%	$6,727	$17,449	$45,259
12%	$9,646	$29,959	$93,050

If you look closely, you'll see that time and interest rates have a greater impact on the amount of money you accumulate than the amount you invest does.

Do you think you can wait a while before you start saving? Think again. Let's say you wanted to invest $1,000 a year at an annual rate of 10 percent. This table shows you the scenario.

$1,000-Per-Year Investment at 10% Interest

Start Saving	Total at Age 65	Cost of Waiting
Age 25	$487,852	
Age 30	$299,127	$188,725
Age 35	$181,943	$305,909
Age 40	$109,182	$378,670

Assume that you save $2,000 a year and invest it annually in a retirement plan, as the next table shows.

$2,000-Per-Year Investment in Retirement Plan*

Interest	20 years	30 years	40 years
8%	$100,845	$246,692	$561,562
10%	$128,005	$363,887	$975,704
12%	$163,397	$542,585	$1,720,285

For illustration purposes, all figures are calculated assuming a tax-free investment.

If these examples don't inspire you to start on your investing program, I don't know what will. Nothing can stop the power of compound interest except your unwillingness to become financially independent. So use it to your advantage by putting money aside today!

Smart Small Investments

If you're impressed with the growth potential of savings, it's time to think about investing. It doesn't matter if you don't have a lot of cash start with, you'll still be setting up an investment program that has a future.

With as little as $25 a month, you can accumulate a substantial amount over the years by letting compound interest work for you. Here are some of the best ways to invest small sums of money to get the maximum returns over time:

Cheap Trick

How about some fast money? Pay off the balances on your credit cards. There's no better way to make a quick 18%–21% in interest. If your balances are high on several cards, use some of your savings to get them paid off now.

➤ Take a specified dollar amount and invest it in a no-load mutual fund every month. (No-load funds are explained later in this chapter.) If you plan to keep the money in the fund for six years or longer, put it in a growth stock fund. That way, you'll take advantage of the natural ups and downs in the stock market. Historically, the market has outperformed any other type of investment over the long term.

➤ Buy a U.S. savings bond. Even though the interest rate is generally low, they're a good way to get started in investing, especially for the kids' college education. You can buy Series EE bonds for half the face value and redeem them at maturity for full value. Many companies even allow automatic payroll deductions for savings bonds, with no commissions to pay.

➤ Make extra principal payments toward your mortgage. By paying a small amount every month on the principal, you can dramatically reduce the length of your mortgage (by as much as ten or fifteen years; see Chapter 9). Just write out a separate check to your mortgage company marked "principal only." For example: If you have a $100,000, 30-year mortgage at 9 percent interest, and you pay an extra $50 per month toward principal, you'll save about $50,000 in interest, and pay the mortgage off seven years earlier. Keep your canceled checks so you can verify how much you put toward your principal at the end of the year; mortgage companies are notorious for crediting these payments incorrectly. When you decide on the amount to pay toward your mortgage principal, remember that you'll need to keep some liquid funds available for emergencies and long-term financial goals. Paying down your mortgage should not be your only means of saving.

Frugality Footnote

Join a local investment club. These groups get together and invest their pooled funds. Members are usually non-professionals, but there's often a pro at the helm. Surprisingly, many clubs have had stunningly successful results. I guess two (or more) heads are definitely better than one. You can find out about investment clubs in your area by calling the National Association of Investors Corporation at 810-583-6242, or ask your banker or investment advisor if they know of any good ones.

➤ Go to a discount book store once a month and invest in a book on personal finance. If you read one book a month on money matters, you'll be well-educated by the end of the year. Better yet, just go to the library and get books for free. Most libraries have extensive book and periodical selections on personal finance matters. The more you learn, the easier your investment decisions will become.

➤ Swap money-saving investment ideas with friends and neighbors. If you're adventurous, start your own cheapskate club. Have members jot down ideas for saving and investing, and meet once a month to share them. Ideas can be free-wheeling because you're not making investments, just sharing your thoughts about them.

➤ Buy stock directly from a company in which you may already have an investment interest. Most major companies offer a dividend reinvestment plan through which shareholders can buy additional shares of stock without paying commissions. Some companies even offer discounts on quoted rates. The Standard and Poor's Annual Directory lists all the companies that offer dividend-reinvestment plans. You can find the directory at your local library or access it on the Internet.

The Earnings Are Mutual

There are a lot of reasons to invest in mutual funds.

➤ They are among the simplest investments to get into and manage.

➤ With some funds, you can make an initial investment with as little as $50, if you sign up for automatic monthly investing.

➤ What you invest is part of a huge pool of money which is invested wisely by professional managers. All you do is pay an annual fee of roughly 1 percent of the

Cheap Talk

A *mutual fund* is the pooled funds of thousands of people, invested for them by a professional manager. In a mutual fund, even small investors can have their money distributed in several different stocks, so there's much less risk.

fund's value for professional management of your investment. The fee is taken out of your holdings in the fund, so you don't need to write a check.

Most of us don't have the time or, in some cases, the inclination to track the market and our investments on a regular basis. Mutual funds are a smart investment because they do it for us.

Before you start investing in mutual funds, decide what your investment objectives are. You can consult an investment adviser or do it on your own by reading some good publications on investing. Are you looking for growth, income, capital preservation, or a combination of all of them? When you've crystallized your objectives, you can narrow down your mutual fund choices.

➤ Look at the 3- and 5-year performance records of the fund.

➤ If you're a long-term investor, try to find the 10- and 15-year performance records as well.

➤ Never invest in a fund that has recently skyrocketed, but has an average record for previous years. Odds are it's a shot in the dark.

You can find performance records in financial periodicals and on the Internet.

Take the Load Off

No-load (no commissions) mutual funds are an excellent choice because, on average, their performance is every bit as good as that of commissioned funds, so you may as well have all your money working for you. Some load (commission) funds charge as much as 8.5 percent. Stay away from funds that are either too small (below $50 million) or too large (over $2 billion). Very small or very large funds aren't adequately diversified.

Keep an eye on the performance of your fund and make sure you're keeping up with the averages for your particular mutual fund industry sector. If your investments continue to lag behind typical performances, you may want to reevaluate your fund investment choice.

These high-quality mutual fund families are my favorites:

➤ American Century, 800-345-2021

➤ Vanguard, 800-851-4999

➤ Fidelity Mutual Funds, 800-544-8888

➤ T. Rowe Price, 800-638-5660

Call any of these mutual fund companies for more information, including a prospectus.

Frugality Footnote

Some discount brokers now offer no-load mutual funds through one account that you set up with them. The benefit is that you can trade several mutual funds out of one account for easier bookkeeping. The funds pay the broker's fee for your investment, so you pay nothing. Two good brokerage houses that offer hundreds of mutual funds under one roof are: Jack White and Company, 800-233-3411, and Fidelity Investments, 800-544-7272.

Five Investments to Avoid

There are lots of investments out there, and it's not easy to judge which ones may be the best for you. But here are some investments that are just no good for anyone under any circumstances. Memorize this list, and don't get taken:

1. CMOs (collateralized mortgage obligations): CMOs are pools of mortgages issued by government agencies, like Ginnie Mae, Fannie Mae, and Freddie Mac. The agencies guarantee payment of principal and interest. Many unscrupulous brokers give these investments a AAA rating, meaning that they're very safe. No such rating exists for this type of debt obligation.

   The trouble begins when institutions start to carve up the mortgages, dividing the principal payment from the interest, and then putting the mortgages back into some type of accelerated bond pool. The more slices in the bond pool, the worse it is for the average investor. The real winners here are the institutions that did the slicing. Their "leftovers" are then sold to us, or you could say, thrown to the hogs.

   CMOs are pools of home mortgages, and when mortgage interest rates fall, homeowners refinance. If interest rates drop 2 percent, an 8 percent CMO that was sold to you and estimated to mature in 1999 may indeed mature in just a few years. But then you'd be forced to invest at lower rates. When interest rates rise, mortgage prepays slow down. The broker can only guess at the average mortgage life on your CMO. Brokers make these guesses sound like a guaranteed bond maturity date. With a 2 percent rise in interest rates, the CMO that was estimated to mature in 1999 wouldn't come due until 22 years later! To make matters worse, rising interest rates dramatically erode the value of the CMO, leaving you high and dry down the road.

2. Initial public offerings (IPOs): An IPO is nothing more than the first block of stock offered to the public. The newspapers are full of great IPO successes, but the little guy rarely wins. The simple fact is that, if a broker is offering the stock, something is terribly wrong. It's common knowledge on Wall Street that only the big boys (pension funds, institutions, mutual funds, and large traders on the floor) get the hot IPOs. You don't stand a chance of buying in and making a safe profit unless you have some major bucks. The main thing to keep in mind is that just because a company is about to go public doesn't mean it'll make you rich.

3. Brokerage WRAP accounts: They're called WRAP accounts because all your investments are wrapped into one account. They charge a flat percentage of your balance to cover all commissions and fees. I don't like WRAP accounts because cheapskates are often charged as much as 5 percent just for the privilege. You can get the same stock-picking expertise in a good mutual fund for less than 1 percent, and tracking the performance of a mutual fund is much easier. More and more brokerage firms are starting to mix the institutional investors' performance with performance of private portfolio accounts. This mix helps firms show off their strong track records, but finding your true rate of return is almost impossible. Stick with much simpler and less expensive mutual funds.

4. Options and Futures: Options are simply contracts that allow you to buy or sell shares of a stock in the future at an agreed-upon price. Futures are similar, but involve contracts on commodities, such as sugar or silver. You pay for the contract up front, which allows you to control a highly leveraged amount of the underlying stock or commodity. The smart cheapskate stays miles away from these investments. They're just a legitimate form of gambling.

Cheap Trick

If you are absolutely convinced that an IPO is a great buy, wait until several months after the stock has come onto the market and its fluctuations have evened out; then you can buy it at its true value. This way, you know whether the stock is another Microsoft or just a flash in the pan. You have no reason to rush into any stock; good companies remain good over time.

Frugality Footnote

No matter how you look at it, even with a great trading system, options and futures are a foolish way to invest. So if anyone ever tells you about a great way to make a killing with some hot options or futures—run!

5. Penny stocks: Penny stocks are simply shares of stock that sell for $1 or less. The definition can be stretched to include stocks selling for up to $5. The rule here is that you get what you pay for. Generally, stocks that are lower priced carry a much higher risk factor. So, unless you want to be a high-risk gambler, you should stay away from any low-priced stock.

Meet the Money Managers

Professional money managers come in all different shapes and sizes. There is the stockbroker, the commissioned financial planner, the fee-only financial planner, the mutual fund manager, and more. In a world full of investment management options and thousands of products, making good choices can be difficult here.

You don't have to have someone else manage your investments, but if that's your choice, here are some pointers on what to look for:

➤ Look twice before you leap at a manager who shows you slick brochures and promises a 20 percent to 30 percent annual return on your money. Odds are that the figures are doctored in the manager's favor, not yours.

➤ Don't buy individual stocks unless you can diversify heavily, and have superior advice. If you insist on buying individual stocks, educate yourself about the market and go to a discount broker to make your own trades. Most stockbrokers can't pick stocks any better than you can, but they charge hefty fees for their advice anyway.

➤ No-load mutual funds are a great way to get professional money management for almost nothing.

Cheap Shot

Be careful of the financial planner who charges commissions in the 8% or higher range. This is too much to pay for financial advice. Quite often these people recommend products that pay high commissions. A fee-only financial planner is a great route to go if you want honest, unbiased recommendations about where to put your money.

269

Seven Great Questions To Ask Your Money Manager

1. Does this investment match my goals, as you understand them?

2. How much risk is involved in this investment, and what are the things that could go wrong?

3. How much commission do you charge, and can I get a discount?

4. Is there a comparable investment that would cost me less?

5. Are any hidden fees involved in this transaction?

6. Taking the commission into consideration, how far does the investment need to go up before I start making money?

7. How liquid is this investment? How fast can I sell it if I want to?

The Cheapskate's Retirement Recipe

There's really no specific time or date to start saving for retirement. To think it through, ask yourself:

➤ How much money do I have now?

➤ What Social Security and pension benefits will I receive?

➤ What kind of lifestyle do I want when I retire?

Some people start saving for retirement in their 20s, which gives them a tremendous leg up. Others don't even think about it until it's just around the corner. For every dollar you set aside at age 35, you'll need about three dollars at age 55. The advantage of starting young is—you guessed it—compound interest. The longer your money's working for you, the more there'll be when retirement rolls around. The earlier the better, but the latest date by which you should start saving for retirement is fifteen years before you plan to stop working.

Frugality Footnote

Most Americans begin their disciplined retirement saving in their 40s. If they're smart, they start adding to the amount they save in their 50s, when household responsibilities begin to decrease and their kids' college expenses are behind them.

When you're investing for retirement, take a long-term approach. The best long-term growth is in the stock market, so you should be exploring conservative stocks and mutual funds. If your return over the years is good, you'll have a long, worry-free, and fulfilling retirement. Put as much into pension plans or 401(k)s at work, and any IRAs or SEPs (see next section) that you have available. They all can be tax-deductible or provide before-tax investing, and the best ones enable you to make your own investment choices. Don't buy the argument that you shouldn't contribute to a retirement plan if you can't deduct the money; your money still grows tax-free until you withdraw it at retirement.

Don't put all your investment eggs in one basket, and as you get closer to retirement age, be careful to have investments that can be removed without affecting your portfolio's overall performance. View your retirement portfolio as an ongoing financial plan, because retirement is not the finish line. Life can go on for many years, and to live it well, you have to have a good plan.

Your Retirement Rainbow's Pot of Gold

Chapter 18 points out that the best way to save for retirement is through tax-advantaged retirement vehicles such as a 401(k), 403(b), IRA, Keogh, or SEP-IRA. The power of tax-deferred savings is unparalleled. Here are some more details about them.

➤ IRA (Individual Retirement Account) or Roth IRA: You can establish an IRA on your own through any mutual fund family or brokerage house, decide how much to contribute, and make all the investment decisions yourself. Contributions may be tax-deductible depending on your situation (as discussed earlier in this chapter). All money grows tax-deferred. Your maximum contribution is $2,000 per year for an individual or $2,250 for you and a non-working spouse. The fees usually run about $15 to $20 per year to manage the account. A fully funded IRA is the foundation of your nest egg, especially if contributions are fully deductible. If your contributions are nondeductible, you may want to fully fund other plans instead. Roth IRAs are nondeductible but have other important features. See your tax adviser, financial consultant, or go on the Internet for further advice on which IRA would be best for you.

Cheap Shot

When you invest in any type of tax-deferred retirement plan, don't put your money in tax-free investments such as municipal bonds. Your return will be lower, and you already get tax advantages by investing in the IRA account. Invest in higher returning vehicles to get the maximum benefit from the tax-deferred nature of the plan.

➤ SEP-IRA (Simplified Employee Plan): A SEP-IRA is similar to an IRA, but it doesn't have all the restrictions. SEP-IRA is an option if you have any self-employment income. All contributions are fully deductible, and your money grows tax-deferred. You can contribute up to 15 percent of your earnings and a maximum of $30,000 per year. The cost is generally about $30 annually. A SEP-IRA is a simple way to contribute the maximum to a retirement plan. You can use it along with other investment plans.

➤ Keogh: If you have any self-employment income, this plan is also available to you. Keoghs enable you to contribute a higher percentage of your income than any other plan. All contributions are deductible, and your money grows tax-deferred. You can contribute 15 to 25 percent of your self-employment income up to $30,000. Most Keoghs cost less than $75 annually. You receive the same benefits of a SEP, but a Keogh requires considerably more paperwork that you must file with the IRS. Keogh is the best plan if you want to contribute more than 15 percent of your income.

Cheap Thrills in Investing

➤ Mutual fund marketing can be very misleading to the average investor. Many funds advertise heavily when the fund has performed well for two or three years. A barrage of ads in financial newspapers and magazines can generate millions and millions of new investment dollars. Don't be taken in; research the fund's performance over the past five to seven years, not just the last year or two. The reality is that many funds that do well for just a few years may be dogs later on. Always check out a fund's average performance over three, five, ten, and fifteen years before you invest.

➤ Don't forget your home, which can be an important asset when you retire. Owning your home has valuable tax advantages as the years go by. If you plan on staying in a house a long time and paying off the mortgage, make sure the house has a lot of equity. Then you can sell it for a substantial profit—and fast—come retirement time. If the house does not have good value, at retirement time it will only be a burden.

➤ If you're one of those people who like to invest in individual stocks, remember that it's easier for a stock to lose value than to recover from a loss. If a stock drops 10 percent, it needs to rise 11 percent just to attain its original value. A stock that drops 50 percent needs to rise 100 percent to attain its original value! Not many stocks double in value in a short period of time. You can see that the key to successful investing is to avoid the big loss. When you're shopping for a stock, figure out the biggest loss you can afford. Set a stop loss at about 8 percent under the value at which you buy the stock. You're smarter to take the loss and move onto greener pastures than to ride the stock lower thinking it will rebound. Keep losses small and let winners ride, and you'll come out ahead even if you pick more losers than winners. This strategy works just as well for mutual funds.

➤ When it comes to finding the right mix of equities (stocks) and fixed-income securities (bonds, CDs, etc.) in your retirement portfolio, use your age as your guide. The farther away from retirement you are, the higher percentage you should invest in equities. The closer you are to retirement, the more you should invest in fixed-income securities. As a rule, 100 minus your age is the amount you should invest in equities. As an example, if you're 55, you should put 45 percent of your nest egg in equities. The other 55 percent goes into fixed-income investments such as bonds. Adjust your percentages every five years.

Cheap Trick

After you've maxed out your company plan or IRA, one of the best and safest tax-shelters is the variable annuity. It allows you to save tax-free for retirement purposes until you withdraw it. Use variable annuities for high returns and the ability to make your own investment choices. Check with Fidelity Investments, 800-544-7272, or Vanguard, 800-851-4999.

➤ Mutual funds make oodles of money. Stay away from funds that try to extract more than a 1 percent or maximum 2 percent management fee. Also watch out for 12b-1 fees. They pay for nothing more than marketing the mutual fund. Higher fees cut into your return. If the fund asks you to vote for a higher fee, write them and ask how you can help the fund cut costs. The reason that there are over 3,500 mutual funds is that they're low-overhead, high-return propositions.

Be aware of these pitfalls, and you'll be on more solid ground when you invest.

The Least You Need to Know

➤ Put the magic of compound interest to work today by setting aside money every month for your future. Your nest egg will grow astonishingly fast.

➤ Avoid the five worst investments outlined in this chapter or else you could lose your money fast. The best place for a cheapskate to start investing is in mutual funds.

➤ If you have a lot of money, or are totally confused about investing, your investment adviser should be an important ally in your financial plan. Be sure that he or she is not charging excessive fees and commissions to your account.

➤ If you aren't currently investing in no-load mutual funds, give them serious consideration. Contact a mutual fund family to receive performance results and a prospectus.

➤ If you haven't started saving for retirement yet, start today by opening an IRA account with a no-load mutual fund company. Even $25 a month would be a great start.

Cheap Talk:
The Complete List

Annual Percentage Rate (APR)   The actual annual interest rate you pay on the money you borrow. This rate is usually higher than the "rate" you are quoted because all fees for the loan have been added into the principal amount.

Balloon Note   A loan that allows for a large lump sum to be due at a specific time during the loan.

Bartering   Trading-out goods or services with another person. You give them something, they give something back. No money changes hands. The best thing is that it's free! Bartered goods and services can be taxable, so be sure to note conditions when you file your taxes.

"Can't Beat This" Ads   Ads for stores that guarantee the lowest prices anywhere. If you find the same product elsewhere for less money, they will match or sometimes beat that deal. Generally, "can't beat this" stores have the lowest prices anyway.

Chapter 7 Bankruptcy   Creditor protection through straight bankruptcy that liquidates most of your assets and frees you of all debts. You can generally retain the equity in your home, car, household goods, and jewelry.

Chapter 13 Bankruptcy   Creditor protection through development of a plan to repay debts over a period of three to five years, during which the court keeps a watchful eye. A household budget is formed, and creditors receive what is left after your basic expenditures. You may be able to keep part or all of your assets.

Cheapskate   "n. chep-skat (long e and a); a miserly or stingy person; *esp* one who tries to avoid his share of costs." However, today's cheapskates are as wise as they are miserly; they save with zeal and live beneath their means. Generally, they are smart consumers who have figured out how to save more than the average American but still live well.

Credit Life Insurance   Life insurance attached to a loan. It is paid for by the consumer but protects the finance company or bank that is issuing the loan in case the insured passes away before the loan is paid off.

Disability Insurance   Provides monthly benefits if you are injured or contract an illness that keeps you from earning an income. In exchange for premiums paid, a policy will generally replace all or a portion of your income for a set period of time in the case of an injury or illness.

Deductible   Amount of medical or accident expenses you will be responsible for before the health or life insurance company begins to pay.

Durable Power of Attorney   Legal document giving someone the right to act in accordance with someone else's wishes. For instance, an elderly cheapskate may be unable to take care of their finances because of health reasons. They can appoint someone else through a durable power of attorney to write checks, sign documents, and do anything else that is in the cheapskate's best interest.

Gross Income or Pay   Total amount of money your employer pays you before any taxes or other deductions are taken out.

Home Equity Loan   Loan obtained from a bank or other financial institution, secured by the equity in your home. Often, people use the money from these loans to pay off bills or finance a needed family purchase.

Invoice Cost   On a car, it's the amount the dealership paid the manufacturer for the car. They then mark up the price of the car and resell it. Anything they get between the invoice cost and sale price, they pocket.

Implicit Percentage Rate or Yield   On a car lease, it's the actual percentage rate charged annually. It is calculated using a complex formula similar to Egyptian hieroglyphics. Just make sure you ask for the annual yield if you are dead set on getting a lease.

Money Market Mutual Fund   Administered by a mutual fund family and usually offering a higher rate of return than a bank money market account. Always put your idle cash in a money market mutual fund for liquidity (ability to get the funds) and higher returns than you'd get from a standard savings account.

Mutual Fund   Investment where thousands of people pool their money and have a professional manager make their investments for them. By doing this, even small investors can have their money spread out over several different stocks to decrease risk.

Net Pay   Amount of money left over after all deductions are taken out of your gross pay. Net pay is the actual amount of money you deposit in your bank.

Pre-tax Income   Income you receive before anything else is deducted. It may also be referred to as gross income. It's the total amount of money you get paid by your employer on a regular basis.

Simple Interest Loan   Loan that calculates interest compounded on a monthly, rather than a daily basis. Always ask for a loan calculated with simple interest.

Stop-Loss   In a health insurance policy, it's the percentage of medical expenses you remain responsible for after your yearly deductible is met.

Store Brand and Generic Products   Often, just repackaged name-brand products. If they are not exactly the same product, they are likely to have been manufactured at the same factory as the name-brand product, and have similar product traits.

Tax-deferred Savings   An accumulated investment return on your retirement account, which is not taxed until you withdraw funds. It doesn't always mean that your contributions to the account will not be taxed. Check with your employer to find out the tax consequences of the account you have.

Term Life Insurance   Straight death protection written on yourself that covers your family in case you pass away. It's always much cheaper than whole life or credit life insurance.

Web TV   Special service that allows you to hook up to the Internet and also have world-wide e-mail for a connection fee of about $300–$500. You then pay a small monthly fee for your Internet access. There are several companies that sell systems, such as Philips and RCA.

Whole Life Insurance   Fancy term for a life insurance policy that has a savings element attached to it. Whole life insurance is a broad term covering Universal Life, Variable Life, etc. If it's life insurance with a savings element, it's whole life.

Index